The Complete
Steelheader

The Complete Steelheader

Successful Fly-Fishing Tactics

JOHN LARISON
Photographs by James R. Larison

STACKPOLE
BOOKS

Published by
STACKPOLE BOOKS
5067 Ritter Road
Mechanicsburg, PA 17055
www.stackpolebooks.com

Printed in China

First edition

10 9 8 7 6 5 4 3 2 1

Illustrations by Dave Hall

Library of Congress Cataloging-in-Publication Data

Larison, John.
    The complete steelheader : successful fly-fishing tactics / John
Larison. — 1st ed.
        p.   cm.
    ISBN-13: 978-0-8117-3466-0
    ISBN-10: 0-8117-3466-8
    Includes bibliographical references and index.
    1. Steelhead fishing.   2. Fly fishing.   I. Title.

SH687.7.L37   2008
799.17'57—dc22

                                                            2007019311

To the Anglers,
For the Fish

In memory of Liam Wood:
you are missed.

Contents

Acknowledgments

This book would be nothing but an idle dream if it hadn't been for my wife, Ellie Rose. Her unrelenting (and likely misplaced) confidence in me worked better than any coffee. I should probably back up and begin by thanking Cupid for arrowing me a mate who understands the significance of a chromehead's river time and who has never once asked me to skip a day of steelheading. I'm grateful every day for Ellie. All my thanks begin at her feet.

My father deserves a gargantuan thank-you—most notably for donating several months of his valuable time to the procurement of the book's photos. Without his keen eye for light, lightning-fast shutter finger, and unrelenting determination to get the best shots possible, this book would be little more than an oversize pamphlet. I'm as thankful for the photos as I am for the time we spent together traveling through steelhead country. Let's do it again soon.

This book would be completely unreadable if Ted "Tightlines" Leeson hadn't taken me under his wing and spent hours of his life—hours he could have been fishing—teaching me how language works. Ted must have scribbled away a dozen perfectly good pencils on that first, horrendous draft. (I can't imagine the damage to his eyes.) And in my dour moments when inspiration was nowhere to be found, all I had to do was crack open a copy of *Habit of Rivers* or *Jerusalem Creek*. For as long as I scribble sentences, I'll be grateful to Ted, for his tutelage and his words.

Two Oregon fly shops and their chromehead owners proved invaluable in the writing of this book. The McKenzie Angler in Walterville and its owner, Brian Marz, helped me not only collect flies but also find fish. In the early days of my addiction, Brian gladly passed on the secrets of his homewater—a gift that provided the confidence necessary to explore other watersheds. The Scarlet Ibis in Corvallis and its owner, Matt Vander Heide, donated countless flies and a wealth of technical information. Moreover, Matt's enthusiasm for the fish and their protection has been a source of inspiration for me. Brian and Matt are two of the finest steelheaders this side of the Mississippi. I feel lucky to fish with them both.

A few fishing friends kindly allowed me to borrow pictures from their own collections. Peter Betjemann, Nate Koenigsknecht, Tom Christensen, and Brian Marz, I owe you several pints apiece. Take me up on the offer.

I also owe the MFA Program of Oregon State University a huge thank-you, specifically Tracy Daugherty, Marjorie Sandor, and Keith Scribner. First of all, thank you for letting me in—a mistake, I'm sure you realize. Fishermen don't make good students. Also, thank you for your hours of guidance and support. I'm forever indebted. Specifically, I'd like to thank Marjorie for her insistence the book get finished. Her footprint is permanently on my rear end.

Thanks to Lyons Press for the use of quotes from Ted Leeson's *Habit of Rivers* and Roderick Haig-Brown's *Fisherman's Summer* and *Fisherman's Fall*. Also, thanks to Sierra Club Books for the use of a quote from David James Duncan's *My Story As Told By Water* and to Random House Inc. for the use of a quote from Thomas McGuane's *The Longest Silence*.

And finally, as promised more than two decades ago, thank you Mrs. Ramadan.

"We have reached the time in the life of the planet,
and humanity's demands upon it,
when every fisherman will have to be a riverkeeper,
a steward of marine shallows,
a watchman on the high seas."

THOMAS MCGUANE, *THE LONGEST SILENCE*

Introduction

Somehow steelhead, those enigmatic salmonids, have managed to swim their way into our heads. Once there, they finned up the gravel of common sense and laid a few million eggs of red-hot obsession. Now nonfishing thoughts are murky at best and contain flashes of chrome at worst. Our yards are overgrown. Our bosses are pissed. Our spouses are organizing interventions.

But despite our obsession, steelhead fly fishing is plagued by a dirty little truth: Many of us don't catch the numbers of steelhead we should. We know the river. We know the fish. We know what we're doing. Yet most steelheaders don't get a fraction of the hookups a neophyte gear fisher does. For decades, we've accepted this as the consequence of fly fishing for an anadromous fish. We distract ourselves with little clichés like "We're after more than just fish" or "We're not meat hunters; we're artists." But deep down, we feel the pain of repeated skunkings. These skunkings, I believe, stem from an outdated angling strategy.

The angling strategy most commonly employed on western rivers today came of age in the 1960s and 1970s. At the time, anglers frequently enjoyed wild runs of steelhead in their local rivers. And these steelheaders experienced little if any competing angling pressure. Feisty fish—spread more or less evenly throughout the river—eagerly chased flies. And a pair of buddies could spend the day leapfrogging each other without seeing another soul.

But times are a-changing. The twenty-first century's dawn glow has revealed a drastically different world. Hatchery fish have replaced most of our wild stocks, resulting in schools of fish clumped into a few runs with largely empty water in between. And now steelheaders are everywhere. Often a pair of buddies must wait in a shoreside line six rods deep for a chance to ply the water. With all this pressure, any feisty fish are plucked quickly from the river, leaving only the more dour and contemplative ones behind.

But there is hope. We know more about these fish than ever, resulting in a clearer sense of their biology and behavior. New technology has allowed the classic techniques to be refined. And it has also allowed the development of new techniques that both persuade tough fish and effectively cover water that was once the sole domain of gear fishers. These changing times call for an evolved angling strategy, one that more accurately matches the modern fish, the modern knowledge, and the modern gear.

The world of trout fishing has experienced some of these same changes. Intense angling pressure on iconic rivers like the Madison and Bighorn has changed the behavior of the fish, making them more shy and selective. But concurrently, technological advances have allowed new presentation options, from smaller flies in increasingly delicate situations to heavier flies in more hardy situations. It seems trout anglers have adapted more readily than steelheaders to the twenty-first century.

So why have we steelheaders dragged our cleats? The answer, I believe, lies in steelheading's romantic past.

Our sport has its roots in the Atlantic salmon fishing of nineteenth-century Europe, a place ruled by classism. Only the richest and most "proper" were allowed to pursue these regal fish. Anglers of the time valued aesthetic form as much as they did catching their quarry; their form separated them from the commoners. Over the years, their genteel manners of presentation grew into an overall approach to the river, one based heavily on the romance of tradition. When Atlantic salmon fishers headed

Facing page: Steelhead: They're more than a fish, they're an addiction.

west and discovered steelhead, they were quick to apply not only the same techniques to these new fish, but also the same aesthetically-based approach to the sport.

The current steelheading paradigm still wears the tweed of its past; our approach to the river still puts tradition above practicality in many situations. We are taught to fish only a few presentations, the "classics," and we are told to resist innovation. Innovation undercuts tradition. So we continue to approach the fish and the rivers as we did forty years ago. By failing to adjust our angling strategy as the world around us changed, we've hindered our ability to consistently catch steelhead.

But worse, we've allowed ourselves to be pulled apart by minor disputes over form. How many times have you seen a fly fisher balk at another angler who is fishing in a nontraditional manner? Frequently the balking angler bases the criticism on a concern for the quarry. But I wonder if the real harm to the fish isn't such divisiveness between anglers, both conservationists who, because of a relatively minor difference of opinion, might resist uniting in their shared quest: to protect their beloved steelhead. It is this divisiveness that is most detrimental to the sport and the fish, in my opinion. By steadfastly resisting any technique that breaks tradition, we fail to make gains in the effectiveness of our approach. As a result, many anglers don't catch the numbers of steelhead they think they should and eventually give up on the pursuit, the rivers, and the fish. And when this happens, steelhead lose a potential friend—someone who might have worked to help save the fish and its rivers—at a time when steelhead need all the friends they can get.

The Complete Steelheader: Successful Fly-Fishing Tactics presents a different approach to the sport, one that brings our romantic traditions into the realities of the modern world. The book's intention is to provide anglers with the knowledge they need to consistently catch steelhead on a fly rod. Thus the book breaks from tradition—when such a break is warranted by fact—and gives anglers an honest account of what is necessary for consistent success on twenty-first-century steelhead rivers.

The Complete Steelheader grows from a swelling counterculture within the steelheading community, a group of guides and other serious chromeheads devoted to the fish. They've been whispering for years in the backs of fly shops and at streamside bars about the limitations of the classical approach. This book sprouts from those conversations.

For an angler to be consistently successful, he or she must have a sound understanding of the three equally important aspects of the sport: river knowledge, steelhead behavior, and effective presentation techniques. The book details the guides' tricks for developing river knowledge as quickly as possible, provides an in-depth look at steelhead behavior throughout their months in the river, and carefully outlines each presentation technique—including the required casts, mends, leaders, flies, and other vital details—commonly employed by successful fly-fishing guides on the West Coast. But more than this, it presents a different way of approaching the river, a methodology that is more aptly suited to the habits and habitat of modern steelhead. In the end, the book should help struggling steelheaders catch enough fish to keep their minds—and possibly their wallets—focused on the fish.

PART I
Approaching the River

*"I don't fish in order to sit atop some predatory or evolutionary hierarchy.
I fish to hook into an entirety. I fish to trade self-consciousness for creek-consciousness."*

DAVID JAMES DUNCAN, *MY STORY AS TOLD BY WATER*

A nine-pound winter steelhead ready for release.

1

We launched the boat in the fog of dawn, the water glimmering sky orange. Spring chinook splashed in the big pool, sending concentric ripples over the tailout and beyond. Our steelhead rods sat rigged and ready on the gunwales. As I oared the boat into the current's grasp, Matt poured a cup of steaming coffee and handed it back. He smiled like a treasure hunter a few steps shy of the map's X.

The rapids lapped against the boat's sides. A strong starboard stroke and two heavy digs moved us around a Volkswagen-size boulder; a port stroke straightened us out. I tucked the oars under my knee and took the piping hot coffee as we glided through the run. Dark trees clawed their way over the water, casting black shadows on the river's metallic finish.

"Over there," Matt said, pointing to a nondescript slice of water forty feet downstream. I chugged the coffee, tossed him the empty cup, and slowed the boat.

"Here," he said. "Drop the anchor here." I did as he said, but I was a little late on the release, and we drifted downstream farther than he wanted. Five feet too far, maybe ten. Not a gross difference, but in steelheading, place—down to a specific rock—is everything. He cringed and forced a "This will be fine."

Matt lived a five-minute drive from the river and fished it daily. He'd fallen in love with the stream years before, as a college student in a city downstream. Upon graduating—or dropping out, I never asked which—he rented a house with some other guides and took to romancing the stream full-time. From May to November, he worked its flows, putting paying customers on fish and spending his days off plying its best lies. I'd fished with him before, on my homewater, and now he was returning the favor. And what a favor indeed. Even in the dim dawn light, he knew every rock, every crevice, every hidden trough.

"The fish move up through the heavy water there," Matt said, pointing to a V of soft water extending into the white violence of the rapids. "Cast to the upstream side of that big rock."

"The one on the left?"

"No, the one on the right, with the tuft of grass growing on top."

We traded places, and I unpinned my favorite rod, a long 8-weight rigged with a floating line and a size 6 Enlighted Green Butted Skunk. "How's this?" I asked, lifting the pattern.

"Ideal."

The water boiled on the front of the rock before spinning around and into the rapids below. I stripped off a pile of line, rolled it airborne, and shot it tight over the water. A big mend slowed the swing, and I held my breath as the fly moved toward the rock. It passed a few feet out in front, untouched by a fish.

"Hit it again. This time strip out another foot." Matt tossed me a corner-of-the-eye look. "I got a feeling."

My cast landed awkwardly, but I corrected with an oversize mend. The bright line painted a neon arrow on the dark water, pointing at the invisible fly.

He jumped onto the oarsman's seat for a better view.

The fly hung in front of the rock for a long five seconds, then slid toward the bank. I tightened for another cast, just as a slab of chrome slashed from the depths in front of the big rock, engulfing the fly in a violent swirl. The rod bucked and the reel squealed.

"You got him!" Matt said, spilling his coffee, as stoked as if he'd hooked the fish.

The steelhead fought to stay in the pool, running upstream under the fast current. The fly line sliced the water behind him, hissing wildly. Near the head of the pool, the fish exploded into the air, contorting her silver body in the mist. I saw her hanging there long after she'd vanished back into the depths, a flash burned into night-trained eyes. She gave one more halfhearted run and tired. Matt and I met the fish on the rocks, beached and on her side, gulping in the air, the fly glowing in her lip. A wild hen of no more than twenty-four inches. A small, perfect fish. With a twist, I unpinned fly and gave her back to the current, where she quickly regained her strength and surged for the obscurity of deeper water.

Matt flashed his eyebrows, beaming white teeth in the growing light. "I had a feeling about that spot." He snagged the rod from my hand and climbed back into the boat. His loops rocketed tight and settled like a fluttering leaf.

"We get hit in front of that rock seven out of ten mornings," he said. "We didn't get one yesterday. Had a feeling about today."

I poured him a cup of coffee and jumped onto the oarsman's seat, intently watching as his fly quivered just under the surface.

Spend much time pursuing steelhead and you'll quickly learn that steelheading—unlike trout fishing—is less a game of theories that can be mastered and readily applied with success to new rivers and more a game of practice. But not "practice" the way your piano teacher meant the word. Steelheading is a game of practicing a place. To be consistently successful, a steelheader must learn the intricacies of a specific location. The best steelheaders have a river or two they understand intimately. They can predict the clarity of the water after an evening's rain. They can judge how long it will take the steelhead to move upstream once they're reported in tidewater. And they know which lies steelhead are using based on light, water clarity, water temperature, and time of year. Steelheaders with an intimate understanding of and relationship to a specific river are the ones who can average two or three fish a trip on the fly. Instead of searching long sections of water, they're able to move from likely lie to likely lie; every cast puts the fly in a honey hole. Catching steelhead on a fly rod depends on developing a relationship with a specific river. Success depends on finding a homewater.

Besides its practical benefits, developing a homewater relationship with a river provides the essential core to the steelheading experience. For some, contemporary society's divorce from rivers and mountains leaves us longing. Maybe we long for a more sustained connection with the natural world. Or maybe we simply long to clear our minds of their workplace clutter. Whatever it is we desire, developing a homewater relationship with a steelhead river has a surprising way of bringing satisfaction into an angler's life. Knowing a river intimately gives us an anchor in the swaying sea of contemporary existence. It provides something to hold on to, something to provide meaning and substance to the passing seasons. July might signify the beginning of the summer run, for instance. March, the best month for catching big, wild winter steelhead. And fishing your homewater makes fishing even more pleasurable. When you know you're swinging your fly through prime holding water, a lie where you've hooked four steelhead in your last six trips, your knees rattle with anticipation. The world outside of your vision—work, stress, even time itself—blurs into nonexistence; the entire universe consists of that lie and your fly and the anticipation of a take.

For some of us, anyway, it is the experience of understanding something about a river—an ecosystem—that keeps us dutifully casting year in and year out.

But developing a homewater isn't easy. It takes an avid fisher at least a season of devotion just to get a handle on the superficial details. The most beneficial knowledge will take several more seasons. Time well spent—in terms of both pleasure gained and fish caught. The coming chapters are aimed at helping shrink the learning curve by establishing which rivers make the best homewater, presenting trusted techniques the savvy angler can employ to turn a new river into a homewater as fast as possible, and detailing the effects of certain environmental conditions on your homewater. ■

CHAPTER 1

Selecting a Homewater

What to Look for in a Steelhead River

For a trout angler, any little creek, raging river, or duck pond can make an ideal homewater. The only requirement of the place is that it have a population of trout. And in trout country, even a good-size mud puddle can have riseforms.

But for the steelheader, selecting a homewater is more complicated. Not just any stream will suffice. It needs to be of the proper disposition, be accessible, and most important, have a healthy run of fish. More is at stake for the steelheader than for the trout fisher. When Derrick Dry Fly shows up to a new trout stream, he can quickly determine the quality of the fishery with a few hours spent casting. If he sees bugs in the air, observes trout rising, and maybe catches a few, he'll have a firm idea of what the river has to offer. But a few hours spent steelheading on a new river will reveal little or nothing. Some casts will be made, some flies lost, but most likely—even on the greatest steelhead stream in the world—not a fish will be hooked. Thus where trout anglers can dilly-dally their way to discovering a quality homewater, steelheaders must first do their homework.

A Few Features of Healthy Steelhead Rivers

The Bow River in Alberta and the San Juan River in New Mexico are both examples of superb trout streams. Anglers frequently catch rainbows over twenty inches in both places. What allows the trout to grow so large is the fertility of the watershed. The Bow becomes a haven for insect life downstream of Calgary, the San Juan downstream of Navajo Dam. This insect life in turn produces large fish. And though steelhead don't require a fertile natal stream to become healthy—they'll put on their bulk in the ocean—they do require certain features from the watershed. Knowing what these features are can help you sort out which rivers are potential homewaters and which are better passed by.

For healthy stocks of wild steelhead to be present in a stream, extensive sections must have a gravel bottom. Steelhead, like many salmonids, prefer to spawn over a cobbled bottom. The hen fish digs a nest, or redd, in the stones in which to deposit her eggs. Most steelhead seem to prefer substrate that ranges from the size of a quarter to that of a barroom coaster. And most prefer that this substrate lie under one to three feet of water. Unfortunately, the headwaters of many rivers in steelhead country have faced extensive clear-cutting and road building, frequently resulting in silt draining from the bare hillside into the feeder creeks and eventually into the river itself—burying that gravel under a layer of sediment. The silting of spawning gravel has been shown to both suffo-

Above: Dawn on a coastal steelhead stream.

5

Healthy steelhead streams are few and far between. Those that remain need all the friends they can get.

cate the eggs still tucked between the stones and discourage future spawning in that area.

After their eggs hatch from the gravel, young steelhead require sections of river that offer safe harbor from predators while they gather the food they need to grow. Such places are commonly referred to as rearing areas. Young steelhead don't have the ability to survive for long periods of time in riffles and runs. Their bodies don't gain the hydrodynamic features with which anglers are familiar until they are several months old. Therefore, young steelhead need slower currents. But slower currents alone don't offer adequate protection from predators such as herons and resident trout. Hence sunken

debris is a necessary component of any steelhead rearing area. Both logjams and beaver ponds have traditionally offered ideal debris structure. But in the early days of sport angling in the Northwest, many fishers actually blasted such structure free from the river channel in the name of easing the upstream migration of returning adult fish. And in many of those rivers where anglers didn't clear the channels, logging companies did to allow timber to be easily transported downstream. Logjams and beaver ponds have returned to some places in steelhead country, but not all. If your potential homewater has these features, mark that as a check in the right column.

Besides spawning gravel and rearing habitat, every wild steelhead river also needs intact shorelines. The shade offered by streamside trees and brush offer young steelhead protection from both aerial predators and overheating. If the sun bakes a section of river, the water temperature can rise. Once it reaches a certain level, which varies based on location, the young steelhead can actually die. Also, healthy shorelines offer a buffer of protection against the runoff that can bury spawning gravel. In recent years, safer logging practices have called for retaining streamside brush. Most of us will find it along the main stems of our local streams. Take note of the feeder creeks that pour into the river, however. If too many tributaries bake in direct sunlight, the river itself may reach lethal temperatures during the peak of the summer.

In general, rivers that flow through intact forests offer the best chance for steelhead populations. Watersheds with a minimum of clear-cutting typically have long sections of usable gravel, unbroken logjams, and healthy shorelines. Moreover, these rivers tend to clear faster after a deluge, providing more fishable days during the year.

While healthy steelhead populations require many other features, these three are the most observable to the angler's eye. If a river has these three, the odds of a healthy population existing in the watershed increase dramatically.

Summer steelhead have additional requirements for their watershed because of the duration of their stay in fresh water. Like all steelhead, summer fish spawn in the spring. But summer steelhead typically enter the river between May and September, requiring them to spend up to a year in fresh water. This time in the river exposes them to severe predation risk, especially considering how low river levels can get in the late summer. Also, summer heat raises the water temperature of rivers, which in turn decreases oxygen levels. For summer steelhead to remain safe and happy until spring, they need rivers with extensive sections of heavy water. In big, fast rivers like the

Rogue, heavy water is everywhere. A steelhead can easily find adequate protection in nearly any run. But on smaller rivers, like those little coastal streams divoting the coastline from California to Alaska, heavy water is typically found only in canyon sections. The structure of canyon water, with rapids and deep pools, offers steelhead protection from predators as well as oxygenated flows. A fish can hold under the whitewater for months without being threatened.

A natal river's character has certain noticeable effects on adult steelhead behavior. In the era of unmolested steelhead rivers, when healthy populations of wild fish inhabited nearly every river from San Mateo, California to Port Heiden, Alaska, the behavioral differences of steelhead were profound. Each watershed contained unique fish. Thousands of years of evolutionary pressures carved out steelhead perfectly suited to the demands of their environment. In the years since, most steelhead rivers have seen the introduction of hatchery fish in some form or another. And studies reveal that even in rivers where hatchery steelhead have never been stocked, stray hatchery fish from other rivers manage to find their way to the spawning grounds. The result is an averaging out of the fish throughout their range. The unique characteristics and behaviors of wild steelhead have been greatly diminished. In some places, however—rivers where the fish have seen a minimum of hatchery-gene dilution—the wild steelhead retain much of their originality.

For instance, rivers with long sections of heavy water select for the most physically agile and aggressive steelhead. These fish need their physical prowess to ascend the rapids that separate them from the spawning grounds. Anglers will most notice this agility once the steelhead has felt the hook. Just ask any angler who has fished the brutal Skeena watershed or between the rapids along the Umpqua. Steelhead from rivers with heavy water will bend your rod like no other. These rivers are the reason common wisdom recommends two hundred yards of backing on a steelhead reel. Besides their ability to whoop an angler's ass, steelhead from fast rivers also seem more willing to travel a great distance for the fly.

Juvenile steelhead are dependent on intact shorelines and the shade they provide.

Whereas most steelhead will rarely move more than a couple feet to strike, heavy-water steelhead frequently rush six feet or more at a provocative pattern. Most likely this aggressive demeanor has to do with the energy stocks stored in the fish. A fly, like a rapid, has the ability to surge the fish into action.

The fertility of a steelhead's natal stream can also have an effect on its behavior as a returning adult. Fertile rivers in the West tend to have prolific populations of caddisflies, which, depending on the location, hatch from the beginning of the spring to the very end of the fall. Most of these caddis species deposit their eggs by bouncing over the surface of the river. Trout anglers have certainly observed this behavior on countless occasions. The female caddis, a ball of eggs attached to the end of her abdomen, drops from the air onto the surface of the water, then hops back into the air, only to drop back down. Since most river breezes flow upstream during the day, these bouncing caddis frequently hop their way upstream. Young steelhead seem especially enamored of this behavior, likely because of its blatant nature—there's no hiding for an egg-laying caddis. Smolt-size fish frequently rise in frantic splashes at these little morsels. For a juvenile steelhead, two years spent chasing these bugs leave their mark as the fish returns to the river as an adult. Wild adult steelhead from fertile rivers are frequently convinced by active fly-rod presentations, most notably the skated dry-fly presentation. Whereas an angler on an infertile stream might find success only with indicator tactics, his buddy over the ridge on a fertile river will often find equal or better success swinging flies.

But the fertility of a natal stream has nothing to do with the size of the returning adult steelhead. All other factors being the same, an adult fish from an infertile river is just as likely to reach twenty pounds as a fish from a fertile river. The size of an adult fish has every-

Wild steelhead from rivers with heavy rapids tend to be more aggressive than fish born in tamer rivers.

thing to do with the amount of time the individual fish spent gorging itself on the ocean's buffet. And the specific factors controlling the frequency at which steelhead stay in the ocean for prolonged periods of time remains a mystery. But as any serious chromehead will tell you, wild steelhead from healthy watersheds are the most likely to return absurdly large.

Finally, a note on river sources. While most rivers throughout steelhead country gain the majority of their flow from snowmelt and other versions of annual precipitation, a handful of notable rivers—the Dean and Sandy, to name just a couple—gain a large proportion of their flow from glaciers. We're all familiar with the mechanics of rivers that are based on annual precipitation: When it rains, they rise, often dramatically. Based on local hydrology, glacial rivers may also be susceptible to rain-induced flow increases. They also are controlled by another variable, however: the speed at which their icy source melts. Depending on their latitude, winter may see their glacier frozen, but the flows frequently run high as a result of rain. And in summer, while the sky is blue, the river might run turbid because of the receding glacier. Hence steelhead in many glacially fed rivers have become uniquely adapted to turbid water. These fish retain their impulse to strike even as fish from other rivers would have gone dour hours before. For the angler, this means that instead of heading home to tie flies, you can simply latch on a bigger, more visible pattern and keep casting.

Understanding what features help create a healthy steelhead river, and what features affect the behavior of fish from that river, is an important step to finding a homewater and understanding it once you do.

Wild Steelhead Rivers versus Hatchery Steelhead Rivers

As the experiments of fish management agencies throughout the Northwest have shown, hatchery steelhead can return in large numbers to even the sickest rivers. A small coastal stream near my house is a prime example. This river used to have a healthy wild fish population, but habitat degradation systematically lowered the population of returning adult fish. Instead of putting safeguards in place to ensure the wild fish a healthy river in which to spawn, a hatchery was built along the headwaters to mitigate the losses. In the years since, the wild fish population has been co-opted by the deluge of hatchery fish—a strain of steelhead completely foreign to the watershed, selected for its ability to grow well in cement tanks. Now the little river has an average return of nearly three thousand fish, which by some estimates is four times the number of wild fish that ran up the river before the degradation of the watershed.

Steelhead naturally return to their acclimation point within a river. Find that point and you'll find steelhead.

The ability of hatchery programs to produce large runs of steelhead in damaged ecosystems sparked a wave of hatchery construction in decades past. If the steelhead produced in these facilities were comparable to the river's wild steelhead, more anglers would be pleased. Most anglers, however, find hatchery fish to be a weak alternative to wild runs. One of the reasons for this is how hatchery fish act when they return to their "natal" stream.

All steelhead are instinctually driven to return to their acclimation point, the place in their natal stream they know best. For wild steelhead, the acclimation point is usually an extensive area, because as a juvenile, the fish traveled up and down the river's riffles and runs. For a hatchery steelhead, however, the acclimation point is usually a precise location, either the hatchery, if the facility is on the streambank, or the point where the fish was stocked. Moreover, wild steelhead are spawned in many different patches of gravel throughout the river system, whereas hatchery steelhead are generally stocked in just a few spots. Adult steelhead more or less stop once they reach their acclimation points, so hatchery fish tend to pile up in specific places. Because of these behavioral differences, it's vital that steelheaders know whether their homewater's run is composed of mostly wild or hatchery steelhead.

For an angler new to a river system, hatchery steelhead offer a certain benefit: Locating the fish will be relatively easy, as they will be piling up at their acclimation points. Discover where these points are, and you know where to find fish. Such points are rarely a secret, however. Odds are good you'll be sharing the water with lots of other anglers, many of whom might not appreciate the river space needed by a fly fisher.

Rivers with runs composed of mostly hatchery fish can be tough on anglers. Creel surveys have year after year revealed hatchery fish to be more reluctant biters than their wild cousins in the same water. A recent study along the Deschutes River conducted by the Oregon Department of Fish and Wildlife, which counted the number of steelhead caught by anglers, revealed that wild steelhead were caught more often than hatchery steelhead by sport anglers. The exact ratio was 1.64 wild fish for every 1 hatchery fish. Yet total fish counts for the years studied revealed that on average, wild fish consisted of only about 30 percent of the run. For whatever reason, hatchery fish seem to be less responsive to the fly.

Conversely, rivers with runs composed of wild steelhead offer a grossly different angling experience. Instead of clumping up at common acclimation points, wild steelhead spread throughout the system. Once you have located a good section of water, say a three-mile section of classic rapids-pool-rapids water, you can expect to find fish holding more or less evenly throughout. Certain sections contain more fish than others, and finding these spots takes time. But because wild fish tend to be more prone to aggressive reactions to flies, you can cover the water more quickly.

Besides the differences in how wild and hatchery steelhead behave in the river and the effects this has on the angling experience, a larger difference still pervades. While a hatchery fish is certainly a prize, something that puts a wide smile on every chromehead's face, landing one might not offer the essential experience of steelhead fly fishing. To hook a wild steelhead, on the other hand, connects the angler to something much larger than a simple fish. As the line comes tight, the angler becomes privy to an entire ecological relationship—one that includes not only the fish, but also the river, its tributaries, the surrounding forests, and the vast Pacific Ocean. For many anglers, it is this connection that makes steelheading steelheading.

Exploring Unknown Waters

Steelhead country is wet country. A sky's worth of water drains from the land, creating a bouquet of rivers for the eager angler. Some of these are well-known fisheries, written up in magazines and probably discussed in the local newspaper. But with any luck, a few will be largely unknown and unexplored. For many of us, these unpres-

Some of steelheading's finest pleasures are to be found along remote streams.

When possible, determining the run count of a river can reveal whether it has a fishable population of steelhead.

sured gems are exactly why we fish. It is here that we are most likely to find wild steelhead existing as they did 150 years ago.

But how do you decide which streams are worth exploring? In my neck of the woods, there are eighteen streams of fishable size within an hour's drive. But only a few of them are worth fishing.

The first step to determining which waters are potential quality waters is to try to determine each river's run count, the total number of steelhead that enter a given river. Many fishing books provide information on the total number of steelhead caught from a stream, steelhead caught versus hours fished, and so on. But this data is of little use to the angler checking up on an unknown river. Sometimes the best steelheading is where others don't fish, so catch-rate data won't be of much help. On the other hand, run count totals will be.

The agency in the state or province responsible for managing the fisheries usually determines run count information through a process known as a redd count. A spawning hen steelhead creates a depression in the substrate of the river about the size of a small car door in an effort to provide her eggs cover from the current. Because the fish spawn in shallow water, the depression is easily visible from the shore or even a helicopter. By counting the total number of redds in a section of river, biologists are able to estimate with reasonable accuracy the number of fish entering a river. The other way biologists determine the run count is by watching the fish passing a barrier, such as a dam or hatchery. This data-gathering method is more accurate, but such barriers are rare commodities on unknown streams—which is probably the way we want it.

Uncovering current run count data isn't always possible, but more often than not you can find the data if you are willing to do a little legwork. Sometimes the fishery management agency publishes the data in either electronic or physical form. If a quick check online turns up nothing, a stop at the local library occasionally will be more productive. If still nothing turns up, a trip to a nearby public university's library can often provide the information. If these options fail, a quick phone call to the fishery management agency will usually result in the name of a biologist responsible for the area. Such folks are frequently eager to talk about streams with passionate anglers; the more people that care about a river, the more volunteer help the biologists will have the next time they need to do a redd count or other conservation project.

But what do you make of run count information? What does five hundred fish in a river really mean? Is the stream worth fishing? Run count information is half the knowledge you need to determine whether the river holds a fishable population of steelhead, meaning a high enough population to warrant pursuit. Besides run count numbers, you also need to know details about the character of the stream, such as how long it is and what the holding water looks like.

When we think of a stream, we usually picture the classic freestone variety with a rapids-pool-rapids kind of structure. Such rivers are a joy to fish, in part because the holding water is obvious and finding fish is easy. But many streams and rivers in steelhead country, particularly those in flatter farming areas, don't have this convenient structure. Instead, the river might be made up of smooth water with little structure to collect resting fish.

Determining the character of a stream can often be done from home. First find a topographical map of the area. My favorite maps for U.S. streams are the quadrangles offered by the United States Geological Survey (USGS). These maps show the terrain in exquisite detail, often precisely enough to locate water features like long pools. But what you're looking for on the map isn't pools, per se. Look at the amount of elevation change over the river's course, specifically in the area you think you might be inclined to fish. The easiest way to determine the elevation change is to mark off a river mile on the map and count the contour lines visible in that mile. With luck, you'll see at least twenty feet of elevation change. On the same map, look for rapids to be marked.

Steelhead slow their upstream migration near heavy water; therefore, rapids collect fish. If you find a steep elevation change, odds are your river's character will be conducive to holding steelhead.

One stream near my house has a run of five hundred steelhead. It's more than forty miles long and usually about a roll cast wide. It contains no dams, heavy rapids, or other obstructions to the migrating fish. Instead, the river has countless deep and long runs where a fish could hold anywhere. With five hundred steelhead in a river that size, an angler can work an entire season and not hook a fish. Five hundred steelhead spread over forty miles of water means roughly twelve fish per river mile. Considering the river's character, finding those twelve steelhead is akin to the old needle in a haystack. Conversely, I fished a river in southeast Alaska that also has a run of five hundred steelhead. That river is twenty-five miles long, made up of the classic rapids-pool-rapids structure, and contains a section of especially heavy water at the ten-mile point—an obstruction sure to slow upstream progress and clump fish together. Considering the character of the river and the numbers of fish, that Alaskan stream is certainly worth exploring.

Most chromeheads agree that five hundred fish is the bottom limit of a fishable population. Less than that and you not only might have trouble finding fish, but also might damage the population by pursuing it. Luckily, in much of steelhead country, there exist countless streams with sufficient runs that are rarely mentioned in local fly shops. Hunt them out, and you'll eventually strike silver.

Learning Your Homewater

How to Find the Right Places to Fish

A friend of mine argues that catching steelhead depends more on picking the right water than on fishing the right technique. And based on this guy's ability to pry big fish out of our local rivers, I'm inclined to agree. His argument makes sense. A fly swung perfectly through fishless water will be ignored ten casts out of ten. But a fly swung badly through fishy water will still occasionally draw strikes. Whether my friend is precisely correct or not, his argument makes a fine point: Picking the right place to fish your fly is vital to consistently hooking chromers.

So you've found an ideal homewater, a nearby stream with lots of eager fish. How do you decide where to start fishing? Not all sections of that river will be created equal; some will hold more fish than others.

Steelhead fresh to the river move upstream quickly. They dash through the lower sections of the river where the current is slow. But as they reach faster currents, their energy reserves begin to be depleted. Soon they need to rest and regain strength. They'll find a lie and hold as long as they need. The point where the steelhead opts to rest is commonly called the slowing point. Steelhead generally tire more or less in the same place along a river; what is the slowing point for one fish is likely close to the slowing point for another. Once the fish begin to slow, their upstream progress ceases to be mea-

sured in miles. Now they pick their way up through a few rapids and hold, then a few more. Fish that are actively traveling rarely strike a fly. They have other things on their minds. Resting steelhead are the ones most inclined to strike. Therefore, locating the slowing point on your homewater is an important step in the quest to find willing fish.

To identify a river's slowing point, you need to have a sense of its geography. If the map you used when scouting the stream shows major rapids, start your search near the lowest one. Traveling steelhead need to store energy before beginning a serious push through any heavy water. Sometimes fish will hold below rapids for a few hours, sometimes for a few days. But in any case, the water below the rapids will collect steelhead. Once the fish pushes through the heavy water, it will need to rest again, meaning the water above the rapids will also collect steelhead. The first heavy set of rapids on a river is often the slowing point.

Above the slowing point, fish can be anywhere. But certain river features will collect more fish than others. Every major set of rapids upstream will probably have a

Above: Steelhead are never spread evenly throughout a river's entire length. Learning where large numbers of fish pause to rest is an essential step to consistently hooking chromers.

13

few fish holding below and above it. If the river possesses rapids of serious size, Class IV or bigger, certainly give the surrounding water a thorough look.

Dams act as the ultimate rapids, drastically slowing the upstream progress of migrating steelhead. Those dams without fish ladders will stop steelhead altogether, effectively topping off the river. Most modern dams have fish ladders, but finding these ladders can be problematic for instinct-driven steelhead. The center of the flow is a focal point for any migrating salmonid; it helps keep the fish in the main channel.

In the days before flood control and riprap channels, many western rivers braided out over their flat valleys and deltas, creating a complex capillary structure of pathways. Some of these braids were small enough to impede the migration of the fish, making them more susceptible to predation. Those fish that stuck near the main flow made it to the spawning grounds more consistently. Over thousands of generations, steelhead developed a propensity for following the center of the current's flow. At most dams, the center of the flow is in the middle of the dam, where the water pours through the release doors. But the fish ladder is usually off to the side of the dam. The migrating steelhead are driven to jump straight up into the cascading water near the middle of the dam. Eventually the fish tire and wander shoreward, with luck finding the ladder. It takes some fish weeks to discover the ladder, resulting in large clumps of holding fish just downstream of the dam.

Once you've located the initial slowing point and the major upstream obstacles to fish migration, you're in a prime position for selecting an ideal fishing section. You're after a section of river with the most ideal holding water in the smallest area. Compressed holding water means more time casting and less time traveling. When on a potential homewater, I boat, hike, or drive as much of the river above the first slowing point as possible. Such reconnaissance paints a clear picture of what the river offers, helping me pick the best section.

But why pick just one section? Why not fish lots of different water? For the same reasons you want to focus your efforts on a single river, you want to focus your casts on a single section. Steelhead tend to hold in the same spots from week to week and year to year. Knowing the location of a likely holding area is the most cherished knowledge in the sport. Fishing a single section allows you to learn the exact spots that consistently hold steelhead—down to the individual rocks.

Learning where on the river steelhead slow their migration provides a starting point for locating your homewater section.

Hatchery steelhead densities will be highest six pools above and six pools below the point on the river at which they were stocked as smolts.

After seasons of fishing the same section of river, you'll be able to show up on the water and move from known hot spot to know hot spot, showing your fly to this rock and that seam. You'll know the essential subtleties of presenting effectively to each spot: cast here, mend there, swing. Each cast will carry with it a heightened sense of anticipation. Moreover, your time between hookups will shrink drastically. Instead of hooking a fish every few trips, you'll eventually be hooking several fish a trip. This is the reward for concentrating so diligently on a single stretch of a single steelhead river.

If the run of fish on the river you've selected is composed totally or partially of hatchery steelhead, the job of selecting a section to fish is much easier, as hatchery steelhead move quickly back to the specific point where they were acclimated. Slowing points affect them just like they affect wild steelhead, so heavy rapids or a dam will still be worth checking out. But to stay consistently in fish, you need to locate the points of acclimation on the river—usually the place the fish were stocked as smolts. A quick chat at the local fly shop will sometimes reveal the answer. If not, a fast phone call or email to the supplying hatchery should do the trick. Hatchery managers aren't in the business of hiding fish from anglers. Smolts are typically stocked at boat ramps and bridges in popular fishing areas, and the returning adults will hold most densely nearby. A golden number for hatchery steelhead is six: The first six pools above and below the stocking point are likely to hold the highest densities of fish. Focus your energies there.

If the river has a hatchery along its banks that raises the juvenile steelhead prior to their stocking as smolts, it

Brian Marz, professional guide and owner of the McKenzie Angler Fly Shop, scouts for holding steelheading during the middle of the day. Memorizing the specific lies that consistently collect steelhead allows you to "edit" the water and concentrate your angling efforts on the best spots.

too will draw fish. Many ichthyologists believe that steelhead are attracted by the scents of their natal stream, meaning the stream where they spent the first years of their life. A hatchery can be thought of as a mega natal stream, drawing hordes of fish to a very specific location. Most hatcheries filter water from the river, through their tanks, and back into the river. This outflow will attract fish like no other feature on the river. Again, remember the golden number: The first six pools above and below the hatchery's outflow will hold the highest densities of fish.

Once you've located a prime section and are fishing it often and consistently hooking steelhead, you may want to start exploring new sections of the river. Many steelhead bums use their homewater sections as barometers of the fishing, helping them determine how well the steelhead are taking on a given day, before branching out and trying lesser-known sections. If the fishing is difficult on the home section, meaning the fish are slow to cooperate, you'll probably be best off staying there and working the water you know best. But if the fishing is hot, with steelhead consistently chasing flies, you'll be able to explore new sections with confidence.

Techniques for Finding Steelhead

Unfortunately, one of the slowest ways to learn where steelhead hold in your chosen section of river is to fly-fish for them. A fly is just damn hard to present effectively; it requires a slow and attentive pace. Though steelhead can be found efficiently in small streams, where the holding water is limited, mid- to large-size rivers often call for a more radical approach.

Scouting for holding steelhead—without a rod and reel—is one effective technique. When the water is clear, steelhead are often visible holding along the bottom, especially when you are substantially higher than the water's surface. Steelhead bodies will always point upstream and usually appear as glowing ghosts rather than solid blocks of color. The best scouting condition is full sun, when a dark shadow will follow under any steelhead. This shadow is usually easier to see than the actual fish. Employing a quality pair of polarized glasses will help you spot substantially more fish.

The most effective way to scout for steelhead is from a drift boat that is being oared slowly downstream. A boat provides elevation and mobility, the two essential factors in spotting lots of fish. If you pair up with a friend, one of you rowing and the other standing on a forward seat, steelhead will become relatively easy to spot downstream of the boat. Any fish too camouflaged to be seen while holding will certainly become visible as it bolts. Most fish sprint upstream when alarmed; watch for them to zip past you. When you spot fish, memorize their locations for future drifts. Next time, you can put a confident cast to that spot. Some anglers carry a small notepad in which they sketch rough outlines of pools and runs, marking an X every place fish seem to hold.

If a boat isn't available and the river is of small or medium size, scouting from the shore is a good backup. The higher your position on the bank, the better your visibility will be. To spot the most fish, you are best off moving upstream while searching. Doing so will allow you to get closer to holding steelhead, as the fish will be looking upstream. Also, working upriver offers a clear view of the lies that happen to be tucked up under fast water. The view from one of the banks usually is more revealing than the other because of the position of the sun. Locating yourself so as to diminish the sun's glare is worth the effort.

For spotting work, some anglers carry a bag of pebbles. Many times you will see obvious fish, whose location you can memorize. But more often than not, you will see something that merely looks fishy. A quick toss of a small pebble upstream of the fishy object will reveal the answer. A steelhead will flinch, often rising off the bottom slightly. Avoid throwing anything more disruptive than a pebble, which can harass the fish unnecessarily. The point isn't to spook steelhead, but to trick the fish into revealing itself.

Spotting fish from a boat or bank is effective, but neither guarantees a decisive view of the river's contents. Steelhead are sneaky little buggers. Sometimes they'll hold so tight to a boulder that they're invisible from above. If you've ever caught one out of shin-deep pocket water, you know how elusive they can be. No matter the skill of the spotter, some fish won't be visible from above. The only way to get a clear view of the river's contents is to complete a snorkeling assessment. By donning a mask, snorkel, and any cheap wet suit at least four millimeters thick, you can obtain a precise assessment of what a section of river has to offer. Fisheries biologists make such floats frequently, counting the numbers of juvenile fish in a river. As you float, look for adult fish moving out of your way and note their locations.

Besides looking for the fish themselves, a lot can be learned by searching a river for certain structural characteristics. Winter steelhead, for instance, are attracted to the troughs in otherwise even runs. A depression of six

inches or more that is located just upstream from heavy water is absolutely prime holding water. But finding these troughs in the winter is nearly impossible because of the high water. Many great winter steelhead streams are just trickles in the summer, so a trip to your section of river in August can pay huge dividends come February.

Other anglers can be a great help to locating common fish lies. Some clearly have a sense for the river. Such fishers often move from spot to spot quickly, putting a few casts here, a few there. They always seem decisive in their actions. When you see such anglers on your section, be they gear plunkers or fly fishers, watch carefully. Study where they lay their casts, where they seem most alert during the drifts or swings. Whether they're competent anglers or not, pay exquisite attention anytime anybody hooks a fish. Mark the spot in your mind for a future trip. No matter how discouraging it is to see others on "your" section of water, watching them can help you learn the river in less time. If you're lucky enough to see a fly-fishing guide on the water, study his or her movements. Guide boats in most states are required to have marks clearly identifying them. When you spot a guide, pay double attention not only to where the client is casting, but also to where the guide is looking. Many of my guide friends have eagle vision, regular ospreys with fly rods, and much of the time while the client is fishing, they're looking for fish. If they stare at a spot for a bit, likely they've seen fish there before. Remember the location. They know the river like you hope to someday. Take advantage of the free lesson.

Better yet, hire a guide. Fishing with a guide is by far the fastest way to learn your section of river. These people have years of knowledge on that section and have a powerful impetus for knowing exactly where the fish hold—their baby's next meal depends on it. The dollars spent on the guide are a sound investment, if only in terms of gas money. In a day spent on the river, you can learn a decade's worth of information, especially if you play your cards right.

Most important, hire the right guide. Guiding in steelhead country is a fly-by-night affair for some. There is no talent or knowledge requirement for getting a guiding license. To ensure that you've found a quality guide, ask at least the following questions: How long have you been guiding fly fishers? How long have you been guiding on this river? How many trips did you run last year? Do you have a list of references I can call? Using the outfitter services of a local fly shop can help filter out the hacks from the pros.

Once you've found the right guide, you can be up front with him or her. A fast way to learn a river is to let the guide know you're more interested in learning where the fish hold than you are in catching fish that day. Saying such a thing takes the pressure off the guide to produce hookups, a pressure that often requires serious fishing at the expense of substantive learning. Most guides are willing to share the locations of some prime holding lies in exchange for a low-stress day on the river. When the guide points out a hot spot, say a trough in the middle of a steady riffle, ask what techniques tend to hook fish there. Ask where he or she would recommend standing. Ask at what water level and time of day fish tend to hold there. These are the crucial details you need to know. The money spent on a good guide can pay huge dividends for years to come.

Besides scouting the section, watching other anglers, and hiring a guide, there is another effective way to learn the intricacies of your section of river. But it isn't for everyone. Nevertheless, many of the most successful chromeheads in the Northwest do it.

Fly fishing requires such a slow and methodical pace in order to cover the water effectively that it isn't the most efficient angling tactic for learning a new midsize to large river. If you want to gain knowledge of the water faster, and in turn catch more steelhead on your fly rod, fishing light gear is a very successful way to do so—especially in the winter, when steelhead can be hard to spot from the bank. By light gear, I'm referring to spinners and jigs fished off a common spinning reel with 6- or 8-pound-test line, not bottom-dredging bait or pulling plugs. Light gear is able to cover huge amounts of water effectively in a fraction of the time it would take a fly rod to do the same. In fact, a well-fished jig can arguably cover an entire run faster than any other technique. Employing a spinner or jig is by no means easy. But the skills required in fly fishing are readily applicable to these techniques, meaning in just a trip or two, an intermediate fly fisher will be able to successfully take steel-

The money invested on a guided trip can produce lucrative dividends in the long haul, especially on big rivers.

In the United States, the federal government protects anglers' rights to access some rivers. Learning which rivers qualify can help you find unpressured steelhead.

head on the spinner or jig. Spending a little time on your section of river with light gear will teach you notebook-fuls of valuable information—quickly.

U.S. River Access Laws

A note on river access laws might prove helpful as you explore your homewater. Many streams and rivers in steelhead country flow through private property, especially farm- and ranchland. Extensive lengths of river are completely bordered by private property, excluding those anglers without a landowner friend. But ubiquitous No Trespassing signs can work in your favor, if you're aware of the subtleties surrounding U.S. river access law.

In 1845, the U.S. Supreme Court ruled in Pollard v. Hagan that any new state admitted to the Union had "rights of sovereignty, jurisdiction, and eminent domain," including rights of ownership to "navigable waterways." This decision, known as the Equal Footing Doctrine, guaranteed public access to any stream or river deemed "navigable" by the state, so long as that state was admitted to the Union after 1845.

In 1892, a second decision, this one in Illinois Central Railroad v. Illinois, ruled that "navigable waterways"

couldn't be bought and sold like a piece of dry land. Rather, the state held the waterways in trust and could use that trust only for the public's own good.

The decisions of 1845 and 1892 have profound impacts on steelheaders today. Our navigable rivers are owned by the state and cannot be sold to private parties, no matter what they're willing to pay. The only thing the state can do with the waterway is help the public get more economic and recreational use from it, such as by building boat ramps and trail systems. And more important, these two decisions guarantee access to the waterway, no matter who owns the land surrounding it.

The first catch in the law is the term "navigable waterway." If this truly meant "runable in a drift boat," eager steelheaders would line up to prove that any river in the West could be handled. Unfortunately, "navigable waterway" means a river deemed boatable by the state. And there is a substantial disconnect between what anglers consider navigable and what the state considers navigable. The state feels profound pressures to keep many rivers classified as not navigable. Navigable status restricts the ability of big landowners to exclude the public from what some of them see as their land. Many fine steelhead streams are currently owned by big re-source-extraction companies, which have powerful lobbyists at the state capitals. A lot of money supports the effort to keep these rivers closed to the public. As a result, not every river that can be run in a boat has earned the status of navigable. But occasionally victories are won. Most notably, in 2002, the Sandy was deemed navigable from its mouth upriver 37.5 miles, thanks to the hard work of angling and whitewater advocacy groups. To determine whether your homewater is a navigable river, contact your state Department of Water Resources.

The second catch in the law is that not all states are in complete compliance with the federal decisions. Some states have laws that contradict the federal statutes. Though these inconsistencies may be ironed out in time, you probably don't want to be the catalyst for change. Again, check with your state Department of Water Resources for accurate information pertaining to your area.

If your homewater is a navigable river—at least the section you want to fish—and your state is in compliance with the Equal Footing Doctrine, you're in luck. You have unfettered access to the river up to the high-water mark, which is the top of the normal channel. If private property borders the section you want to fish, simply drop down to the water at a public bridge, and you can move upstream or down as far as your legs will take you. Just be sure to stay within the normal channel.

Many times, at least in the areas I fish, landowners will post the stream's bank with No Trespassing signs, even on a navigable river. On one river, a rancher dared to put a fence across the water. The barbed wire didn't survive the weekend. I've had more than one encounter with self-righteous landowners, but a calm and kind explanation of the laws has won them over each time. Knowing the name of the Supreme Court decisions certainly helps. Before ignoring a No Trespassing sign, it would be wise to consult with the landowner, if only to remind him or her that this is a navigable river.

The advantages of the Equal Footing Doctrine to steelheaders are numerous. Knowing the ins and outs of the law can help open up miles of fishable water.

CHAPTER 3

Keeping Tabs on Your Homewater

How to Determine When the Fishing Will Be at Its Best

Besides learning where steelhead hold in your homewater, another crucial step to consistently catching fish is deciphering how your river interacts with the larger world. Knowing details such as when the fish arrive in the river, how much rain is needed to raise the levels, and how much time after a freshet is needed to clear the river will help you not only come to understand your river more fully—a noble goal for its own sake—but also focus your fishing time on the most productive moments. An intimate knowledge of the river and its interactions with the world helps you spend your fishing time when the fishing is at its best.

For many serious steelheaders, the most satisfying relationship they have with their homewater is the one that allows them to know what is happening on the water by simply checking a weather report. Such knowledge is not only deeply satisfying, but also of utmost utility. Most of us don't have the luxury of fishing more than once or twice a week. Some of us can't get out more than once or twice a month. With river time so valuable, it's best allotted wisely. After a couple seasons of keeping an attentive eye on the weather, the river, and the runs of fish themselves, you'll be able to determine the best fishing times with increasing accuracy. More and more often, you'll find yourself casting to aggressive fish.

Many chromeheads keep logbooks of their homewaters, fishing journals of a sort that allow them to record the data they feel are important. Some employ calendars instead of traditional notebooks, filling in the data in the daily spaces provided. Such a document becomes infinitely helpful for its ability to predict when your section of river will contain steelhead. A quick look at last year's records will reveal not only the dates you hooked your first and last fish, but also how the river responded when certain weather conditions arrived, such as freezing air temperatures or heavy rains. And more important, the logbook will reveal how long it took for the fishing to pick back up after the bad weather. Next time a similar storm hits, you'll be able to look to your journal for guidance. Eventually you'll be able to stand in your yard with a hand in the air and make prophetic statements: "Barometer's rising; rain will stop tonight; the river will fall to 2,300 cfs by morning." Translation: The fishing will be gangbusters at dawn.

The Valuable Data

Steelheaders as a group seem to have an attraction to data collection. And each chromehead has pet data, things he or she thinks are important to document. Some people, for instance, find monitoring the wave size at the

Above: Monitoring how your homewater responds to changing weather conditions allows you to arrive streamside when the odds of catching fish are best.

river mouth to aid in predicting when fish will enter their homewaters. Others believe the moon's phase is vital to predicting how fast steelhead will move upriver. But a few items are essential to measure for all steelheaders, as they consistently help keep you fishing when the fishing is at its best.

All steelhead rivers have periods when fish are present in high numbers and others when the river is nearly barren. Even on those rare streams where fresh steelhead enter every month of the year, a few weeks exist when there aren't fishable numbers in the system. Keeping an eye on the movements of the fish will help you arrive streamside at the right time. Some of the most interesting data to document is the date of the first hookup in your homewater section—with luck, you'll be the one doing the catching. But before that's a realistic prospect, some time with an ear to the ground will be helpful. The fishery management agencies of most states and provinces keep catch-rate data, either the number of steelhead caught per month or, more helpfully, the number of steelhead caught per angler-hour per month. If your homewater is a well-known steelhead

river, catch-rate data can give you a clear sense of when fishable numbers arrive in the stream.

If your homewater is not a well-known river, your own reconnaissance will provide the most accurate information. Instead of fishing as you normally might, covering the water carefully, try hitting only known hot spots, those places that consistently collect lots of fish. The main objective on such recon trips isn't to fish, per se—it's to determine if steelhead are present. Talk to other anglers. If people seem to be catching fish regularly, you'll be able to cast your fly with more confidence.

Fly shops are an excellent source of run-timing data, especially if the shop happens to function as an outfitter for local guides. When the fish are in, the guides will immediately let the outfitters know. But fly shops in steelhead country are usually manned by people like us—chromeheads. If you happen to ask about the counter jockey's homewater, you might not receive a straight answer. An afternoon spent streamside talking with other anglers will consistently provide the best information.

However you discover fish are being caught, whether through your own reconnaissance or at a fly shop, you'll

Knowing the precise dates when steelhead enter your homewater helps you consistently find bright and eager fish.

want to mark the date on your calendar. And then you'll also want to look at some other information, namely preceding weather events and fishing reports or dam counts from the lower river, if they're available. The goal is to determine when the fish began moving upstream and how long it took them to arrive in your homewater section.

Steelhead don't just enter a river for no good reason. Typically an environmental change helps bring them into the freshwater flows. A good rainstorm is frequently the motivating factor. When rains start, the rivers' rate of flow in cubic feet per second (cfs) climbs, and steelhead are instinctually driven to move. High flows mean that tough rapids will be easier to ascend and risks of predation will be lower. Thousands of years of evolution has selected for steelhead that take advantage of such conditions. If you know the first steelhead were caught on June 7, for instance, and a freshet caused the river to bump on June 1, you have a pretty clear sense that it took the fish six days to get upstream. If the lower river has a dam with a fish ladder and a counter tracking the number of fish passing, as on some inland rivers, you can rely on the fish counts for highly accurate information. Knowing how long it takes steelhead to reach your section of river puts you one step closer to knowing exactly when your river will be fishing best. Next year, when a similar weather event arrives, you'll know precisely when to free up some fishing time.

One of my regular haunts flows through Oregon's rugged Coast Range. Winter steelhead begin stacking up in tidewater just before Thanksgiving. The first time the river climbs above 1,200 cfs after Turkey Day, the waiting fish rush upstream. After keeping nearly a decade of journal entries on this river, I know my homewater section will be worth fishing eleven days later. Such knowledge allows me to give the water a proper, confident plying when I arrive—and is an important part of consistently catching steelhead.

Other valuable data to collect are the conditions of your homewater itself, such as the river level, temperature, and clarity. Excellent data can be gathered on many rivers from the comfort of home. The National Oceanic and Atmospheric Administration (NOAA) and United States Geological Survey (USGS) websites offer frequently updated river level information on many streams and in some cases also report the water temperature and clarity. If your homewater isn't a stream included, pick a nearby stream in the same drainage to use as a relative indicator of local conditions.

The water level of a river affects the fishing in three ways. First, it determines which holding lies the fish will be using. Steelhead hold in certain types of water. What attracts a fish to a specific trough, for instance, might be the current speed. But as the water level changes, the current speed will change too. Eventually it will cease to be a good place to hold. Second, the river level determines which holding lies will be accessible to the fly. Not all holding water can be reached with a fly. Sometimes the overhead current is too fast or the lie too deep. Third, water level (in conjunction with water clarity) determines how aggressive holding steelhead will be. When the water is low, especially in smaller rivers, steelhead tend to be less aggressive. The risk of predation increases as the water level lowers—there are simply fewer places for the steelhead to hide. Conversely, when the water level rises, steelhead frequently become less cautious and more aggressive. Every river has an ideal water level, the point when aggressive steelhead hold in predictable places that are reachable with a fly.

If water temperature and clarity data aren't available on the NOAA or USGS sites, monitor these factors when you go fishing. Simply sticking a thermometer in moving water for a minute will provide an accurate reading of the water temperature. Steelhead, being cold-blooded, are profoundly influenced by the surrounding water temperature. Every strain of steelhead reacts differently to excessively cold and warm conditions. But by monitoring the temperature in relation to the quality of the fishing over time, you'll come to understand the ideal temperature range for the fish in your homewater. To test clarity, try dropping a heavily weighted pink fly, attached to your leader, into a deep pool. How deep the fly goes before disappearing will give you an adequate sense of how much sediment is in the water—in other words, the water clarity. Too little or too much sediment in the water negatively affects the fishing. Drifting sediment can help calm nervous fish, prompting them to respond more aggressively to a passing fly. Every stream and its steelhead act differently in this regard. Some glacially fed rivers fish best when the clarity is four feet. Some spring-fed rivers fish best when the water clarity is ten feet. By monitoring the clarity of the water and the quality of the fishing over time, you'll develop a sense of when your steelhead are most responsive to the fly.

Once you've collected information on river level, temperature, and clarity, a quick check of recent weather patterns will give you a sense of what it took to create those river conditions. Every river responds to a rainstorm in a different way. Some rivers rise and cloud up immediately. Others don't rise or cloud up until rain has fallen for days. Rivers also clear at different rates. Some flow like gin two days after a blowout; others take weeks to settle. Determining exactly how fast your river responds to weather changes will help you time your fishing excursions appropriately.

Water temperature is a highly influential factor on steelhead behavior. And though nothing can replace an actual temperature reading in the stream, monitoring the air temperature in conjunction with the water temperature can, over time, allow you to predict the water temperature with increasing accuracy. Luckily, you can collect air temperature data from home by checking a simple weather report for the area. If you watch river temperatures closely, you'll likely notice that they are profoundly affected by rain. Cold rainstorms from the northwest frequently drop water temperatures out of the ideal range, but warm southern rainstorms often pull them back into the ideal range. Hitting the river as the temperature is rising can result in epic fishing.

Steelhead respond to changes in the river's level, temperature, and clarity in a generally consistent manner within a river. The consistent pattern experienced on one river won't necessarily correspond to another, however. Learning how the fish in your homewater are affected by environmental conditions is key to reliably putting steelhead on the beach.

The details of how your homewater's fish react to environmental conditions can be learned only through experience, but some general guidelines will prove helpful.

The water level has a profound effect on which holding lies steelhead use. By understanding how steelhead respond to various water levels, you'll know where to concentrate your angling efforts. NATE KOENIGSKNECHT

Keeping track of how steelhead respond to changing environmental conditions will help you predict where to find eager fish on any given day.

When the water is murky and rising or when the water temperature is falling, steelhead usually become unresponsive to flies. When the water is clearing and dropping or when the water temperature is climbing, steelhead usually become aggressive.

For some serious steelheaders, keeping detailed records of their homewaters is a compulsion. For others, it's a more casual pursuit. But either way, keeping records over time, and occasionally reviewing those records, will radically affect your catch rate, allowing you to consistently put yourself on the water when the fishing is at its best.

Besides, keeping close tabs on a homewater means that at least one angler is paying attention and will notice sudden changes, such as sediment increases as a result of unsafe logging practices. On a macroscopic scale, the phenomenon of informed citizens keeping an eye on small sections of water ensures a critical mass of vocal riverkeepers fighting for the overall health of steelhead country.

PART II
The Fish

"All salmonids must be saluted for bearing upon their collective shoulders the burden of generations of contradictory theorizing as to what they eat and how they are best persuaded to give up their lives and freedom."

THOMAS McGUANE, *THE LONGEST SILENCE*

A ten-pound buck from an October tailout.

eter and Dave picked me up in the 3 A.M. darkness, a light rain splattering on the black sidewalk. I tossed my pack and rod tubes in Dave's truck and took a seat in the back.

It was mid-January, and we had three hours of hard mountain driving to the trailhead and another hour and a half of hiking after that before we'd reach our destination, a small stream tucked in the safe harbor of a wilderness area. We'd made one journey to the place before, the prior season, and each of us had hooked our biggest fish of the year. Peter pulled his fish from a riffle that sat in a placid meadow section. Dave wrangled his from the deep water above a quarter-mile set of rapids. Mine, the smallest of the three, came from pocketwater, a brute I followed through a logjam—clicking off the drag and threading the rod through the sunken timbers—before finally landing him a hundred yards downstream. As I slid his silver side onto the gravel, a ruffed grouse drummed from a nearby thicket.

"How big do you think these fish average?" I asked. "Seems to me they went thirty-five inches last time."

"In my memory, the average was closer to thirty-six inches," Peter said. "Of course, it's impossible to determine an average with such a limited sample."

Dave shook his head. "They average big. What else do you need to know? What I want to know is how they got so big in the first place," Dave said. "Why so many hogs in one stream and not in the next river over?"

Peter was confident: "The heavy rapids. A thousand years of evolutionary pressure selecting for the strongest of the strong."

"Rumor has it," I cut in, "a baitfisher lived at the mouth for fifty years and killed every fish he caught under thirty inches. A World War I vet with shell shock."

Dave licked his thumb and wiped the speedometer's glass, removing a smear. "I'll go with that answer."

When we arrived at the trailhead, the mountains were still buried in darkness. We tossed on our packs, snatched our rod tubes, and turned up the trail. Dave set a determined pace, flashing his headlamp over the muddy path every few minutes for reassurance.

Peter broke the silence of the hike. "I don't buy it. No guy, baitfisher or not, could affect the size of the fish like that. It's got to be the rapids."

"You're probably right," I said, pacing the words between breaths. "But there are plenty of other rivers with heavy rapids and no huge fish."

"True, but do we spend an hour and a half hiking to them?"

"Touché."

"B.S.," Dave said from the front. "The right dude could do it. Keep that smoker full season after season, on a small stream like this. It could get done."

About an hour after we entered the wilderness area, the trail dropped down to the river's side. The dawn's fuzzy glow gave shape to the splashing water. A blacktail buck watched us from a small meadow across the stream, his antlers black as sticks. We all tossed a quick glance in his direction, but no one voiced the sighting. The stream's dark water was too close.

Dave crawled into his waders and had his rod rigged with a sink-tip twice as fast as Peter and me. "I'm going to take this run, unless y'all want to roll for it."

"You'd better be tied into one before I'm dressed," Peter said.

We spent the morning hopscotching upstream, covering miles of prime water. But by noon, we still hadn't felt a bump. Besides a couple dark fish in the shallows, the river seemed devoid of life. We met up on a narrow bridge over the water, just the three of us and an empty wilderness valley.

"We're doing everything we should." Peter watched an osprey circling above.

"We jinxed it in the car," I said. "All that talk of big fish, 'nothing under thirty-five inches.' . . . What were we thinking?"

Dave took a bite of his sandwich and spoke between chews. "Who needs a jinx not to catch fish? We're steelheading."

Peter seemed to see something in the water. His gaze suddenly focused, serious. "Have you guys hit that tailout?"

We shook our heads no. "Doesn't look as good as the next one downstream," Dave said. "And I pounded that one."

Without a word, Peter rushed off the bridge and waded into the fast water below us. He shot his line skyward, dropping an egg pattern and an indicator near the far shore. The fly dropped to the bottom instantly, and after one stack mend, the rig dead drifted flawlessly toward a midstream rock in the tailout.

Dave stopped chewing.

The drift passed on the far side of the rock, along a small section of deep water there, then floated out of the pool and into the rapids. Another cast put the flies two feet closer, set to pass along the near side of the rock. A tricky swirling current caught the line, twisting it, threatening to ruin the entire drift. But with a subtle and precise mend, Peter flicked the line out of harm's way, and the flies continued toward the rock.

"That guy can fish, can't he?" Dave said.

This time, as the cast neared the rock, the yellow indicator slipped underwater. Peter delivered the hook with a strong raise of the rod.

Instead of the deep bowing arcs of a large steelhead's violent headshakes, Peter's rod showed delicate twitches in the front half of the blank. A plate of chrome flashed underwater, and then a small fish—no longer than the distance from an elbow to a fingertip—punched through the surface. We rushed down to find Peter cradling the chromer. With a green back and glowing red cheek, it looked just like the huge steelhead we'd caught on the river the year before, minus a dozen pounds or so.

"Is that a half-pounder?" I asked, not believing my eyes.

"Sure is," Peter said. "Fresh from the salt."

Dave took another huge bite of his sandwich, crumbs landing in his beard. "That sure f——s up your average, now don't it?"

Steelhead are enigmatic fish. The simple facts of their life cycle can defy the bounds of our comprehension. And when they pulse their way upstream, mystery is only a riffle behind.

Thanks to the catch rate steelhead offer even the most determined angler, each landed fish only spawns new perplexing questions. Whereas trout give themselves so freely to the fly that an angler can quickly come to conclusions about the fish's ideal food, preferred holding water, even average size, steelhead remain elusive enough to resist such conclusions.

Besides, conclusions kill the glorious wonder of speculation. They steal the mystery from the natural world and replace it with categories of comparably boring facts. Steelhead, and steelheading, dodge conclusions like no other freshwater fish. The river will give up only enough fish to keep us obsessed, never enough to result in any solid determinations.

What steelheading offers is an endless arena for questioning. Each cast is a question: Does a willing fish hold in that water? And every take breeds more questions: Why did the fish want that fly? Why did it choose that lie? Such self-sustaining, self-generating questions keep steelhead tucked in the dark recesses of the unknowable—and keep steelheaders gleefully casting our flashlights. ■

CHAPTER 4

The "Typical" *Oncorhynchus mykiss*

A Brief Life History

What is known about steelhead can be summarized quickly. And the story starts not with steelhead, but with rainbow trout. The rainbow trout, via genetic analysis, has been revealed to be nothing of the sort. A rainbow is actually a type of salmon, as is the cutthroat. The genus name of both rainbows and cutthroats is no longer *Salmo,* the genus of trout. Instead, it's now *Oncorhynchus,* a designation shared by all Pacific salmon. Some rainbows stay in fresh water their entire lives, much like the landlocked kokanee of inland lakes. Landlocked rainbows live off freshwater foods and spawn near where they feed. These are the fish we catch all over the continent, from stocked ponds in New Jersey to fertile streams in New Mexico to deep lakes in British Columbia. But not all rainbow trout are of the landlocked variety. Due to factors ichthyologists don't quite understand, some rainbows are inclined to travel to the ocean. It is these oceangoing rainbows that we call steelhead.

Only two of the six subspecies of rainbow trout have anadromous forms: the coastal rainbow *(O. mykiss irideus)* and the redband rainbow *(O. mykiss gairdneri).* Coastal rainbows inhabit streams as far south as San Diego County; as far north as Port Heiden, Alaska; and as far west as Russia's Kamchatka Peninsula. Meanwhile, redband rainbows inhabit the Columbia River drainage,

east of the Cascades and north to the Finlay River in British Columbia.

Steelhead are simply rainbows that went to the sea, and as such, they actually share more genetic material with the landlocked rainbows in their natal streams than they do with other steelhead from distant drainages. For instance, a steelhead from the Clearwater River shares more genetic material with a Clearwater rainbow than with a Grande Ronde steelhead. In fact, recent genetic analysis of resident trout and anadromous steelhead from the Deschutes River found no genetic distinctions between the two, whereas similar analyses of steelhead from two different rivers do reveal a genetic distinction.

Such similarity between the resident trout and the anadromous steelhead in a river suggests the distinction between the two so adamantly applied by anglers isn't as clear-cut as we may believe. Recent analyses of the otoliths—tiny ear bones that can reveal details of the parents' life cycles—from several trout and steelhead in the Babine River revealed the shocking truth: One of the twenty-four steelhead examined had a resident rainbow

Above: This steelhead spent three full years at sea, likely traveling as far as the Asian coastline, before returning to its natal stream. PETER BETJEMANN

trout as a mother, and two of the nine resident trout examined had a steelhead mother. Thus the steelhead we see spawning in a river may actually produce resident trout. And likewise, the trout turning up the gravel may produce steelhead. Equally interesting, ichthyologists have documented repeated cases where female steelhead actually spawned with large male resident trout, further blurring the line between the two forms of fish. Evidence for such blurring dates all the way back to an 1883 stocking in New Zealand. Nearly all the rainbows on the islands today are descendants of steelhead eggs from the San Francisco Bay's Sonoma Creek, yet no oceangoing steelhead ever emerged. Such bizarre life history details are but a few examples of the enrapturing enigmas that follow steelhead—enigmas that can occupy steelheaders' minds when they should be, say, working.

The Steelhead Life Cycle

The life cycle of the steelhead, whether of the *irideus* or *gairdneri* subspecies, has three phases: the freshwater phase, the open-water phase, and the spawning phase. Each is characterized by unique features, threats, and unanswered questions.

The Freshwater Phase

The freshwater phase begins the moment the young steelhead, still in egg form, are deposited in the springtime gravel. Once the fish hatch from the egg—or, more accurately, grow out of it—they are called alevins. These awkward little fish are attached at the neck to the rich yolk sacs of the eggs and look like a trout that has had its neck superglued to an orange playground ball. After two to four months of living such a life, the alevins use up the yolk and are forced from the gravel into the river. At this point, they are called fry. Fry are one to one and a half inches long, with a solid black line running up the front ridge of the dorsal fin. These fish spend their time living in the tenderly currented areas along the edge of the stream, depending on small insects for the bulk of their food. When they reach three to four inches, they're considered parr. Parr have white-tipped dorsal fins and circular "parr" marks on top of their heads; both characteristics differentiate them from salmon parr. It is at this stage in a steelhead's life that it is most dependent on submerged debris, such as logjams and beaver dams, for protection from predators.

Steelhead share more genetic information with the resident rainbows of their natal streams than they do with the steelhead of other drainages.

Come the high water of spring, smolts move downriver in massive groups.

Some juvenile steelhead migrate to the sea after spending only two years in fresh water. Others decide to migrate after four years. The amount of time the young fish spends in the fresh water depends on the fertility of the fish's natal stream. For instance, in the northern end of *irideus*'s range, where the rivers have their origins largely in glaciers and run through a landscape characterized by granite, the rivers tend not to be very fertile. Such landscapes produce rivers characterized by cold and barren water conditions, the type of conditions that don't facilitate rapid piscatorial growth. The juvenile steelhead in these infertile areas often spend up to four years in fresh water before heading downstream to the ocean. Fish in the southern end of *gairdneri*'s range, where the rivers tend to be warmer and more fertile, spend less time in fresh water as juveniles, usually descending in their second year.

Independent of the time it takes, the first spring in which a steelhead finds itself six to eight inches in length, it begins smoltification, a process of physical change that prepares the young steelhead for life in the salt water. One of the more noticeable changes a smolt undergoes is the loss of its trout coloring in exchange for a silvery finish. Smolts are eager little buggers that move in big schools down the river, feeding with abandon to prepare for the demands placed on them in the dangerous estuaries. If you've ever swung flies in the early spring, you've likely encountered a barrage of smolts. They sneak up on you. One minute you're minding your own business, wondering why no fish are striking, and the next you can't keep the things off your line. As the last thing steelheaders want to do is make life for smolts any harder, you'd be doing the population a service if you moved to new water once the smolts showed up.

The movement of smolts to the salt water is an event that draws many predators. Ospreys, seals, and an assortment of other piscivores show up annually in the spring for the predictable and easy meal the smolts offer. Unfortunately, current hatchery practices have only encouraged these predators, and at the expense of wild steelhead populations. When the big schools of smolts move downriver, they collect other smolts that were holding in smaller groups. Because hatcheries get such small returns for the number of smolts they put in the rivers, usually less than a 1 percent return rate, the hatchery must stock huge numbers of smolts into the river. These giant waves of fish move downstream, collecting any wild fish along the way, and then deliver the smolts in a big wave to the awaiting predators. Over the years, the great numbers of hatchery fish have supported a much larger population of oceangoing predators than would naturally exist there. And as hatchery smolts tend to be put into the river during short windows of time, all these predators show up at once, claws ready. The end result is added pressure on the already burdened wild smolts. Luckily, many hatchery managers are aware of this problem and are working on ways of avoiding it in the future, including more challenging hatchery environments for the parr that will produce a more capable smolt, a higher return rate, and eventually smaller numbers of smolts dumped into the rivers.

As if migrating smolts didn't already have enough to deal with, human-made dams provide another hurdle. The dams' reservoirs are killers for young fish because of the unnatural loss of a steady current. The smolts use the current to find their way to the ocean, and once in the lake behind a dam, they are often unable to find the outlet. The more time they spend in this slow water, the more susceptible they are to predation from reservoir fish and the birds that collect there. Moreover, the decreased levels of oxygen in the stale water can actually suffocate the delicate smolts. Dams also tend to funnel steelhead through the turbines, as the fish try to follow the current when it is available, and a dam's current typically leads to the turbine's biting jaws. In their calculations, Northwest fisheries biologists estimate that each dam along the Columbia, the biggest steelhead river in the world, kills 10 percent of the descending smolts. With at least nine dams to transcend, every upper Columbia smolt making it to the ocean is a lucky smolt indeed.

The Open-Water Phase

The open-water phase of the steelhead's life is shrouded in mystery. Until the latter part of the twentieth century, biologists believed that steelhead didn't travel far from their native estuaries. Some thought the fish fed within two miles of fresh water. But research done since then paints a drastically different picture.

We now realize that once in the ocean, steelhead travel thousands of miles. In one study that used the help of both commercial and sportfishers, steelhead were marked at sea with small numbered tags. When the fish were caught months later by freshwater anglers, their natal streams were located. The results were eye-opening. Steelhead tagged off the Alaskan coast turned up in Oregon streams. Even more impressive, smolts implanted with small wire tags showed up along the Aleutian Islands. And as if these examples weren't enough, a six-pound steelhead marked by Japanese researchers off their coast turned up in a Columbia River tributary. Likely the fish move up the U.S. West Coast, along the Aleutian Islands, and finally to the Russian shores, following their prey of herring, shrimp, and other high-energy foods. Young steelhead grow rapidly in the ocean environment, putting on inches faster than seems possible to an angler familiar with the slow growth rates of streambound trout.

Interestingly, little is known about the migrations of Kamchatka steelhead. The fish there are known for their size and strength, but little to nothing is known about how they gain that size and strength. Are they feeding along Asian shores? Maybe the Canadian coast? Or are these fish striking out for waters unknown? Conclusive answers have yet to be found. Likewise, little is known about the steelhead of South America. Some fishers familiar with the area claim the fish stay near their natal streams, but we've heard that argument before. Could these fish be feeding off New Zealand's coast? Or maybe even Uruguay's? Why not?

Such questions are of paramount importance. If steelhead are to be saved from human threats, their time in open water must be protected. Any plan to save an endangered stock of Californian steelhead, for instance, must include protections along British Columbia's coast. And maybe, if Californian steelhead frequent the Asian coast in great enough numbers, their protections will have to extend that far.

Steelhead spend varying amounts of time in the ocean, ranging from a few months to five years, before returning to their natal streams. Half-pounders, immature *irideus* steelhead typically ranging from fifteen to nineteen inches, spend the least amount of time in the ocean. The smolt may enter salt water in April and be back in just as little as sixty days. Half-pounders are possible in any run of *irideus* steelhead, independent of their locality, but the runs of California and southern Oregon contain large numbers of these eager fish.

Half-pounders are immature irideus *steelhead. Every healthy* irideus *run contains a few half-pounders, but nowhere are they as prolific as in the streams of northern California and southern Oregon.*

Steelhead typically spend one or more complete years at sea. A fish that returns after one year is usually twenty to twenty-four inches. A fish that returns after two years is usually twenty-five to thirty-two inches. A fish that returns after three years is usually thirty-three to thirty-six inches. And a whopper that returns after four or five years will be in excess of thirty-six inches, possibly forty. Steelhead over the forty-inch mark are caught each year throughout their range. A forty-inch fish can be twenty or thirty pounds or even more. Steelhead just short of fifty pounds have been caught in tribal nets in Washington and British Columbia. The sport angling record is forty-two pounds, two ounces. It is certainly the *irideus* fish that attain these enormous sizes. *Gairdneri* steelhead top out at twenty-five pounds, with most fish being substantially smaller. The difference may have something to do with the length of the migration. *Gairdneri* fish must make long trips up their streams to find spawning water. Such an endurance race may select for fish less than twenty-five pounds.

In technical writings on both steelhead and steelhead streams, the age of the fish is represented in a specific manner. Each fish is given two numbers: The first is the amount of time the fish spent in fresh water, and the second in salt water. For instance, a 2.1 (or 2/1 fish; some people use the period, others use the slash) spent two years in fresh water and one year in salt. Various other marks can identify other features of the fish's life history. For instance, a plus, as in 2.1+, means the fish spent two years in fresh water and one and a half in salt.

Individual river systems select for fish that are most perfectly suited to that river environment. This fact, coupled with the varying ocean conditions experienced by different fish, results in the wide range of steelhead sizes. Rivers near the southern end of the range tend to select for smaller steelhead, the 2.1 and 2.2 fish, while rivers near the northern end of the range tend to select for bigger steelhead, the 4.3 or 4.4+ fish. But on a healthy river, there is a wide range of sizes in adult steelhead. A half-pounder could be caught on one cast and a four-salt fish (a steelhead that spent four years at sea) the next.

Traditional hatchery practices have long selected for fish that grow quickly and return consistently. Because of this, hatchery steelhead often appear as if they were cut to shape with a cookie cutter. Most hatchery steelhead are 2.2 fish and range in size from twenty-six to

Hatchery steelhead are typically marked by clipping the adipose fin. The fish on the left is of hatchery origin; the fish on the right is native.

thirty inches, although these sizes can vary depending on the strain used by the hatchery. Also, most hatchery steelhead—especially those on short streams—enter the river in the beginning of the run, thanks to years of hatchery personnel grabbing all the fish they need from the first returners. From the hatchery's perspective, grabbing the breeders early ensured enough stock for future smolt stockings. If they waited and selected fish from throughout the run, the hatchery might end up falling short of its quota. But as a consequence, hatchery steelhead have become highly predictable. This early return of hatchery fish does have an advantage from a conservation point of view. Statistically, early-returning steelhead are more likely to be caught before spawning, hence helping keep inferior hatchery genes out of the redds. But of course, not all returning hatchery fish are caught by anglers.

Moreover, traditional hatchery practices have eroded the quality of the wild steelhead, not only on the rivers where hatchery fish are stocked, but also on neighboring rivers where stray hatchery fish frequently wander. Traditional hatchery practices favor those steelhead stocks that grow most quickly and can survive the arduous fry-parr experience inside the hatchery's cement tanks. On many rivers, hatcheries have used steelhead from hundreds of miles away as the breeding stock. For instance, Skamania steelhead, from Washington's Skamania River, developed

a reputation for their ability to survive in the hatchery and put on weight once at sea. Thanks to these traits, Skamania-strain steelhead are now found all over the West and are even common in Great Lakes steelhead programs.

Stocking out-of-basin fish in a river with a wild run has profound impacts on the health of the native fish. Each river is different, tossing unique challenges at the steelhead that inhabit it. Over thousands of years of adaptations, the steelhead native to a river become especially suited to that stream. These adaptations allow the stocks to survive drought years, flood years, heat waves, cold snaps, and other catastrophic natural events. And from an angler's point of view, these adaptations ensure two important characteristics: that fish enter the river over many different months, providing a longer season, and that they are of varying sizes, with some steelhead being tremendously large. Also, wild steelhead carry a well-earned reputation for fighting harder than their hatchery cousins.

But when out-of-basin fish are stocked in a river, these advantageous adaptations become diluted. Not all returning hatchery steelhead are caught by anglers. Many survive and end up spawning with wild fish in the spring, ensuring that the offspring will be less suited for survival. Because juvenile hatchery steelhead have their needs cared for in the cement tanks, being fed and protected from predators by hatchery managers, the less adept members aren't weeded from the population. Out-of-basin fish are also built for the unique demands of another river. These two factors ensure that the offspring of hatchery steelhead won't be as well suited to the river in which they end up spawning. When these less adept fish survive and spawn with wild fish, the wild fish's offspring become less likely to survive than they would have been if they'd spawned with another wild steelhead. Over many generations of such dilution, the entire wild stock becomes impaired and weakened—putting the whole population at risk. And of paramount interest for the angler, the wild steelhead start to lose their range of size. More and more wild steelhead will start to be of that cookie-cutter mold, two-salt fish of twenty-six to thirty inches; fewer and fewer wild steelhead will be large three- and four-salt fish that often break twenty pounds.

Many Northwest hatchery managers have realized the faults with the traditional system and are developing ways to create better hatchery steelhead. One new hatchery plan, called a brood stock program, is being tested extensively on Oregon rivers. The program calls for in-basin fish, steelhead that are native to the basin in which their offspring will be stocked. The in-basin steelhead are often collected with the help of anglers. When a wild steelhead is caught, it is quickly put into a portable live well and rushed to the hatchery, which keeps the fish until it is ready to spawn. After the fry emerge, they are placed in a new type of holding pen, one that more accurately mimics the natural river environment. By using this model, hatchery managers are able to increase the return rate of their smolts from less than 1 percent with traditional practices to upward of 8 percent. And because the wild fish were caught throughout the season, the hatchery steelhead offspring return over a wider time range.

But some anglers fear the brood stock program and other innovative hatchery practices even more than they

A recent study suggests that the average wild steelhead is more likely to strike a fly than the average hatchery fish. Here Peter Betjemann leans into a wild winter buck on a remote stream.

fear the traditional programs. First of all, the brood stock program calls for the slaughter of wild steelhead so their eggs can be harvested for hatchery purposes. These are fish that in all likelihood would have found the spawning grounds themselves and produced more wild fish. Instead, the hatchery intercepts their eggs and uses them in a manner designed to produce more smolts than the wild fish could have on its own. To succeed in its goal, the hatchery can't subject the eggs, alevins, parr, fry, or finished smolts to the same risks of predation they'd experience in the wild, nor can it force them to forage in the same way they would in a natural environment. As with traditional hatchery practices, the result is a returning adult that hasn't been tested as nature intended and therefore has an increased chance of carrying deficient genes to the spawning grounds. Except now these dangerous fish are returning throughout the months of run, which increases their chances of spawning with wild fish; increases competition for limited spawning grounds; and exposes the remaining wild fish to dangerous baitfishing methods normally employed only in the early part of the season, when hatchery fish traditionally composed the majority of the run.

Many anglers see hatchery programs as the catch-22 of modern steelheading. We've obviously depleted the number of wild steelhead in most rivers to levels that can't sustain a catch-and-kill fishery. Yet many of us chromeheads want to take a fish home to our families every now and then. Without hatcheries, the common logic goes, we'd be left with a catch-and-release steelhead fishery at best—and no fishery at worst.

But an emerging group of anglers, led by several prominent conservationists, including Bill Bakke of the Native Fish Society, believe the common logic is wrong. In the few rivers where hatchery programs have been abandoned, the numbers of wild steelhead returning to the watershed have increased. And in several of these streams, the speed of the resurgence has surprised everyone. For instance, on the Clackamas River above North Fork Dam, the summer hatchery program was abandoned in 2000 after decades of dumping up to two hundred thousand smolts into the river. A study conducted by the Oregon Department of Fish and Wildlife in the years following the hatchery closure found that the hatchery fish had reduced the spawning success of the wild steelhead by 22 percent on average. The example of the Clackamas River and others like it suggests

Facing page: Hatchery programs do irreparable damage to wild steelhead. Study after study has revealed that when hatchery stocking programs cease on rivers with native populations, wild steelhead numbers increase.

that hatcheries are systematically suppressing the recovery of our wild stocks of steelhead.

Thus contrary to what many anglers have thought for years, hatcheries appear to be part of the problem—not part of the solution. Like habitat degradation and overharvest, hatcheries seem to be one more challenge wild steelhead face in their road to recovery. Until wild fish aren't competing with hatchery fish, we can't expect the wild steelhead in our homewaters to have a shot at returning in healthy numbers. Instead of supplying high numbers of hatchery steelhead, the goal of fishery management agencies should be resurrecting wild populations until they can sustain a limited catch-and-kill fishery. And more and more anglers believe resurrecting wild populations means shutting down the hatchery facilities on those rivers with native steelhead. As Bakke puts it: "Hatcheries are a technological fix for an ecological problem. The fix does not fit the problem and cannot solve the problem."

But of course, closing hatcheries won't instantly bring wild steelhead back in their original numbers. Wild steelhead require healthy watersheds. And healthy watersheds don't exist where the ecosystem has been grossly disturbed. Therefore, change begins with us. Watershed protection demands concerned anglers banding together and making our voices heard.

The Spawning Phase

The spawning phase of the steelhead's life cycle begins once the fish have entered fresh water. Their upstream migration begins quickly, with a speedy move through tidewater and the lower sections of the rivers. Once the faster currents of the upper river are encountered, with their ideal holding conditions, steelhead will slow their migration. The Oregon Department of Fish and Wildlife recently tagged several winter Umpqua steelhead in an effort to establish just how fast and far the fish travel. The steelhead often moved several miles during a twenty-four-hour period, and amazingly, some traveled as much as eighteen miles in a single day.

Steelhead continue moving upstream, sometimes taking tangents up tributaries for the cool oxygenated water they often provide, until the fish reach the general location of their spawning grounds. Usually they pass the area where they will eventually spawn, hold upstream of it for some time, and then drop back down as the spawn approaches.

A hen fish ripe with eggs typically digs a redd in gravel under about one to three feet of water. Males will gather downstream of her, competing for the opportunity to spill their milt onto her eggs as she releases them in small bursts. The most fit male available will stay close to the female, biting at any other fish that come near. Once the eggs are released and the milt makes contact, they fall to the stones below, where they stay until the alevins emerge.

Steelhead do not die after spawning, as do other pacific salmon. Rather, the spent steelhead often attempts to return to the sea after depositing its milt or eggs. Male fish have a tendency to stay near the redds, waiting for that one last willing female, until they are too weak to make it back to the sea. Because of this, male steelhead rarely survive to spawn a second time. Female fish, however, often head back downstream immediately after spawning. Depending on the distance from the sea, the number of dams present, and a host of other factors, these fish may or may not survive the trip. If they do make it back to the sea, they feed quickly to regain their energy, and then ascend the river again the following year. These fish rarely gain much more size when they get back to the ocean. Instead, their efforts serve to reestablish their original proportions.

The life cycle details of a specific steelhead are easily available to the angler. All a person has to do is collect a scale from near the tail of the fish and put it under a microscope. Like a tree, the scale shows the growth of the fish in rings, the thicker rings showing freshwater winters the fish endured. With a little bit of practice, scale reading can be an intriguing way to learn the life history of the fish in your favorite rivers. But scale collection shouldn't be done on wild steelhead by the novice. The

Once the female steelhead releases her eggs, they make contact with the male's milt and fall into the cracks between the stones, where they stay until the juvenile steelhead emerge as alevins.

wound left on the fish can leave the animal susceptible to fungus and disease, which might hamper its ability to successfully spawn.

Adult steelhead don't feed in a river like trout do. The fish do have a striking reflex at foodlike items, but they don't feed in an effort to put on weight like a resident trout. Rather, the steelhead depend on conservation of their energy. It is a rare stream that can produce enough food to support an eight- or ten-pound trout. Such streams are even rarer in steelhead country. If a steelhead were to actively feed in its natal river, the fish's energy and body weight would diminish more rapidly than if it did not feed at all. By not moving around trying to catch prey, a fish is able to minimize its movements and hence slow its metabolism to a crawl. This strategy ensures that the fish will keep its energy deposits for the highly taxing spawning period.

There are two main types of steelhead: summer fish and winter fish. The *irideus* subspecies is composed of both, whereas the *gairdneri* is entirely summer-run—minus one Oregon stream where a *gairdneri* and *irideus* hybrid returns in small numbers in the winter. This summer and winter classification is helpful for anglers because of the difference in fish behavior and therefore angling strategy. Steelhead often do not lend themselves willingly to this simple division, however. Some rivers have fresh fish each month, like Washington's Kalama. And even on rivers that have only a summer or winter run, there are fish that enter outside the arbitrary time boundaries prescribed by anglers.

Summer steelhead tend to enter the rivers in the late spring, summer, and early fall. These fish do not spawn until the following spring, meaning that some of them hide out in the river for up to a year. To survive such a stay, these fish need rivers that provide adequate cover, even during the low flows of late summer and fall. In a big stream, finding such cover is not a problem. But in a smaller stream, such water can usually be found only in extensive canyon sections. Because of this, very rarely do small streams have wild summer steelhead.

Winter steelhead do not have the same restrictions, however. These fish enter the rivers from midfall to midspring, when the rivers are typically higher and flowing with more sediment. These conditions allow the winter steelhead plenty of cover. Plus, winter steelhead spawn in the spring, meaning that they don't have to survive for a long period of time in the river environment. These factors allow even the smallest of streams to host healthy runs of winter steelhead. In fact, practically every little coastal stream from northern California to southern Alaska has a run of winter steelhead, although the numbers might be too low to allow for angling. Nonetheless,

Rarely do small streams have wild summer steelhead. Lisa Wassgren works a dry fly over one of the few streams that do.

little is more exciting than stumbling upon a healthy run of unknown wild steelhead within sight of the ocean. Any fish caught will be chrome bright and still mad from the ocean's brine.

Both summer and winter steelhead—and resident trout, for that matter—spawn at roughly the same time in the river. The specific date varies with geography, but all *O. mykiss* fish—in their native range—spawn in the spring when the daily water temperature gets above 43 degrees Fahrenheit. Fish in South America also spawn in the spring, although that corresponds to North America's fall.

Of course, a book can be, and has been, written on the life history of the steelhead. But that isn't the aim of this book. What is important to glean from a lesson in the life history of the species, in my opinion, is an understanding of the interrelations among the steelhead and its rivers and oceans and its human suitors. If we're not careful about how we treat the many environments the steelhead inhabit, our children will see fewer wild steelhead than we've been privileged enough to see. And once a wild run is lost, it can't be adequately replaced by some hatchery concoction.

CHAPTER 5

Holding Water

Where to Find Steelhead in the River

I pushed my boat down the slide in the morning darkness, river mist still glowing in the moonlight. As the boat slapped the water, an owl lifted from a limb and sailed soundlessly across the river. For a moment, I saw its wings silhouetted like a kite against the sky.

I'd chosen to fish early, and alone, because the trip carried a tinge of seriousness. The river was new to me, a beautiful freestoner with a strong run of summer steelhead. A guide friend had recommended it. "You've got to get up there. Seriously, the fish are nose to tail and eager as hell." But twice now I'd made the long drive, and twice I'd been skunked. Something wasn't right. Maybe I'd assumed the fishing would be easy. Maybe I wasn't working hard enough. So after the last trip, during the long, long drive home, I'd decided to come back earlier next time and give the river a serious going over. No messing around.

By legal casting light, I'd anchored above a long run, the rolling water splashing for seventy-five yards below me. With each cast, mend, and swing, I held my breath, confident that eventually a fish would take. The river worked the line for me, bringing the fly around in textbook arcs. "How could a fish resist this?" I wondered.

As the sun touched the mountaintops and sucked the river mist toward the sky, I worked a nymph and Glo-Bug in a prime section of pocket water. Fish had to be there. I could feel them, one of those inexplicable sensations anglers get when they just know a fish is about to strike. But nothing did.

At noon, as the summer sun beat on the back of my neck, I loaded the boat on the trailer, fishless again. As I cranked the winch, I heard the coughing bark of a friend's truck. Brian slid to a stop, a client in the front seat. "You must have crushed them today," he said.

"Hardly," I replied. "Skunked."

He waited for me to break into a laugh, tell him about the fish I'd landed. "Come on?" he finally said.

When I cleaned the cement with my toe, he realized I wasn't joking. He stepped out of the truck and came nearby so the client wouldn't hear. "Is everything all right?"

"Fine," I said.

"At home, I mean?"

"Yeah, fine," I said again. "Everything's fine. I just had a tough day."

"Did you have a fly on the end of your leader?"

Above: Steelhead hold in specific types of water. Knowing what to look for will help you find fish when you explore new rivers.

I refused to answer.

"Where were you fishing?" he asked.

As I told him, he nodded like a doctor who had just realized his patient's disease. "That's it. The right area, but the wrong spots."

Over the next five minutes, despite the frustrated sighs of his client, Brian told me of specific boulders and troughs that collected fish. The tan rock on the left side of the tailout. Under the fir branch that just tickles the water's surface. The trough in the middle of the fast run where the current slows to a walk's pace. These were the spots.

"If I didn't have this guy," he said with a toss of the thumb, "I'd take you up there right now."

"Probably for the better," I said. "I should head home anyway. It's a long drive."

But as I started the truck and pulled out onto the road, I could feel dread coming over me. Any steelheader is used to a few trips without a fish, especially when on new rivers. But something about my expectations for that stream and my inability to connect had gotten under my skin. I needed to set the record straight. Take my tail out from between my legs. I turned the truck around. Hell with it. I'd drift it again.

The river in the heat of the day looked impossible, so clear and shallow every steelhead would be in a constant state of panic. But I stuck to Brian's plan, to the spots he'd outlined for me. And sure enough, a steelhead finally took as my Easy Egg drifted through a trough in the middle of a run—exactly where Brian had told me to try. It wasn't a big fish, but it was a steelhead nonetheless, and its three jumps were enough keep a smile on my face the whole drive home.

Unlike trout, which can be found in any stream by an out-of-towner with a basic knowledge of trout holding water, consistently finding steelhead requires more than just a sound understanding of theory. It requires an intimate knowledge of the river, the kind of knowledge developed after seasons spent on the same water. If you're serious about catching steelhead, the importance of developing a homewater can't be understated.

But steelheaders like to travel. We like to see new rivers and catch new fish. And we can't turn every one of these rivers into a homewater. Luckily, there are logical reasons why steelhead hold where they do, and by understanding their motivations, you can not only find steelhead more quickly on new rivers, but also find more fish on your homewater.

Hooked up on a Rogue River summer run.

Characteristics of Steelhead Holding Water

Trout hope to get at least four things from their holding water: respite from the current, protection from predators, a supply of well-oxygenated water, and easily attainable food. These four requirements force the majority of river trout into a single type of river feature: the seam, or the place where a fast current meets a slower one. (It's easy to see why trout guides' favorite mantra is "hit the seams!") Because trout on any river are dependent on seams, an eager angler can travel the world over with a rod and find fish relatively easily.

Steelhead, on the other hand, need only three things from their holding water: respite from the current, protection from predators, and a steady supply of well-oxygenated water. Since steelhead don't need a conveyer belt delivering food to their front door, they aren't as dependent on seams; steelhead are able to spread out more evenly throughout the river. This is important to the steelheader for a couple reasons. First, given this ability to spread out and the generally low number of steelhead in a section of river, the fish can be very hard to find. And second, steelheaders who think of fish concentrating in seams—the old habit of many trout fishers—might neglect many other, more productive types of lies.

Steelhead are able to find exactly what they're looking for in a lie—respite, protection, and oxygen—from two ubiquitous river features: midstream rocks and cobbled bottoms. Midstream rocks divert the current's flow, creating lees around the stone. Most obviously, a midstream rock creates a patch of still, or nearly still, water directly behind it. As the lee extends downriver, it narrows. Eventually the lee completely disappears, giving way to the full force of the river's current. Like trout, steelhead rarely hold in the center of the lee directly behind the rock. Both fish prefer to hold along the side of the lee, on the edge of the fast and slow water, in the seam created there. The ideal holding water behind the rock is the downstream point of the lee, where the two seams meet (see the figure on page 45). But a steelheader who focused exclusively on the seams behind rocks would miss many, if not the majority, of the steelhead. Unlike trout, steelhead typically bypass these seams below the rock in favor of the cushion of slow water directly in front of it (see the figure on page 45). As the river meets the rock, the current splits to move over and around it. At the point of the split, the water is nearly still. For a steelhead, this is prime holding water. The fish has plenty of respite from the current in the calm water. It is protected from preda-

Midstream boulders offer ideal holding conditions for tired steelhead.

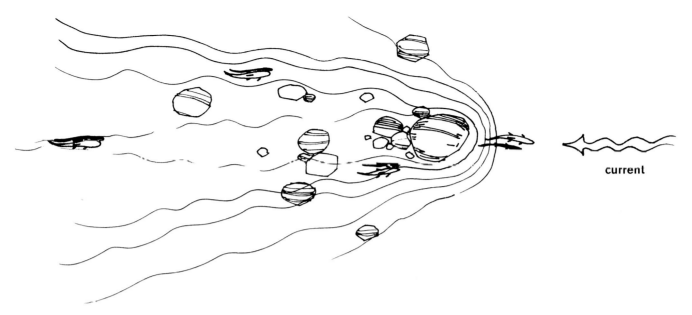

Steelhead frequently hold around midstream boulders, selecting lies that provide protection from predators, respite from the current, and oxygenated water.

tors by the flowing water overhead and its ability to see everything upstream. And the flowing water guarantees a steady supply of well-oxygenated water.

Not all midstream rocks that hold steelhead will be visible. Only a fraction of the midstream rocks in a river create ripples or disturbances on the surface. Some serious fish magnets become apparent only on closer inspection.

Cobbled bottoms are common formations on western steelhead rivers, frequently appearing in riffles, runs, pools, and tailouts. Steelhead take advantage of the shelter cobbled bottoms offer. When water runs over the river bottom, the stones act like sandpaper, applying friction to the current. The bigger the stones, the more friction is applied. The friction causes the water to actually slow down, creating a pocket of slower water near the bottom. Anglers often refer to this process as the triangle effect (see page 46). The triangle effect can take any patch of stones and turn it into prime steelhead holding water. The fish can find respite in the slower water and obtain protection and oxygen from the faster water overhead. The bigger the rocks along the bottom, the slower the water will be. Depending on the speed of the river's current, rocks the size of baseballs or prize-winning pumpkins could create the ideal holding lie.

As the current splits to move over and around the rock, a cushion of slower water is produced, creating the ideal holding lie for steelhead.

fastest

fast

slow

The bottom's stones apply friction to the passing current, slowing it and producing prime holding water.

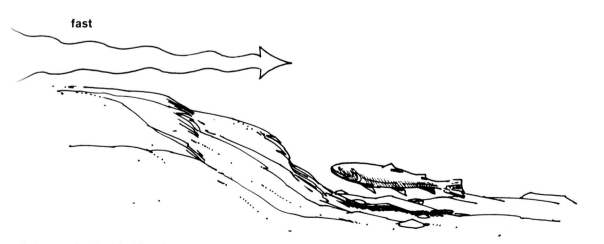

fast

Shelves make ideal holding lies. Try searching for them on sunny days when the water is low and clear.

Although less common than cobbled bottoms, submerged shelves act as steelhead magnets. Some rivers, like the North Umpqua and other coastal streams prone to heavy winter flows, have sections where the current has cleaned the river bottom of its stones, exposing the river's bedrock foundation. Frequently these shelves appear in runs below heavy water. Usually the exposed bedrock is flat and offers little shelter for the holding steelhead. But every once in a while it has shelves, places where the rock falls away for at least eight inches (see page 46). Shelves running both parallel and perpendicular to the current provide soft spots under the heavy main current flow, ideal steelhead holding conditions. Though shelves can take time to locate, they are rarely filled back in with stones. Once you find one, it's likely to be there year after year. If that shelf happens to be a steelhead hot spot, you may have stumbled upon the kind of secret that will pay dividends for years to come. The best time to search for such features is when the water is low and clear and the sun is overhead. Many successful steelheaders scout their winter rivers during the summer for just this reason.

Troughs, indentations in the cobbled substrate of the bottom, also collect holding steelhead. For whatever reason, rocks frequently get shifted around along the bottom during floods, often leaving channels that run parallel to the current. Steelhead are attracted to troughs because they offer a pocket of slower water under the mass of fast water above (see figure below). Some troughs are two feet deep and as long as the entire riffle, run, or tailout. Others are only eight inches deep and three feet long. But whether small or large, these features collect

holding steelhead. Like shelves, they are best found during periods of low water when the sun is overhead. But unlike shelves, they often reveal their location during normal fishing conditions. Troughs frequently appear as blurry places along an otherwise discernible bottom.

Midstream rocks, cobbled bottoms, submerged shelves, and troughs are the four main types of bottom structure that attract steelhead. But just any random midstream rock, cobbled bottom, submerged shelf, or trough is unlikely to house a fish. Few steelhead, for instance, want to spend a warm, sunny day holding behind a midstream boulder in motionless water. Steelhead look for more than just bottom structure when searching for a lie; they also look for certain current features. To consistently find chromers, first find the ideal current features, and then pinpoint a midstream rock, cobbled bottom, submerged shelf, or trough within them.

When a steelhead holds, it wants to use as little energy as possible; recharging its energy reserves is its main objective. But because the fish also needs protection from predation and a supply of well-oxygenated water, it can't hold in stillwater. Depending on certain environmental conditions, steelhead will select currents of varying speeds and depths. The clarity of the water usually determines how deep the fish hold—whether they sit in the deepest flows available or spread out into more varied depths—because murky water acts as a camouflaging mechanism for the fish. Murky flows make steelhead feel safer from predators. Clearer flows make them more cautious. Under normal conditions, when the water is slightly off-color, steelhead prefer

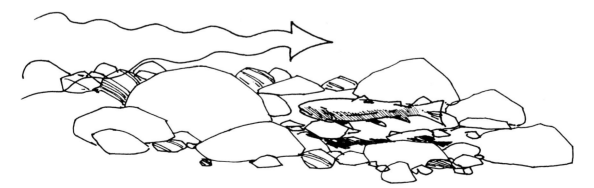

Troughs are depressions along a cobbled bottom, and frequently collect resting steelhead.

Identifying key bottom structure is only half the game. To consistently find chromers, you need to target places where the key bottom structure and ideal currents come together.

water that is between three and six feet deep. Meanwhile, the temperature of the water usually determines the speed of the current in which the fish hold. Warm water contains less oxygen than cold water, so the warmer the water, the faster the current needs to be for the steelhead to feel comfortable. Cold water contains more oxygen, but it also slows the metabolism of the fish, leading them to prefer slower currents in which to hold. Under normal conditions, when the water is within the ideal temperature range, steelhead prefer to hold in water moving at roughly the same speed a human walks down a city street. Extremes in either water clarity or temperature can cause extreme behavioral adjustments in the fish. For instance, when the water is clear and very cold, steelhead often hold in the deepest and slowest-moving water available. Conversely, when the water is murky and very warm, they'll often prefer shallow and fast areas.

Depending on river clarity and temperature, steelhead will hold anywhere within a river, from rapids to pools. But under normal river conditions, fish prefer riffles, runs, and tailouts, as these places are the most likely areas in which they will find water of the preferred depth and speed. Moreover, these places have even currents.

Steelhead prefer water with a uniform current direction—not swirling or upwelling—as such water doesn't require the fish to constantly correct its position with its fins. Keep in mind that the steelhead wants to use as little energy as possible when it holds; constant adjustments make a lie more work than it's worth. Riffles and runs are of special importance to anglers because they are typically easy to fish. The riffle's uniform current helps anglers control their drifts and swings, and its shallowness makes the fish easy to reach. Runs are usually faster on the outside edge, allowing an angler that stands on the inside edge to swing with ease. After the cast, the river will essentially do all the mending. Both riffles and runs have a well-earned reputation for holding eager and explosive fish. Tailouts are important to the angler because they tend to collect the most fish, especially in the low light of morning. Steelhead move up through fast water during the night and immediately want to rest and regain energy. Also, tailouts are the last places on a river to blow out when the heavy rains come. Some tailouts remain fishable way after the river is considered out of shape.

Riffles, runs, and tailouts can hold steelhead anywhere the fish can find shelter. But every riffle, run, or tailout has a best place—the spot where the water most matches a steelhead's desires. Since most rivers have few steelhead present at any given time, fish rarely have to compete for ideal holding lies. If a steelhead is in a particular section of the river, it is most likely to hold in the ideal spot. In small to medium-size rivers, the ideal spot is typically where the water is at its deepest while still maintaining the ideal current speed. Anglers who look for the ideal spot in each riffle, run, or tailout they fish—and concentrate their angling efforts accordingly—will end up catching more fish at the end of the day. Some chromeheads fish only these ideal spots, bouncing from one to the next all day long. They'll cover three times the water during a day—and often end up catching three times the fish. These anglers arrive at a riffle, run, or tailout, and before making a cast, they locate the spots

where the current is moving at the ideal speed. Of those several places where the current is moving perfectly, they pick out the deepest one or two spots and fish them most intensely. If no fish takes, they move on. Of course, they end up passing up those fish holding in less-than-ideal places, but if there aren't many people on the river, the trade-off might be worth it. Even if you fish a riffle, run, or tailout in its entirety, concentrating your efforts in the prime water isn't a bad idea.

Some sections with the ideal speed, depth, and structure will consistently produce steelhead; others won't. I know a guide who hooked steelhead behind a small midstream rock in the middle of a run sixteen out of nineteen trips one season. But another spot just downstream that looked identical in every way produced only one fish in those nineteen trips. Though the

Tailouts collect steelhead throughout the night and can offer superb fishing come dawn.

reasons for such inconsistencies in steelhead behavior are sure to remain mysterious, at least we can understand some of the logic.

A steelhead's journey upstream follows a precise rule: Stick to the path of least resistance. The river from the steelhead's perspective is a steady rushing current directly in its face. Though the fish's body is aptly suited to such an environment, moving upcurrent still requires substantial energy expenditures. To maintain energy reserves for the spawning grounds, steelhead need to take the path upstream that will tax them the least. On most sections of rivers, the fish's adherence to the path of least resistance means that the majority of steelhead follow the same specific course, or migratory route, upstream. Locating the migratory route can help predict which lies will be the most consistently successful.

If you've ever rowed a canoe upstream, you have some idea of what a steelhead is up against. When the canoe slips into the lee behind a rock, substantially less energy is required to move the boat. Likewise, as the canoe moves up the soft side of a bend in the river, you don't need to work very hard to cover water. The steelhead experiences the river in a similar manner. Certain features, such as rocks and soft bends, affect the current, allowing for minimal energy expenditure and maximum upstream progress.

Locating current-breaking features requires a macro view. One strategy for developing such a perspective is to think of the river from the position of an osprey. From the air, the soft spots connect together. The lee behind a rock connects, or nearly connects, to another lee, which connects to the soft side of a bend. From the aerial position, the migratory path is often obvious. And because most rivers are slow to change their design, the path is likely to stay generally consistent from year to year.

When a steelhead tires, it slips out of the migratory path and into a lie. Holding lies on the opposite side of a heavy current from the migratory path are less likely to attract the fish than those nearby.

One common exception to the general utility of the migratory path theory comes when the section of river being fished is at the terminal end of the steelhead's mi-

Once you have determined the migratory path of steelhead, the most logical lies become apparent.

Under certain conditions, steelhead seek out the oxygenated flows and protection from predation offered by rapids. Knowing what conditions drive steelhead into the rapids can keep you catching fish on tough days.

gration. Wild steelhead that have reached the water in which they plan to spawn mill around, crossing the current frequently and taking up quality lies anywhere. Likewise, hatchery steelhead that have reached their acclimation point leave the migratory path and mill around aimlessly. In both cases, a fish could appear anywhere quality holding water is available.

Environmental Effects on Holding Water

Typical summer conditions are tough for steelhead. Rain becomes less common, starving the rivers of their essential ingredient. The sun glares down on the water, making every nook and cranny visible. As the water warms, the oxygen levels diminish substantially. Steelhead need to take immediate action.

The general guidelines to holding-water preferences, as discussed above, hold true in the summer. The steelhead are still looking for the same things in their lies. But with tough summer conditions, the fish are able to find these things in some strange places—places common steelheading theory tells us to avoid.

Pocket water, especially in smaller rivers, is often the ideal place for steelhead to find oxygenated water that still provides respite from the current and protection from predators. Steelhead often hold directly under the whitewater created by the splashing currents. They also hold in the deeper troughs located throughout the pocket water. A careful approach with a short-lined presentation can be hugely successful. Pocket water also offers you a chance to spot fish. If you crawl up on a midstream boulder on the shaded side of the river, the fish often become apparent, allowing you to present flies to sighted steelhead.

Besides pocket water, rapids also hold fish in the summer. The heavy water provides plenty of oxygen and protection from predators, while the occasional midstream rock or submerged shelf affords respite from the current. The fish in such situations are often tough to spot, but by locating likely rocks and submerged shelves, you increase your odds of finding a taker. As in pocket water, short-lined presentations will be the most productive.

Winter brings easy living for steelhead. The higher flows and suspended sediment mean plenty of protection from predators. The colder flows allow the fish to find well-oxygenated water in even the slowest currents. A sluggish metabolism can cause the fish to favor the slower water offered by the river's deeper runs. Still look for currents moving at a walk's pace, but also don't hesitate to try slower water. Even deep pools collect steelhead when the water gets cold enough. Any pool or run located above a set of rapids that also happens to have a series of midstream rocks or a submerged shelf is sure to attract the big fish of winter.

Heavy angling pressure also affects the holding water steelhead select. When hordes of anglers, especially gear fishers with their thick lines and bouncing slinkies, descend on the water, many steelhead quickly take the cue and leave the area. These fish may move to an entirely new riffle or run, or if the pressure is great enough, they'll probably move into the fastest water immediately upstream. No water is too fast for a shy steelhead. The rapids above a popular gear-fishing hole often contain several dislocated fish. The steelhead look for the same features to hide near in the rapids—midstream rocks, cobbled bottoms, submerged shelves, or troughs. But reaching them here can be difficult. The rapids will probably have a roaring current over the top and a flow clouded with white bubbles underneath. You'll need heavy flies, a short line, and repeated casts to the same likely area to take fish. But steelhead in the rapids can be roused up. Once they enter the fast water, they often lose the lockjaw tendencies forced on them by the heavily pressured downstream water.

CHAPTER 6

Convincing Steelhead

The Science Behind Fishing Effectively

Picture this: An eight-pound wild steelhead enters its natal river and swims quickly upstream. A tributary dumps its cool flows into the water, filling the river with complex and provocative smells. The fish tosses the tributary a glance but pushes on, tail working determinedly. It comes to its first big rapids, the water roaring white. Instead of hesitating, the steelhead bolts, kicking harder than it ever has before. Slowly, ever so painfully slowly, it crawls up through the rapids, finally bursting into the quiet water above. There our fish finds a boulder-strewn riffle several feet deep, the perfect place to hold. In the next twenty hours, it only flicks a fin here and there to stay righted, using as little energy as possible.

During those twenty hours, our steelhead enters a trance, where it ceases to see the environment as it did only days before. In the salt water, the fish saw the world as a hungry predator should, filled with various food items waiting to be chased. But suddenly our steelhead's mind slows. The river environment is filled with food, yet the fish is content to just sit and zone out. Our steelhead's senses turn inward, the outside world becoming less vivid, less prompting. The fish has begun a process of mental reclusion, akin maybe to Zen meditation.

It can be useful for anglers to think of holding steelhead as piscatorial monks. They travel between lies determinedly, and once there, they rest meditatively, conserving their energy. Their daily actions are directed by a desire to rest, not to feed.

Steelhead maintain this pattern until spawning time, sometimes almost a year after entering the river. Trout, on the other hand, are the human equivalent of teenagers on sugar. They dart around in a near panic, never slowing, never resting. They are directed by a desire to feed, to consume as many calories as possible, to put on weight. The behavioral differences between a resident trout and a holding steelhead couldn't be more profound. Yet most beginning steelheaders fish as if they were pursuing a large trout.

Fly fishing for trout is the most scientific of the piscatorial pursuits. Most of the science that informs fly fishing for trout revolves around matching the hatch. Trout live by a simple rule: Get the most calories possible with the least amount of effort. A stream trout has very little time to look at an object before deciding to eat it or let it pass by. Hundreds of food-size items drift past every minute, so the trout must make up its mind quickly. The resident trout wants to choose an item that will provide

Above: Holding steelhead frequently drop into a reclusive trance, where their predatory instincts take a backseat to energy conservation. For our flies to be effective, they must spark the fish awake.

the highest number of calories for the least number of calories expended while capturing it. In many situations, this means selecting a single type of insect amid dozens of other equally edible types. The trout's strategy, reinforced by natural selection because of its efficiency, is to key in on certain physical characteristics of the selected food item. And it is this strategy that produced in trout anglers the "match-the-hatch" mantra. For a fly to be effective, its physical properties must more or less match those of the trout's insect du jour.

Most fly-rodding steelheaders also are, or were, avid trout fishers. It's natural then that these anglers would still have "match-the-hatch" residue clouding their judgment. But the effects of such thinking can be detrimental to a steelheader's catch rate. Attempting to match the hatch results in your not varying your techniques enough, simply changing flies instead of your overall presentations.

Steelhead that are not actively feeding rarely become selective eaters. A steelhead strikes for a completely different reason than a trout. A trout is eating to put on weight. A steelhead eats out of compulsion. Whereas a teenager eats a whole pizza pie to fuel his growth spurts, a college kid eats a whole pizza because he got used to eating a whole pizza as a growing teenager. A steelhead strikes a drifting stonefly as thoughtlessly as you would block a ball coming at your head; it's the ingrained reaction to a certain stimulus.

After a fish refuses your initial presentation, instead of adjusting the minutiae of your pattern in an effort to

Instead of adjusting the minutiae of your patterns to convince dour steelhead, you are better off changing presentations altogether. Switching to indicator tactics convinced this winter buck.

As long as a sighted fish appears active, it is worth presenting flies to it.

match the hatch, you should show the holding fish something absolutely new, be it a completely new pattern or a completely new presentation.

Sight Fishing

Usually we steelheaders blind-fish likely looking water, meaning we spend our days casting because the currents and bottom structure look fishy—not because we see a fish in that spot. But occasionally we do spot a steelhead holding before it spots us.

Imagine you're on the river. There is a steelhead holding in three feet of water out in front of you. Every minute or two, the fish slides to one side and opens its mouth. This is an eager fish, one likely to strike a fly. Yet it refuses your Lifter as it dead drifts by. After five good presentations where the fly comes within six inches of the fish, the steelhead still isn't interested. What's your next move? Should you switch to a smaller Lifter, or a different color or pattern? Or should you change presentations completely? Maybe try hanging a wet fly over the fish?

A located fish presents the steelheader with a unique problem, one that confounds many anglers. Not all steelhead are willing to take a fly. How do you determine whether the fish is a taker? The fish's behavior in the water can be a clear indicator of the likelihood that it will eventually strike.

From the angler's perspective, there are two types of fish: dour ones and active ones. Dour steelhead are so lost in their meditative world that they seem impervious to our finest advances. The greatest angler can place the greatest fly in a dour fish's face and it won't even notice. Active steelhead, on the other hand, will often swim across the entire riffle just to swallow a badly swung pattern. Luckily, the fish's level of activity can easily be determined by an observant angler. Active steelhead frequently move small distances from side to side. It might be just two inches here or there, but those two inches signify that the fish is paying acute attention to the world around it. Also, an active steelhead frequently opens and closes its mouth. You will see this as a flash of white near the fish's lips. If a steelhead moves to one side and opens its mouth, you've found yourself a highly active fish, one that should see a fly as soon as possible. A dour steelhead, on the other hand, is content to sit motionless along the bottom. Often the fluttering of its pectoral fins is its only movement. Its mouth won't open and close, and it surely won't move to the side to take a drifting morsel.

As long as a fish appears active and eager, it's worth continuing to deliver casts. Show it patterns a few times before you switch, and when you do switch, make big adjustments. If the fish doesn't take swung flies, try dead drifting. If dead drifting doesn't work, go back to swinging. Keep working the fish until it takes, goes dour, or spooks.

If, however, a sighted fish doesn't appear active, you're better off showing it a few flies and then moving on. The following is a process developed by Northwest guides for attempting to convince dour steelhead. The driving principle behind the process is to show the fish as much diversity of presentation in as little time as possible, helping you either elicit a strike or know to move on.

Step 1. When you locate a dour steelhead, especially in shallow water, you should always assume the fish to be spooky. An obtrusive presentation could send the fish racing for deep water. The most inconspicuous way to present a fly is by dead drifting it. The river is full of sticks, twigs, and insects moving downstream with the current. Even a cautious steelhead will usually be comfortable with natural-looking objects drifting by. A dour fish typically won't be willing to move very far to take a fly; therefore, it's best to dead drift the pattern as close to the fish as possible. Indicator tactics are usually the most reliable means for delivering flies close to holding fish.

Step 2. If the steelhead doesn't respond to your dead-drifted fly after five good presentations, go ahead and switch patterns. If you started with a Dr. Evil Stonefly, for instance, try a Steelhead Prince or an egg pattern. Remember, you're not trying to adjust the minutiae of your flies to match the physical characteristics of the food items in the river. You're trying to trigger the fish's striking reflex, which is best accomplished by tying on a totally different fly. Whichever fly you choose, make sure it is drastically different from the one you just tried.

Step 3. If the steelhead doesn't respond after a couple switch-ups, you're usually best off changing presentations altogether. Though you might eventually elicit a strike to one of the patterns in your dead-drifting box, odds are pretty good you won't. But by switching presentations, you have a better chance of sparking the dour steelhead's latent striking reflex. If the dead drift fails, try a swinging presentation. Depending on the water type and conditions, the best option will likely be a broadside rise, a classic swing with a floating line, or a sink-tip swing. Whichever swing presentation you select, try to hang the fly over the fish for as long as possible. The longer a dour fish sees the fly, the more likely it is to strike. I once hung a wet fly over an especially dour fish and pulled out my lunch. Halfway through the sandwich, the fish finally struck.

Step 4. If the fish still doesn't respond, move on. Sticking with it all day might produce a hit, but odds are good you'll accidentally spook the fish first. Moving on allows you to present your flies to more fish and in the long run will result in more fish hooked.

You've likely noticed that except for step 2, this process doesn't call for changing patterns. There is a clear reason for this. You are usually better off trying a completely new presentation than you are changing flies. This isn't to say that switching patterns eventually won't produce a strike; rather, switching presentations is just more likely to produce a strike in a shorter amount of time. This is exactly the reason why many guides carry two or three rods in the boat at a time. That way, they can quickly change presentations without cutting a leader.

Prospecting for Steelhead

A located fish is the rarity in most steelheading. Usually we spend our onstream hours casting to water that looks as if it might hold a steelhead, not to the actual fish itself. The tendency, then, especially among former trout anglers, is to spend too much time fishing one section of water. Steelheaders need to stay on the move if they're to find chromers. Yet moving too fast means that some slots, and some eager fish, won't get a look at the fly. The most successful steelheaders have found a balance between effectively covering lots of river and carefully fishing each riffle, run, and tailout.

Successful fishing for nearly any species depends on systematically covering the water. You are better off casting to a new portion of the water than you are casting to the same spot over and over and over. Steelheading is no different. Imagine a wide and long riffle in front of you. Five fish are holding in that riffle, but you don't know where. If you cast willy-nilly to the water, you might put a fly in front of all those fish, but odds are you won't. You'll likely miss some or even all of them. Approaching the water without a systematic plan is literally hit or miss.

The steelheader's task is similar to that of an archaeologist. Somewhere in a promising meadow might lie an artifact from an ancient civilization. If the archaeologist were simply to dig random holes, he or she might get lucky, but the odds are against it. To guarantee that any existing relic is found, the archaeologist will break that meadow into even sections and then dig in one section at a time, ensuring that all of the area is covered. Any artifact present will be found.

Similarly, steelheaders mentally break the water into slots, or even slices of the water. Breaking a run into slots allows you to cover a big section of water perfectly, with a cast to every possible lie.

By effectively covering as much water as possible, you can show your flies to the maximum number of steelhead. The more fish that see your fly, the more fish you'll put on the beach.

The shape of the slots applied is determined by the technique being fished. If the angler is using a dead-drifting technique, such as indicator tactics, the slot will be a band of water running parallel to the current (see page 58). If the angler is using a swinging technique, such as a skated dry fly, the slot will be a band of water running in an arc across the current (page 59). Throughout the rest of this book, I will talk about presentation in terms of slots. It's a concept essential to successful steelheading.

Strike Zones

Whereas the shape of the slot is determined by the technique being fished, the width of the slot is determined by the fish's horizontal strike zone, the distance it is willing to travel in one direction or the other to take a fly. If a fish will move one foot to either side for a fly, its horizontal strike zone is two feet.

A fish's eagerness to attack a fly is influenced by several factors, the most important of which are water temperature, water clarity, light level, and the condition of the fish. These four factors affect the size of a steelhead's strike zone. Sometimes a strike zone is big. The Deschutes is famous for steelhead eagerly moving four feet or more to take a fly. Steelhead in rivers with more adverse conditions have smaller strike zones, sometimes mere inches.

The strike zone size often changes from day to day and hour to hour. If you are to be consistently successful, you must pay constant attention to these changes and become skilled at determining how they affect the size of the strike zone.

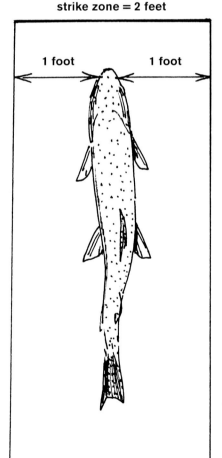

strike zone = 2 feet

1 foot   **1 foot**

slot size = 2 feet

The slot size equals the horizontal strike zone of the steelhead. Determining the correct slot size allows you to cover the maximum amount of water without passing fish by.

The Deschutes River is famous for producing wild steelhead with large strike zones.

ment. It would make sense that the fish would carry the effects of this sheltered existence into adulthood. In general, you can assume that hatchery fish will have an ideal temperature range that is 50 percent lower than that of the wild steelhead in the same river. If wild steelhead in your homewater are most active when the water is between 45 and 60 degrees, the hatchery fish are probably most active at 49 to 56 degrees.

There is yet another temperature-related discrepancy between wild and hatchery steelhead. Whereas native fish remain somewhat active when the water temperature is outside the limits of the ideal range, hatchery fish frequently become dour the moment the water temperature leaves the ideal range. For instance, on one hatchery-dominated river I frequent, the moment the water temperature rises above 53 degrees, guides start calling clients to postpone trips until the temperature drops.

While water temperature is the most important factor in determining the size of the strike zone, other variables such as water clarity, light level, and the condition of the fish work to fine-tune it.

Water Clarity

Water clarity also plays an important role in determining the size of the slot, for obvious reasons: If a fish can't see the fly, it surely can't strike it. Therefore, it's important to determine the clarity of the water.

On most days, the average river runs plenty clear. But there are those times, especially in winter, when the flows are thick with sediment. During such conditions, the best way to determine the extent of the murkiness is to wade into a section of river that has a rock bottom and a slower current. Continue to move into deeper and deeper water until you can no longer see your feet or have waded up to your waist. If your feet are still visible in waist-deep water, water clarity will have little effect on the strike zone of the steelhead. But if your feet disappear before this, the depth at which they disappear can be considered the maximum size of the steelhead's strike zone, and hence the maximum size of the slot.

Most likely your river won't flow so murky you can't see your feet very often. Steelheaders typically fish rivers as the levels are decreasing, when the sediment has begun to settle. On such days, the water will flow off-color, but your feet will remain clearly visible even at waist level. Off-color conditions can still work to decrease the size of the strike zone, however.

Flies cease to grab the attention of steelhead as sediment and debris cloud the river. For the fly to draw a strike, it must catch the fish's eye. Many steelheaders find that under murky conditions, dead-drifting techniques become less and less effective. The size of the steelhead's strike zone to such presentations diminishes as the water clarity decreases. Likewise, the standard steelhead patterns meant for swinging during clear water cease to draw strikes. To help keep the strike zone as big as possible when the river is clouded with sediment and debris, many steelheaders switch to large flies that are swung near the bottom. Big patterns stand out prominently even during murky flows and hence will draw more strikes. While steelheaders find success with both bright and dark patterns during murky conditions, dark patterns produce the best silhouette, meaning more steelhead will see them from farther away.

Light Level

The light level can affect a steelhead's willingness to move to a fly in profound ways. The complication is, depending on the river and the time of year, the light level can have varying consequences. For instance, in the summer months, the sun is typically a bad thing. Steelhead usually have smaller strike zones when the sun is directly on the water at this time of year. But in the winter, the sun can increase the steelhead's willingness to take a fly, actually increasing the size of the strike zone. As a general guideline, when the water is in the ideal temperature range, sunlight on the water diminishes the fish's strike zone. When the water temperature is below the ideal range, sunlight usually increases the strike zone.

Also, the direction of the sun can affect the strike zone of steelhead. If the sun is positioned downstream—

When the water temperatures drop, steelhead become less inclined to move to a fly. To be successful, you need to take your flies to the fish.

When the water is colder than the ideal temperature range, bright light can make steelhead more aggressive. When the water is already in the ideal temperature range, however, bright light tends to make steelhead increasingly dour.

and hence not in the fish's eyes—it will have only minor effects. But if the sun is overhead or upstream—and hence in the fish's eyes—it will have profound effects.

Condition of the Fish

The condition of the fish being pursued also plays an important role in determining the size of its strike zone. A steelhead that has recently arrived from the ocean is typically referred to as fresh. Fresh fish are usually light in color. These fish often are even chrome, the color of polished steel. Fresh fish generally are much more willing to chase down a fly. I've seen fresh steelhead travel across an entire riffle, covering a distance of more than twenty feet, to take a large swinging fly. A fresh fish is likely more active because of its recent exposure to actual feeding situations, where it needed to strike a herring or other food item before another fish did. Also, steelhead fresh from the ocean are at the highest energy level of their lives. All their work in the big seas was to store energy for these moments. The fresher the steelhead, the more susceptible it is to a fly.

As the days turn to weeks and the weeks to months, the steelhead's chrome coloring slowly gives way to a more troutlike coloration, especially in the bucks. The fish's body turns greenish brown, and its cheeks begin to glow red. As a general guideline, the longer a steelhead is in the fresh water, the less active it becomes. There are exceptions, most notably the steelhead that have just spawned and are making their way back to the sea. These fish, called kelts, are notorious for their active feeding. They recover many of the traits they displayed as a smolt, feeding with abandon in an attempt to store the energy they'll need to escape predation within the estuary. Many Northwest trout fishers accidentally catch these steelhead on trout flies in March and April. Besides kelts, winter bucks also become ferocious takers as the spawn nears. These steelhead are competing violently for the attention of females. This competition makes them especially aggressive, and large flies often pull them great distances. Other than these two specific exceptions, the guideline generally holds true: The longer the steelhead has been in fresh water, the smaller its strike zone will be.

When the run of steelhead is just beginning to enter the river, odds are good the majority of fish that see the fly will be fresh. All other things being the same, the strike zones of these fish will be larger, and you will be best served by fishing large slots. But when most of the fish entered the river six months earlier, the strike zone will probably be smaller, and you should fish smaller slots.

One freestone stream near my house has fresh summer steelhead entering from May through July. The river clearly illustrates the effect of run timing on slot size. In May, June, and July, the guides on the river fish wide slots, usually about three feet. As the summer progresses, those slots shrink, and by September, most guides are fishing slots no bigger than a foot. The longer the fish are in the river, the less willing they are to move for a fly.

Certain environmental changes frequently spark steelhead back to life, however. Most notable are the changes that arrive with the fall. Autumn brings desperately needed freshets to much of steelhead country, bouncing rivers up from their summer lows. As the water rises, it often cools, both changes that breathe sudden life back into dour summer steelhead. Many of these fish have spent months in fresh water, but a little rain leaves them as aggressive as they were when sea lice still clung to their fins. The burst of energy is short-lived, however, usually not lasting more than a week or so. Fall also brings spawning salmon and October caddis emergences to many steelhead streams, both events that make chromers especially susceptible to anglers.

This factor is a less consistent indicator of the strike zone of steelhead than the other three. I've had dark fish move a great distance to take a fly, and I've had fresh fish refuse every presentation I put nearby. But there are times when steelhead act as we think they should, and understanding how their condition generally affects their strike zones can be the missing piece to a complex puzzle.

Determining Maximum Effective Fishing Speed

Just how much do these factors affect the strike zone of a steelhead? The answer to this question varies with every river. The more you fish your homewater, the better sense you'll have of how the conditions affect the strike zone. And after each landed fish, you'll be able to fine-tune your fishing speed.

Knowing the steelhead's strike zone is essential for determining the slot size to be fished. And knowing the slot size is essential for determining the maximum effective speed you can fish. In the end, covering water at the maximum effective speed will help you consistently catch more steelhead.

Winter bucks color up quickly once in fresh water and become increasingly aggressive throughout March. This twelve-pounder came several feet to strike an especially large pattern. PETER BETJEMANN

Just recently, I fished a new river for winter steel-head. As is typical that time of year, Oregon had just received a week of cold rain. After drinking a steaming cup of thick coffee, I slid my way down the muddy bank to the water's edge, burying my thermometer in the green water. It was 40 degrees even. I waded out into a slow, rocky run and saw my feet disappear when the water reached the center of my thighs. The sun hid behind thick Pacific clouds, casting a dim light over the water. According to a friend, the bulk of the run had entered the river a month prior, when an early-winter freshet brought the river near flood stage. All signs pointed to small slots. So I divided the riffles, runs, and tailouts into twelve-inch slots. Putting a cast to each slot required a slow, deliberate pace, but I was confident that such a strategy was my best chance of finding a willing fish.

The time spent proved worthwhile. A fish took my swinging Bunny Leech around evening, gave a powerful head shake, and snapped the leader. In the day of casting, I'd forgotten to check for wind knots. But a moment connected to a feisty steelhead goes a long way. Fishing smaller slots that day ensured that my fly would pass within striking range of any fish holding in the run. If I'd fished larger slots, odds are I wouldn't have put that fly inside that fish's strike zone.

On my next trip to the river, the water was warmer, 44 degrees. It flowed slightly jade from recent warm rains, and I could still see my feet in waist-deep water. The sun cast its rays through the overhanging trees and down on the water, giving a warm glow to the surface. Things looked good. I decided to fish two-foot slots. This time I remembered to check for wind knots and

Paying astute attention to the river conditions—and adjusting the size of the slots accordingly—will help put your fly within the strike zone of more steelhead.

Rarely will steelhead take a fly dragging over the stones. Here Nate Koenigsknecht dead drifts an egg pattern through a deep winter trough, making sure to keep his fly six inches off the bottom.

landed a small wild hen late in the day. If I had been fishing twelve-inch slots, I wouldn't have made it far enough downstream to fish the riffle that finally produced that hen.

The importance of slots goes beyond simply allowing you to systematically cover all of a section of water. Determining the right size slot is the key to effectively covering as much water as you can. Remember, the idea is to present your fly within the strike zone of as many fish as possible. And to do this, you must figure out the maximum speed at which you can effectively fish a given section of water.

Determining How Deep to Go

In addition to the horizontal strike zone, the steelhead also have a vertical strike zone, how far the fish is willing to move up through the water column. You can figure this out quickly once you've determined the horizontal strike zone.

Steelhead nearly always rest along the bottom of the river so as to take advantage of the calmer currents provided by the gravel substrate. Such a position gives the fish a clear view of the world above. Any fly passing to the side of a holding steelhead is backdropped by the darkness of the distant shore. But a fly passing overhead is backdropped by the bright sky, giving the fly a vivid silhouette. The added visibility provided by the sky's backdrop will pull a fish about twice as far vertically as it would move to one side. The result is a horizontal strike zone that is roughly the same as the vertical strike zone. (Remember, the horizontal strike zone takes into account the distance the fish would move to both the right and left sides.) Thus if the horizontal strike zone is two feet, the vertical strike zone will also be about two feet.

You are always better off making things as easy on the fish as possible, however. If you can put the fly closer to the fish without slowing your fishing speed, as is usually the case when dead drifting nymphs, you might as well do so. Even if a fish is willing to rise four feet for a fly, it will be more likely to take if it has to rise only six inches.

So why not always put your patterns on the bottom? Some techniques, such as nymphing, lend themselves readily to fishing deep. But others, such as swinging, do not. If you fish a sink-tip instead of a floating line, your ability to cover water will generally be hindered. If you cover less water, you will catch fewer fish. Thus it is usu-

Consistent success on the steelhead stream depends on remaining versatile.

ally better to fish higher in the water column so you can show your fly to more fish.

There is such a thing as too deep. Steelhead rarely take a fly that is on the rocks. A fly among the stones just doesn't spark the striking reflex as frequently as one suspended a little higher in the water column. Imagine a baseball rolling toward you. Are you more likely to bend over and snatch it up or simply move out of the way? Some steelheaders go even further, claiming that adult steelhead actually have a diminished ability to take overly deep flies because of the position of their eyes. These anglers say that unlike resident rainbows, adult steelhead have eyes that are fixed slightly higher on the head, allowing them to focus more keenly directly in front and above—the ideal position for feeding in the ocean. At sea, steelhead frequently chase baitfish into balls, striking up through the mass of fish. This behavior

may have selected for fish with eyes in this position. Who knows? Either way, though, a fly dragged over the bottom will produce a fraction of the hits as the same pattern fished six inches to a foot off the bottom.

Giving Steelhead What They Want

The most successful steelheaders are able to effectively cover lots of river yet still carefully fish each riffle, run, and tailout. Another part of the equation is how to ensure you're fishing the water in a manner that will entice as many steelhead as possible.

Steelhead are like any other type of fish: Some days specific presentations will draw more strikes than others. In trout angling, sometimes the fish will strike only dry flies, other times they'll strike only wets, and some days they'll strike both. The most successful trout anglers show the fish several different presentation techniques on any given day until they discover the one that consistently produces fish. The same strategy of using a diverse array of presentations can be found in some form from the tarpon flats of Belize to the salmon streams of Alaska.

But we steelheaders sometimes forget this most basic fishing lesson. Most likely, some time ago, anglers decided that since steelhead strike out of reflex, rather than because of a need for calories, the fish would hit one presentation just as readily as another. Of course, we now know this to be false. Yes, steelhead strike out of reflex. But sometimes that reflex won't be triggered by the technique we trust most. To entice the fish into striking, you may need to try something different. For instance, often steelhead aren't in the mood for swung flies, but those same fish can be taken on dead-drifted ones. And vice versa.

The most successful steelheaders offer the fish more than one presentation. If they swing their way through a trusted run and don't get a strike, they switch to a different technique and try the run again. By showing the fish more than one technique, they often find a taker where other anglers believed there were none.

This isn't to suggest that you are best off fishing every presentation over a section of water. Doing so would consume an entire day, drastically limiting the amount of river covered and the number of steelhead seeing the fly. Instead, you are better off picking two or three different presentations, ones you have faith in because of the conditions and water type (riffle, run, tailout, pocket water, rapids), and fishing them each once before moving on. For instance, on my homewater, the fall brings a flush of fresh fish into the riffles and runs. On these days, I try swinging with a floating line first, and if that doesn't produce a strike, I fish the same water with indicator tactics. If I still don't get a take, I move on. In this manner, I can cover many river miles and have confidence that I am covering them carefully.

Generally, fly anglers are thought to have three types of presentations: swinging, dead-drifting, and rising tactics. The character of the water determines which of these presentations you should employ. Often swinging and rising tactics might be the best bets. Or dead-drifting and rising tactics. Or swinging and dead-drifting tactics. Or all three. Whatever the combination, you'll find more success by fishing different types of tactics than you will by fishing small variations of the same tactic. Instead of first swinging with a floating line and then swinging the same water again with a sink-tip line, try starting with the swinging technique that best matches the conditions and then using a dead-drifting or rising tactic. Likewise, instead of fishing a dead-drifted dry fly and then a dead-drifted nymph, start with the presentation that best matches the water conditions and then try a swinging or rising tactic.

Many anglers wonder which tactic they should fish first through a likely section of water. Don't give yourself a headache over the decision. It probably doesn't matter. Most chromeheads I know start with the presentation with which they'd be most thrilled to hook a fish. Occasionally a lie holds a fish so hot, so eager, it would strike a bottle opener if you put it nearby. You might as well as hit the water first with your favorite method, so long as it fits the water type, and use other, less favored methods on your second and even third times through. Start with whatever tactic you want, but don't be afraid to try more than one.

To avoid constant rerigging, many steelheaders carry multiple cocked and loaded rods. This way, you can hit new water quickly with various presentations, and you won't lose time in tying knots.

Of course, not all rivers are conducive to all three types of tactics. For instance, small streams frequently don't offer water features that are conducive to swinging or rising tactics. In such cases, you must rely exclusively on dead-drifting tactics. Or conversely, huge rivers offer too much possible holding water to make dead-drifting or rising tactics consistently successful for most anglers. In such places, steelheaders often rely exclusively on swinging presentations.

But the character of most rivers allows you to employ different types of techniques. In such cases, effectively covering lots of water *and* showing the steelhead two or three different types of presentations will consistently allow you to catch the most fish.

PART III
The Presentations

"In a world that rolls ceaselessly underfoot, rocking and lurching like a subway car,
I've found that the cork grip of a fly rod offers a pretty steady handhold."

TED LEESON, *THE HABIT OF RIVERS*

A six-pound summer fish.

We parked the truck on the rim of the canyon, the river's wavy sound mixing with the pattering rain. "Shall we, good sir?" Dave asked with a wink.

"Oh, I believe we shall," I said.

With that, Dave kicked his truck's door shut and stepped over the canyon's rim.

Heavy winter clouds, burdened by their recent trip over the wet Pacific, hovered overhead. I pulled up my hood to stop the cold trail of water running down my neck and into my waders. It didn't help. Dave, on the other hand, a staunch advocate of minimalism, especially when it comes to fishing gear, wore no hood. In fact, he wore no wading jacket, just a wool sweater and a baseball cap. But such is Dave's style. The rod in his wet hand was a further example of his minimalist bent. It was a two-piece made into three by a ceiling fan. Most guys would have forked out the dough for a repair, but Dave—on principle—patched the ragged fracture with half a roll of duct tape. When he handed it to me that morning at his house, he'd said, "Don't wiggle it too hard; I want it strong for today."

Along the canyon floor, we found the river flowing cleanly, green with tints of blue over the black stones. Prime shape. As we stood watching the water, a steelhead appeared in the tailout.

"You take him," Dave said.

But I refused. "I want to see you cast that 'rod' of yours."

"You'll get to watch it do more than cast," he said, boarding a big canyon rock upstream of the fish. With a stout flip, he rolled the nymph and indicator in the current. His eyes went back and forth between the tailout lie and the yellow tuft of yarn drifting toward it. After a precise mend, the two points seemed destined to meet. And as the moment of truth neared, Dave hunched with attentiveness.

Before the indicator could reach the fish, it bounced, then slid under the green current. Dave struck instinctually and the line came tight. Immediately a fish broke the surface—a small fish—then tried to dive. But it was no match for the duct tape. Dave stripped in the fish hurriedly and slid it onto the stones.

I found the two of them there, Dave examining the little creature, keeping its body in the water. The river held lots of cutthroat trout, but not a one over twelve inches. And sure, the river held plenty of juvenile steelhead, even a few resident rainbows, but again nothing breaking into the teens. Dave's fish was an easy seven-teen inches long, wild, and clearly a fish with a history in the ocean—its flanks shimmered silver.

"Sea-run cutthroat," Dave said. He rolled the fish over, revealing two blood red streaks across its throat.

"A beauty."

He let the fish fin off into the river, darting away with the jittery insecurity of a trout in steelhead water. Turning to me, the rainwater running off his hat brim, Dave said, "Don't you get any fancy ideas. I'm not done with the rock."

"Oh, I wouldn't dare," I said. "I still haven't seen that rod of yours tested."

He climbed back up on the canyon stone. "You doubt me," he said. "You just watched me summon a fish with a single cast—on a duct-taped rod, no less—and you still doubt my abilities."

The truth was, I didn't. He rolled another cast into the current, sending a stack mend down the line before the indicator had even landed. His timing and execution were flawless. The cast worked its way through the tailout without hesitating.

Meanwhile, the drizzle had progressed through the shower stage and was now a full-blown rain, pocking the river's surface. Along the shore, I found a thick tree where—if I positioned myself just right—I could stay dry. From my dry spot, I could see rainwater running off Dave's elbows as he worked the rod through the air.

On the mossy ground, a six-inch slug slimed its way toward my boot. Along the creature's back was a gash, healed over and brown. The old scar didn't affect the speed of its crawl. The slug's long antennae seemed fixated on my wading boot. I was about to step out of its way when the grunting struggle of a man hooked to a serious fish echoed up through the rain.

Dave leaped from the rock to the shore, the duct-taped rod bent—rather uniformly—from the tip to the cork. A fish thrashed on the surface, just on the lip of the heavy rapids, throwing green water airborne. Dave managed a strained "It's big!" over his shoulder. But the words obviously taxed his resources, and he returned all his faculties to the massive fish thrashing the pool. He dropped the rod to the side, the duct tape precariously close to a sharp rock, and the fish sprinted upstream. When it should have jumped, when a normal fish would have jumped, this one didn't. Instead, it reversed its direction and raced downstream, straight through the tailout and into the rapids without a fin stroke of hesitation. Dave's reel hissed, filling the canyon air with a reverberating song.

take the majority of their fish using techniques that require precision mending. Getting a sink-tip to dead drift into a deep hole before beginning its swing often requires you to both mend and feed line to a point on the water some distance away. Trying to complete such a thorny tactic with a soft-action rod can be frustrating. Precision mending is more easily accomplished with a fast-action rod. Less movement is required for the same effect with a fast-action rod, and less movement means tighter, faster loops. Moreover, a fast-action rod has the backbone required to throw those precision mends a greater distance. The disadvantage of the fast-action is that for most anglers, it takes a little more practice to cast efficiently. Tailing loops are a frequent problem for those new to the fast-action. But a little time spent watching your backcast is usually plenty of cure.

Fly-fishing steelheaders of years gone, when rods were made from cane, used relatively short rods. The materials weighed too much for the average angler to fish a 10-foot rod all day. But even from these early days of steelheading, anglers knew that a longer rod would be a better rod. And as materials got lighter, rods got longer.

As a rule, steelheading techniques are most efficiently performed with a long rod. Because the presentations are performed in a river, an environment with rapidly moving currents, you must be able to control the fly line. You have to mend the line in order to keep the fly's presentation controlled. The longer the rod, the more line can be kept off the water. During the casting stroke, a longer rod is able to keep more line in the air as it is being delivered to a distant target. If a roll cast is needed, the longer rod allows more line to be delivered in a single attempt. During the strike of a distant fish, a longer rod is able to pick up more slack line, delivering piercing tension to the fly as quickly as possible. Most steelheaders who use single-handed rods trust rods be-

Fast-action rods allow tighter loops to be thrown with greater accuracy, helping you effectively cast and mend at distance.

tween 9¹/₂ and 10 feet long. Such rods are still light in the hand but capable of precise line control at a distance. Rods between 10 and 12 feet are better able to control the line, but their added weight can be too much for many anglers.

Switch Rods

Over the last few years, switch rods, long single-handed rods with an extended fighting butt for use as a grip during short-range Spey casts, have gained in popularity. Switch rods offer the steelheader some supreme advantages, most notably their diverse utility. One minute you can Spey cast along a wooded shoreline, and the next overhead from an expansive beach. Switch rods also lend themselves to advanced indicator tactics, as they can send small stack mends to the far side of a run, without turning your dominant arm to mush.

Switch rods fill a niche left vacant by single-handed and Spey rods. On many small to mid-size steelhead streams, like those common in coastal regions, the forested banks forbid overhead casting. But the overhanging limbs also forbid long Spey rods. Enter switch rods. Suddenly an angler can make short-stroke Spey casts to deliver flies to distant lies without hitting the limbs.

Many manufacturers now produce switch rods, which range in length from 10¹/₂ to 12 feet and in weights from 5 to 10. I prefer lighter rods, as they allow the most versatility.

But switch rods can't cover all situations. When on big water or when backed up against a wall of brush, Spey rods become the choice of most steelheaders.

Spey Rods

In the last two decades, Spey rods have made a thunderous emergence on America's steelhead streams. Anglers from California to Alaska, and even over to the Great Lakes, swear by these tools. And it's easy to see the attraction. Spey rods, which commonly range in length from 12 to 16 feet, allow exquisite line control, both while casting and while mending. They also let less-than-confident overhand casters cover more water in a single day. Moreover, Spey casting allows you to spread the burden of aerializing the fly line between two arms instead of using just one.

Historically, Spey rods were used with double-taper floating lines on rivers where long casts were needed over huge runs to find scattered fish. But modern Spey enthusiasts have realized the rod's utility in other situations as well, including for delivering heavy sink-tips to distant lies. Even more recently, anglers have started using the Spey rod for indicator tactics. As Spey rods are long, they allow you to use longer leaders than with sin-

Switch rods allow you to cast in both an overhead and the traditional Spey style without making any tackle adjustments.

gle-handed rods. A longer leader lets you sink a dead-drifting fly deeper. Hence Spey rods can be used to deliver weighted flies to incredibly deep lies.

Thanks to the demands of different rivers and the casting habits of different groups of Spey casters, there are three major kinds of Spey casting done on modern steelhead streams. Some rod companies currently manufacture rods especially designed for each style of cast.

Traditional Spey casting, which uses a fixed length of line, lifts the line at the end of the swing and keeps it continually moving until it is laid straight again. The traditional Spey cast offers you a major advantage: You

Steelheaders have been quick to realize the advantages offered by Spey rods. They allow long casts and precise mends, all while saving arm strength for the moments after a good fish takes.

don't have to strip in the fly line before it can be cast again. You simply begin the stroke at the end of the swing and end it as the line lands over the riffle. Rods designed for traditional Spey casting tend to be softer, flexing through the midsection. Some anglers call these rods full-benders, after their tendency to bend throughout the blank. A traditional Spey rod is an excellent choice if you plan to use the rod predominantly for swinging tactics that use a floating line, such as greased-line or skating dry-fly tactics.

The Scandinavian Spey casting style, often called underhand casting, is a derivative of the traditional style. It operates on the same principle as the traditional cast: The stroke lifts the line from the water and keeps it airborne until it is delivered back over the run. But Scandinavian casting uses a smaller stroke and produces faster line speeds and tighter loops. Scandinavian casters often employ shooting tapers and running lines, propelling flies incredible distances. Many Spey casters consider the Scandinavian style an advanced Spey-casting skill. Scandinavian casting requires a rod with a very fast action. These rods are best for anglers who commonly swing using sink-tips or need to deliver a floating line

extreme distances. Some modern steelheaders also favor these rods for indicator tactics.

A third casting style, one native to steelheading, is called Skagit casting. Unlike traditional and Scandinavian casting, which keep the line out of the water during the stroke, Skagit casting uses the water's resistance to load the rod. The cast operates on the principle of "unsticking" the line from the meniscus. In other words, the rod loads as it lifts the line from the surface. Skagit casting differs from traditional and Scandinavian casting in another manner as well: The cast doesn't use a fixed length of line, requiring you to strip in line after the swing is completed. The casting motion is designed to shoot that slack line back through the guides as the line unfolds over the surface. Skagit casting generally is done with shooting tapers or sink-tip lines. Rods designed for Skagit casting are usually moderate- to fast-action and often shorter than traditional or Scandinavian rods. A Skagit rod is a good choice for the steelheader who frequently swings deep with heavy sink-tips or dead drifts deep water with indicator tactics. Moreover, Skagit casting is generally considered the easiest Spey casting technique to learn, making it the ideal choice for beginners.

During the salad days of our love affair with Spey rods, their disadvantages didn't get much media attention. But Spey rods do have their limitations.

While a great deal of emphasis is put on "distance casting" in steelheading, much of even a big river's finest holding water is close to shore. A Spey rod can be a hindrance to fishing this nearby water, as the long rods won't load at close range. Also, for anglers who frequently fish delicate presentations, like dead-drifted dry flies or low-water greased line tactics, Spey rods are rarely the best choice.

The ideal rod quiver for a steelheader will likely contain an assortment of rods, from single-handed 7-weights to 8-weight switch rods to two-handed 9-weights.

But in my opinion, what's more important than having a lot of gear is knowing how to get the most out of the gear you have. For instance, one single-handed 8-weight rod in the right hands can do everything de-manded in steelheading—dropping a dead-drifting dry fly in a shallow summer tailout, roll-casting a heavy sink-tip across a winter run, or sinking a weighted egg pattern 10 feet below an indicator. That same rod will land half-pounders on the Rogue and twenty-pounders on the Skeena. If it's a choice between more gear or more on-the-river practice, I'd go with practice every time.

Reels

A steelheader's reel does more than hold line. It also picks up slack and puts the brakes on running fish. Just any reel isn't up to the task. But you needn't mortgage your house for a top-end reel either. More important than the list price of a fly reel are its vital features.

Steelhead live in big water, where distant presentations and long lines are the norm. Often fish take when you have a pile of slack line at your feet. That line must get on the reel before the fish decides to bolt, otherwise a

Prime summer steelhead conditions on the Rogue.

tippet-snapping tangle is nearly certain to occur. Or worse, a small tangle in the fly line might suddenly bust through all your guides. Large-arbor reels are able to pick up line much faster than conventional reels because of their larger diameter. Some large-arbor reels actually pick up line three times as fast as their conventional counterparts. Some anglers, however, find the bulk of a large arbor to affect their rod's balance. The dominant reel manufacturers produce many quality mid-arbor reels that still pick up line quickly but are smaller in stature and lighter in weight.

To stop a running brute—no easy task—a reel needs to have a stout drag system, something sure to stand up to the pressure. But reels made for salt water, like those designed for albacore and tarpon, are not necessary. No steelhead will burn you for two hundred yards without stopping. Plenty of fresh chromers will steal fifty yards, however. Many manufacturers make in-line drag systems that will put the brakes on a fast-running fish without breaking your piggy bank.

Besides being dependable, a reel's drag system should also allow microscopic adjustments in pressure. In a river environment where whitewater and nearly still eddies exist side by side, the pressure the current places on the tippet can vary from moment to moment. When a steelhead gets 150 feet downstream, you'll need to stay attentive to your drag setting, sometimes making tiny adjustments.

Lines

There are more line options for steelheaders today than ever before. It was only a few years ago that most anglers made their own sink-tips out of cut-up shooting tapers. Now there are sink-tips for every type of water, every rod, and every angler's preference. But the excessive options aren't just limited to sink-tips. There are general-purpose floating lines with conventional dimensions. There are steelhead floating lines and even clear lines. And the prices vary as much as the options.

For single-handed rods, no line is more useful than a floating steelhead taper. These lines have a longer front head, allowing for longer casts. Plus the longer head helps turn over bulky indicators and flies even when cast a distance. The increased length of the rear running section, or belly of the line, gives you more room to feed drifts. The belly also makes mending at a distance substantially easier. Steelhead tapers are worth the extra couple dollars.

A good reel is an essential investment for a serious steelheader. Fish like this chrome ten-pound hen put your gear to the test.

Winter can be hard on fly lines.

But any line will quickly lose its utility if not treated properly. Ideally, after every trip, you should clean the line and apply fly-line dressing. Such treatment will keep your line slipping through the guides smoothly, making each stroke of the rod more effective. Also, frequent doses of line dressing helps keep fly line from cracking.

Leaders

A leader is the weakest link. Any steelheader who has logged a few seasons on the river knows what a traumatic event it can be to lose a good fish to a bad leader. One minute you're hooked to a head-shaking steelhead; the next your line is lying limp on the surface and the air is filled with expletives. Occasionally, these break-offs were destined to occur: The fish was just too big or the leader slid along a razor-sharp rock. But usually break-offs are preventable. And the first step to prevention is starting with the right leader.

Though fluorocarbon leader is typically thought of as a tool for duping leader-shy fish, steelheaders employ it for a different reason. Fluorocarbon is more abrasion-resistant than standard monofilament. When fluorocarbon brushes against a sharp rock underwater or encounters the rough teeth of a big buck, it resists scraping better than standard mono. As big fish often take several vicious minutes to land, the leader is likely to do plenty of rubbing. Also, many steelhead presen-

tation techniques call for the fly to be near the bottom. If that fly accidentally snags, the leader will probably rub against a rock or limb. Standard monofilament leaders will collect burrs on each of these encounters, weakening the line. Fluorocarbon will result in more landed fish.

While fishing throughout a day, it's natural to botch a cast here and there. Casting errors, especially collapsing tailing loops, often result in small wind knots in the leader. Each wind knot reduces the strength of the leader by roughly 50 percent. A hooked fish will be quick to capitalize on such a weak point. By running pinched fingers down a leader every fifteen casts or so, you can reduce the chance of a steelhead breaking off at the knot first.

Hooks

Good hooks make a huge difference on the steelhead river. Steelhead have mouths of, well, steel. The bone and cartilage of the jaw are both formidable obstacles to a solid hook set. Though occasionally you may land a chromer that is hooked only in the flesh of the lip, landing a fish usually requires that the hook be buried in the jaw. And only the sharpest of hooks will penetrate such a hard medium.

Typical hooks, like those used for trout fishing, are machine sharpened at the factory. These hooks are com-

A wind knot lessens the breaking strength of a leader by roughly 50 percent. Steelhead are quick to exploit such weaknesses.

pletely adequate for the demands of most species, but they don't cut the steelhead muster. Instead, most steelheaders fish only with chemically sharpened hooks. The chemical-sharpening process allows for a much sharper and harder point. And most of these hooks are produced with higher-quality steel, allowing for a fundamentally stronger hook.

You may want to carry a file to keep a hook's razor point on the river. Every time a fly snags or hooks a fish, you can use the file to touch up the point. A hook sharp enough to dig into your fingernail with minimal pressure is sharp enough to penetrate a steelie's mouth.

Steelheaders are best off using barbless hooks, either fabricated as barbless or made so by the angler. A barbless hook has a narrower penetrating section, allowing for a deeper set with less energy. And as a hook buried in bone isn't likely to come free at the release of tension with the line, the barb brings little advantage. Moreover, steelheaders frequently fish streams with wild trout populations, often fishing the water when trout seasons are closed. As these fish consistently take a liking to our patterns, we should make every effort to release them safely.

Polarized Glasses

Polarized glasses are the steelheader's secret weapon. Quality optics are as essential as our reels, in my opinion. A good pair of glasses allows you to see through the sky's shimmering reflection on the water and helps define the contrasts along the river bottom, making the shades of color stand out. Effective steelheading often depends on spotting holding fish, or at least prime holding water, so a quality pair of polarized glasses is vital.

Many different types of lenses exist for the freshwater angler. They come in nearly every shade from yellow to brown. Because steelheaders spend so much time fishing in the low-light conditions of dawn and dusk, and show no fear of dreary weather, you need a color that remains useful during low light. The best strategy for finding the right lens color is to beg the fly shop to let you try some out on the water. Check to see which pair reveals the most bottom contour on your homewater.

Facing page: Light levels vary greatly in steelhead country. Investing in a quality pair of polarized glasses with versatile lenses allows you to spot likely holding water all day, every day.

Though not realistic on all homewaters, where you can use a drift boat, it can make finding steelhead—and getting within casting range—significantly easier.

I've never found a more consistently helpful shade than copper. Copper lenses allow you to fish right to dark while still getting the benefits of increased aquatic visibility. And they are plenty shaded enough for the brightest Northwest summer day.

Waders and Wading Boots

Steelheading requires plenty of wading. Anglers frequently cover miles of ground through thick brush, and then wade deep in fast water. Just any pair of waders can't hack it. You will get your money's worth from top-end wading gear.

Stocking-foot breathables are the choice of most serious chromeheads. You can use the same pair of waders in the heat of the summer and freeze of the winter by adjust-

ing what you wear underneath. And stocking-foot waders allow you to match your wading boots to the conditions.

Because steelheading so often demands serious wading, wading boots with metal studs are the ideal choice. Boots with a combination of felt and studs on the sole offer the maximum stability over varied terrain. A quality wading boot shouldn't be any bigger than it needs to be. The river applies a tremendous amount of drag on the boot, and any extra size only increases the drag applied.

Many people claim that boot-foot neoprene waders are the best choice for cold winter steelhead rivers, but most Northwest guides I know disagree. Steelheaders do too much hiking to stay comfortable in sweat-trapping neoprene.

CHAPTER 8

Rod Play

teelheading typically is thought of as a pursuit that requires a minimum of casting techniques. Most anglers I've met, either at the fly shop or while guiding, assume that a steelheader only needs to know how to do a couple conventional casts to effectively cover most lies. Nothing could be further from the truth. Effective steelheading requires at least as many casting techniques as the most technical trout fishing. And many of the casts needed for steelheading are significantly harder than those needed for trout fishing because of the heavier tackle.

Part of the reason for the number of casts demanded by steelheading is that the sport employs so many different techniques. A consistently successful steelheader often fishes a skater one minute and a nymph the next. And each presentation requires its own casting and mending tactics.

If you want to consistently be successful, you need to know an array of casts, from the simple overhead to the tuck to the long-reaching double haul. You also need to be able to control the line once it is in the water with effective mends and feeds.

In this chapter, I detail several common casts and mends done with single-handed rods. After much deliberation, I decided not to include instruction in Spey casting, and for good reason: Only in my fantasies am I a good enough Spey caster to teach the subject. But Spey fishers may find value in the discussion of specific mends and feeds, all of which are just as applicable with a Spey rod as they are with a single-handed rod.

With enough practice, the rod will simply become an extension of your arm. When you want to throw a rock, your arm comes back like a spring and then releases, launching the rock into flight. This process does not take any thought. The body instantly understands how to achieve the mind's goal. The throwing of a rock feels to an adult like a natural talent, something that didn't require any tutelage. But if you think back far enough, you can probably remember some lesson you had as a child in the art. Casting, mending, and feeding line with a fly rod are all skills that will become as natural as throwing a rock. The motion will be completed without a conscious thought from the mind. When you want to achieve something, such as a little more distance, your hands suddenly become double-hauling machines. At this point, the fly rod has become an extension of the arms. Casting becomes as natural as throwing a rock. This is the ideal state.

The Casts

The double haul, roll cast, and reach cast all are examples of casts that steelheaders use regularly—most days on the river, in fact. These casts have been detailed in many fine books already. I see little value in regurgitating that information here. But what *is* valuable is learning how you can use these well-known casts to hook more chromers.

Above: Effective steelheading requires at least as many casting tactics as technical trout fishing, except that the casts must be done with heavier gear.

Double Haul

The double haul is a common fly-casting technique, a skill employed from the bonefish flats of the equator to the char rivers of the Arctic Circle. The cast produces faster line speeds than the standard overhead cast, hence propelling the fly farther away.

On many rivers, success with swinging presentations requires covering lots of water. An angler who is able to cast fifty feet will take half as many fish as one able to cast a hundred. A finely tuned double haul can double the distance of your cast, therefore allowing you to show your fly to more fish.

Besides adding distance to your cast, the double haul has other utilities in steelheading. Our rivers are often besieged by unrelenting Pacific winds, which can stop the forward progress of a cast and pile the line at your feet. In such situations, the double haul can drive the line into the wind and keep you fishing while other anglers are heading home.

The double haul allows you to cover more water and, in so doing, show your fly to more fish.

Also, the higher line speeds generated by the double haul turn over bulky flies and indicators with greater ease. When using indicator tactics, the double haul can produce a perfect tuck cast even at radical distances. Whether you're swinging flies on a sink-tip or dead drifting drys on a floater, the double haul is an essential steelheading skill that once mastered will result in you putting more steelhead on the beach.

Roll Cast

The roll cast has three valuable functions for the steelheader. First, it can be used as a fly delivery mechanism. When streamside brush prohibits a standard overhead cast, the roll cast can save the day.

Second, it can be used to help sink a fly more deeply. Several modern steelheading techniques depend on sinking a fly quickly. Many anglers are inclined to add lots of split shot to help their leader sink, but enough drag will keep a shot out off the bottom. Besides, weight on the leader absorbs the often subtle strike of steelhead, causing you to miss many fish. Instead of adding weight to the leader, you can use a roll cast to put a lightly weighted fly on the stones. The standard roll cast is made slightly farther out and upstream of the lie to be fished. Then a second roll cast, this one significantly smaller, sends a roll of line toward the fly, depositing the leader directly on top of it. The leader's position over the fly provides a pile of slack, hence allowing the fly to sink quickly.

Third, the roll cast can be used at the end of a swing, when a sink-tip is deeply under the surface. If you were simply to begin a new cast at such a moment, the heavy line might strike you in the face or break your rod. (Much to my chagrin, I broke two rods this way during my early days of steelheading.) Instead of beginning a new cast at the end of the swing, many sink-tip anglers strip in a pile of slack, then make the next cast. But this stripping in of slack takes a lot of time and increases the chances of a fly-line knot that might take several minutes to untangle. Instead of stripping in slack at the end of a swing, you can use a roll cast to position the sink-tip on the surface. Once it is there, you can begin a standard overhead cast.

Reach Cast

The reach cast is probably familiar to trout fishers, if not by name, then by practice. This cast is commonly used on the trout stream when an angler is trying to dead drift a fly to a lie across the current. Making an overhead cast and extending the rod to the side as the front loop straightens out buy the fly an extra few seconds of ideal drift. The steelheader uses the reach cast to increase the effectiveness of a whole host of presentations, both dead drifting and swinging.

The reach cast acts as an aerial mend, helping you either slow the swing or prolong a dead drift.

Picture yourself standing on a long beach along your homewater. The riffle is flowing at a walking pace from your right to your left, an ideal place to try the wet-fly swing. You wade in at the top and face quartering downstream. If you make a standard overhead cast, the current will instantly form a belly in the line as it lands. This belly will cause the fly to pull across the river at an undesirable speed, possibly even causing it to skip across the surface. A properly timed reach cast can eliminate that immediate belly and therefore slow the swing of the fly. In effect, the reach cast is little more than an aerial mend.

Though the reach cast is typically used to slow a fly's swing across the river, it can also increase the speed of the fly's swing. Instead of reaching toward the center of the river's flow, simply reach toward the bank. In a slow run, a shoreward reach can impart the action to the fly needed to tempt hesitant steelhead.

The reach cast is also invaluable when fishing dead-drifting tactics. A overhead or roll cast that ends in an upstream reach can buy you enough time to start sending stack mends toward the fly without imparting drag on the fly's drift. In other words, a good reach cast can result in longer drag-free floats with either dry flies or indicator tactics.

Ideally, you want to be able to make a double haul or roll cast that ends in a reach cast. If you can make a good reach cast, you will always be one mend ahead of the game.

Tuck Cast

The tuck cast, or pile cast in some circles, helps sink the fly as quickly as possible. Modern steelheading techniques, such as the dead-drifted nymph and broadside rise, require you to put the fly on the bottom while fish-

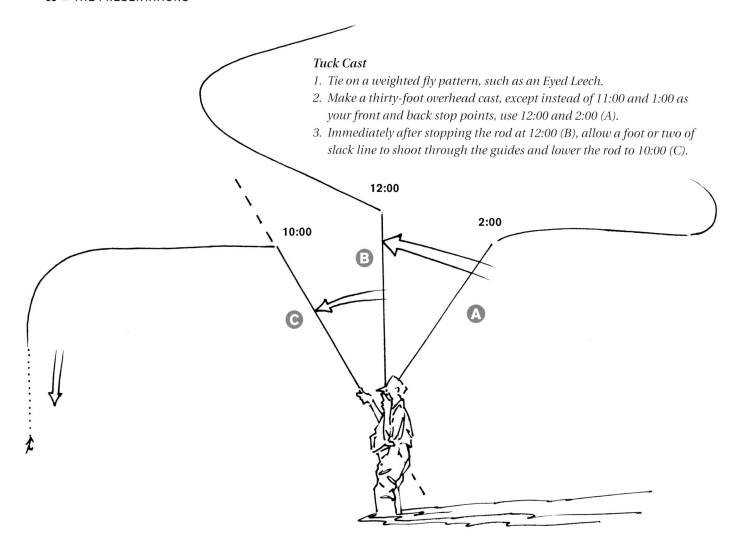

Tuck Cast

1. *Tie on a weighted fly pattern, such as an Eyed Leech.*
2. *Make a thirty-foot overhead cast, except instead of 11:00 and 1:00 as your front and back stop points, use 12:00 and 2:00 (A).*
3. *Immediately after stopping the rod at 12:00 (B), allow a foot or two of slack line to shoot through the guides and lower the rod to 10:00 (C).*

ing a floating line. Some anglers get deep by attaching plenty of weight to the leader or hook. But to avoid the headache and sore arm that follow a day spent casting a shot put's worth of lead, many steelheaders employ the tuck cast. I'll detail its mechanics here, as this cast is rarely explained elsewhere with steelheaders and our heavier gear in mind.

The physics of the cast are simple. When a fly, even a heavily weighted one, lands on the water during a standard overhead cast, the immediate tension from the straight leader and fly line hinders its ability to sink. The tuck cast corrects this problem by delivering the fly, leader, and several feet of fly line onto the same small point on the water, allowing the fly to sink unhindered to the bottom. The cast also gives the fly adequate momentum to break through the surface tension, helping speed its initial descent. When done correctly, the tuck cast helps even a lightly weighted fly plummet like a rock.

The tuck cast is best practiced over a stream, where you can see whether it successfully placed the fly deep within the water column. Here's how to do it:

If done correctly, the fly will hit the water first, followed by the leader and the fly line. The whole pile should land on the same point.

Some anglers have trouble generating sufficient line speeds to turn over a weighted fly and an indicator with the tuck cast. If you experience problems, try employing a double-haul motion to the casting stroke to speed up your line.

Once mastered, the tuck cast will become a standard tool in your repertoire. Its ability to get a fly down quickly often makes the crucial difference, allowing you to take fish in water others just worked.

The Mends and Feeds

Angling historians credit A. H. E. Wood of Glassel, England, with stumbling upon two major innovations, both important to steelheaders, while fishing his homewater early in the twentieth century. Wood, an Atlantic salmon fisherman, developed a technique called the greased-line presentation to persuade dour fish to take. His revolutionary method involved presenting a fly near the river's surface in a nearly broadside manner. One of the novel elements was that this technique required a line that floated. To achieve this, Wood greased his silk fly line with animal fat, hence the name of the presentation. This greased line paved the way for his second innovation, mending. Once the line could float, it could be controlled by precise movements of the rod.

The steelheader uses mending, in the most general of terms, to control the drift of the fly. Every technique used in steelheading requires some form of mending. And techniques like the dead-drifted nymph require a copious amount. Becoming a confident mender is an essential step to consistently catching steelhead.

Successful steelheaders incorporate various mends and feeds on a single cast. The specific techniques you should use depend completely on the unique character of the water you are fishing. Becoming competent at controlling your line will allow you to present your flies effectively in all types of holding water. The more holding water you can cover, the more steelhead you'll land.

If you've ever watched an expert steelheader work, you'll notice the angler doesn't mend excessively. Overmending not only fatigues the arm prematurely, but also can hurt the fly's ability to fish properly. A competent mender uses a few perfectly timed and executed mends to get the job done. And these mends come as soon as the presentation allows, rather than in the middle of the drift or swing, guaranteeing the fly the most uninterrupted fishing time. When on the river, remember this mantra: Mend early and mend rarely.

Line Lifts

The line lift is the easiest of all the mending techniques and is used frequently with swinging presentations such

Mending is used to control the swing or drift of the fly, depending on the technique. In this case, an angler mends to keep his fly line out of the fast water between him and his dead-drifting egg pattern.

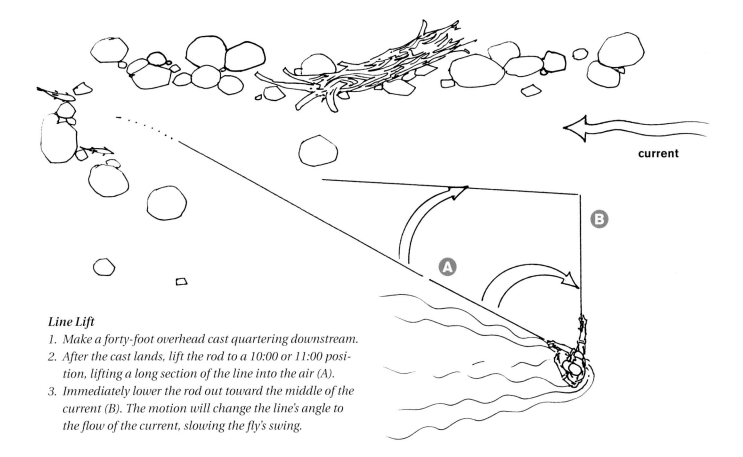

Line Lift

1. *Make a forty-foot overhead cast quartering downstream.*
2. *After the cast lands, lift the rod to a 10:00 or 11:00 position, lifting a long section of the line into the air (A).*
3. *Immediately lower the rod out toward the middle of the current (B). The motion will change the line's angle to the flow of the current, slowing the fly's swing.*

as the classic swing, sink-tip, greased-line, and skated dry-fly presentations. Its task is to control the speed at which at the fly swings.

The line lift is best practiced on the river. Find a riffle or run you think ideal for the classic swinging presentation with a floating line.

The mend is most effective if done in one fluid motion. Stalling at step A can cause the line to slip deeply into the surface tension, hindering an easy lift. Some anglers report steelhead turning away when a fly is twitched by a mend. The mend is best done early in the presentation and as infrequently as possible.

Most often, line lifts are needed to slow the fly's progress, so the rod is lowered toward the middle of the flow. But sometimes, especially when employing a sink-tip, greased-line, or skated dry-fly presentation, the rate of the fly's swing needs to be increased. Lowering the rod toward shore will speed the swing.

Line Flips

Line flips are a variation on the standard line lift. Both mending techniques have the same goal: to reposition the line in an effort to control the speed of the presentation. But the line flip results in a line positioned farther from the angler than the line lift, hence affecting the fly more profoundly. Line flips are best done when a gross

adjustment to the fly line's position is demanded by the character of the river. Sometimes you want to profoundly slow the fly's swing as it nears a known holding area to allow the fish more time to strike. In such situations, the line flip may be your best option.

If done correctly, the line will be placed several feet farther from the rod than if you made a line lift mend. Timing is essential in the mend. After the cast is made, the progression through steps A and B must be a fluid one, with enough power behind the motion to move the line. At step A, think of your elbow as a loaded spring. Step B simply lets the spring loose, flipping line accordingly.

The line flip has two disadvantages. As you perform the motion, the fly has a loose connection to the rod, reel, and you. If a fish takes at that moment, you might not ever know. I once watched a small summer fish swirl on my fly the moment I threw the flip. Once tension came back, the fish was gone. Repeated casts didn't move it a second time. But though a missed fish is a possibility, the slower pace of the swing promised by the line flip often makes the risk worth taking. The occasional missed steelhead will be replaced by two, three, or five fish taking because the swing slowed near their lies.

The second disadvantage of the line flip is that it can't be done without substantially jerking the fly, a practice some believe can put fish down. Completing the flip once early in the presentation can limit the possibility of a spooked fish.

You can also use the line flip to feed line into the drift. When a lie is outside your casting range, or when a sink-tip needs to be allowed to dead drift so as to sink, you can feed line via a line flip. To accomplish this, you simply need to shoot line as the arm is extended from the elbow (step 3, below). Repeated line flips can feed line into the drift for as long as necessary. In this manner, you can reach a lie far outside your maximum casting range or sink a sink-tip into the deepest of slots.

Stack Mends

Unlike the line lift and line flip, which are both used to control the fly's swing, stack mends allow a fly to maintain its dead drift. The mend also allows a slightly weighted fly the necessary slack to sink into the deepest of lies. It works by keeping the slack line off the water without adding tension to the leader. On today's pressured rivers, where most steelhead are shy of flies moving unnaturally, a deeply drifted fly is often the most consistent producer. Being able to proficiently stack-mend will allow you to prolong your dead drifts and therefore cover more water.

Learning the stack mend might take a little time, but the investment will pay huge dividends. For practice, find a run a few feet deep with a current moving at a walking pace.

The stack mend does two important things. First, it feeds the drifting and sinking fly slack. Without this slack, the fly will not reach the desired depth without the addition of tremendous amounts of weight. Second, it keeps the line out of the water so that the current can't form a belly, decreasing drag on the fly. The high rod position coupled with constant mending strokes keep the line in the air and out of trouble.

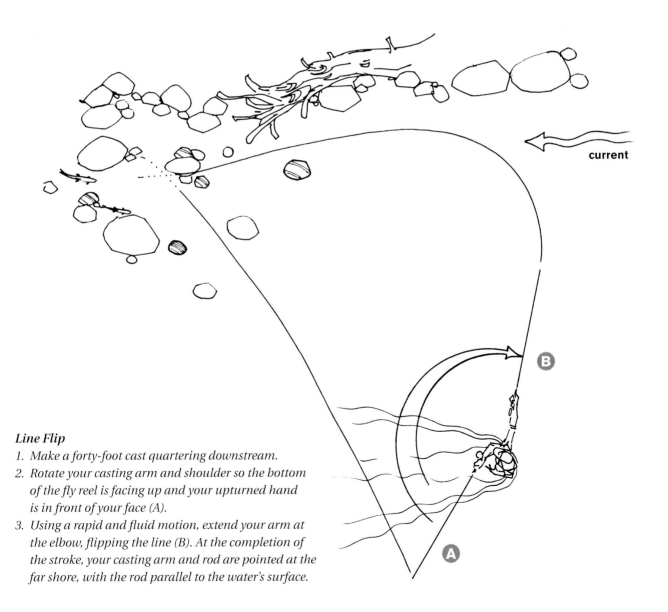

Line Flip

1. *Make a forty-foot cast quartering downstream.*
2. *Rotate your casting arm and shoulder so the bottom of the fly reel is facing up and your upturned hand is in front of your face (A).*
3. *Using a rapid and fluid motion, extend your arm at the elbow, flipping the line (B). At the completion of the stroke, your casting arm and rod are pointed at the far shore, with the rod parallel to the water's surface.*

current

The stack mend is most commonly used to keep the fly line out of the current, helping a fly both sink deep and drift naturally.

Stack Mend

1. *Make a tuck cast that lands twenty-five feet quartering upstream from your position.*
2. *Immediately move the rod to the 1:00 position, rotating at the waist to pace the dead drift of the fly (A).*
3. *Snap the rod from the 1:00 position to the 11:00 position (B). Each snap will send out a small roll of line. Aim the small rolls so they'll land on top of the dead-drifting fly.*
4. *As the fly drifts past your position, continue sending stacks to the fly's slot (they'll start landing upstream of the fly), except now send a few feet of slack with each mend (C).*

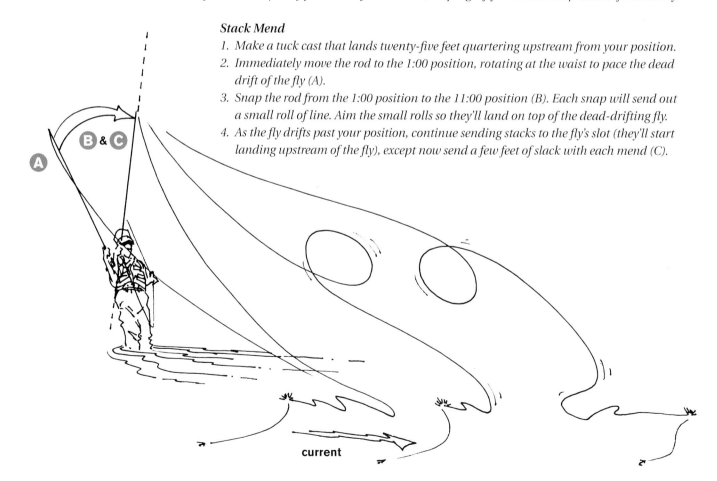

current

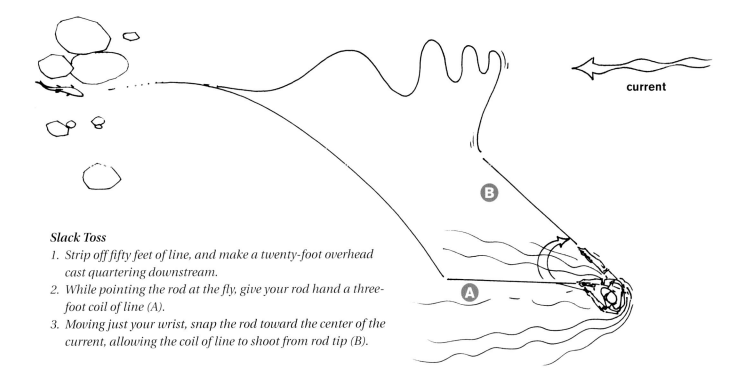

Slack Toss

1. *Strip off fifty feet of line, and make a twenty-foot overhead cast quartering downstream.*
2. *While pointing the rod at the fly, give your rod hand a three-foot coil of line (A).*
3. *Moving just your wrist, snap the rod toward the center of the current, allowing the coil of line to shoot from rod tip (B).*

Slack Tosses

The slack toss is used when trying to prolong the dead drift of a downstream presentation. Most frequently, it is employed to help an indicator and fly float through a long run below the angler. But it is equally practical when fishing sink-tips and the broadside pull when the river's character merits. The technique feeds slack into the line, allowing the fly to escape the tension applied by the current.

Like all mending techniques, the slack toss is best practiced on the river. Find a riffle or run and wade into the top.

If done correctly, the slack will land in the current. To get the best drift, make repeated slack tosses in fast order.

Also, make them land in current that is moving at the same speed as your drifting fly.

Slack tosses are most useful on long riffles and runs while dead drifting flies below an indicator. When done in conjunction with stack mends or feeding line flips, slack tosses can help the flies drift the length of the line unimpeded. And the more time your flies spend fishing, the better your odds of hooking a chromer.

Pressure Pulls

Pressure pulls are used most commonly on the greased-line and broadside-pull presentations to help feed slack into the drift. Instead of using the rod to throw line, as is done with other mending and feeding techniques, the

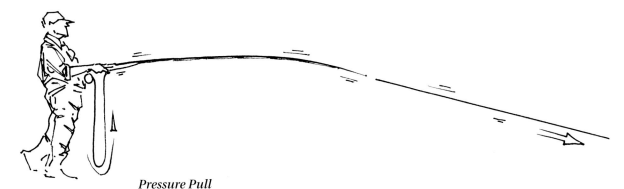

Pressure Pull

1. *Strip off fifty feet of line, and make a thirty-foot overhead cast quartering downstream.*
2. *As the current's drag builds on the line, release your rod hand's pinch on the slack line, allowing a small section of slack to be pulled into the river.*

pressure pull uses the current's drag to take slack from the angler.

The technique is best practiced on a riffle or run with an even current from side to side.

If the pressure applied by the current isn't adequate to pull the slack line from your rod hand, you can raise the rod slightly to help it along. If done correctly, perfectly controlled amounts of slack will be fed into the drift, but you won't lose contact with the fly for more than a moment. If you were to lose contact for too long, a fish could take and you wouldn't be the wiser.

The cast allows you to feed just enough slack into the swing to allow the fly to stop rising toward the surface, as is typical when the line is held tight during the swing. While fishing the broadside-pull presentation, the advantage of slowing the fly's rise is that you can prolong its climbing motion, providing as many fish as possible a view of this tantalizing action. While fishing the greased-line presentation, the advantage of feeding line is that you can prolong the broadside position of the fly as well as keep it from skating over the surface.

CHAPTER 9

Swinging with a Floating Line

For many of us, the transition from trout fishing to steelheading is a logical one. We've caught enough trout to feel a certain confidence in the pursuit, and we're interested in tackling a new challenge. Plus, it doesn't hurt that most steelhead will double the mass of our best trout. The trade-off inherent in steelheading—lower numbers, more size—is an acceptable compromise. Going a few days without a strike won't kill us, and it'll make each hooked fish that much more memorable. Losing the small, consistent bursts of excitement provided by trout fishing will surely be compensated for by the inconsistent but huge adrenaline explosions of steelheading.

But for others of us, the transition between trout fishing and steelheading isn't as obvious. Trout offer consistency in an inconsistent world. They're almost always willing to dance, given we provide them the right incentive. Such constancy breeds a loyal following among some, my father included.

Despite my most arduous attempts—long family functions spent romanticizing the volatile fight of a fresh steelhead, detailing the riveting life history of the fish, and so on—he just couldn't be persuaded. He loved trout. Cool evenings spent reeling in mountain rainbows from pocket water. Dawn patrol on high-country lakes. This was fishing to him, not long days spent casting, casting, casting. "But you only catch one a day, right?" he'd say. "Sure," I'd answer, "when you get it wired, but

that isn't the poi——" "See, that just doesn't sound like as much fun as normal fishing."

As my father reached his later fifties, I ratcheted up my appeals. His friends were starting to retire, to delve headlong into their passions, to enjoy life to its fullest. And as if to compensate for their indulgence, my father cranked up his work schedule. He spent more time at the office slaving away. But more troublesome, he started to say things like "I'll never retire. It's the beginning of a short walk off a high plank."

Finally, with a helpful nudge from my mother, he consented to take a weekend away from work and do a little fishing with his "boy." "The Deschutes," I said. "The fish are in, and they're eager."

"I've got my terrestrial box filled up," he said. "What else should I bring? Will the caddis be hatching?" He obviously had his mind on his 5-weight.

When he showed up at my door a few days later, I casually slipped an extra 8-weight into his truck.

We camped on the lower river, down where the pools are wide and long and there's a chance of hooking a "B strain" fish—Idaho steelhead that sometimes reach more than twenty pounds and hold temporarily in the cool Deschutes flows. That night, as we ate in the lantern light, I

Above: Two anglers use floating lines to swing wet flies along the Deschutes in October.

gave it all I had. "Look, I'll rig the rod and everything. All you'll have to do is fish the fly like you would to a mountain trout, cast down and across and let it swing. That's it. Just pretend you're trout fishing. Hell, in a certain sense you are."

He kept eating his baked beans, his spoon clanking against the tin. "This is one of those things you'll never let slide, huh?"

"Damn straight. You're missing out."

I woke him before dawn, the extra 8-weight loaded with a svelte little Max Canyon. "It's go time," I said. "We've only got fifteen minutes until legal light."

He eyed me seriously, wondering, I could tell, if he were my real father. "At least trout have the civility to wait until after breakfast." Then, after yawning a cloud into the frozen desert air, he snatched the rod from my hand. "Well, since I'm up anyway."

With the towering canyon walls black against the cobalt sky, we waded into a long run just downstream from camp. Submerged boulders churned the surface, and between two, I saw the slivered moon bouncing in the ripples. I took a position upstream from my father, eager to watch him work through his first section of steelhead water.

He figured out the rod quickly and made good casts that allowed his fly to swing slowly, confidently, across the river. The presentation came naturally to him, as if he'd been a steelheader in hiding his entire life. We'd been fishing for close to an hour, the morning sun barely nicking the canyon rim, when a fish rolled on his fly. He raised his rod, and I heard the reel panic and saw a chrome steelie clear the water once, twice, three times. The steelhead turned and rushed downstream, so fast the reel's drag smoothed into a solid harmonizing note. And then he was off.

To say the man was shaken wouldn't do his mental state any justice. Shaken would imply a certain level of underlying consistency, a bedrock foundation (name, rank, serial number) still intact somewhere within. No, that fish had rocked him to his core, caused in him a mental earthquake that would leave the entire man, bedrock and all, cracked for eternity.

He wouldn't stop casting. Once through the run, he started again at the top. As the sun hit the river, I grew worried. And as the morning gave way to midday, I pleaded that he give the river a break and come to camp for some food and water. Maybe the only reason I eventually maneuvered him back to camp was that his dehydrated body could no longer perform the tasks his fish-obsessed mind demanded of it.

He spent at most fifteen minutes in camp, chugging water and forcing granola into his open mouth, never once letting the 8-weight out of his grip. "Did you *see* that?" he'd ask every couple bites. "I mean, that was no normal fish. Did you *see* the size of him?"

After he'd taken care of his body's physical demands, his fish-obsessed mind resumed control.

"What, you don't want to go trout fishing?" I asked as he marched through camp. He grinned and grabbed my steelhead box off the truck's hood.

We didn't hook another fish that night or the next morning, and then because of my work commitments, we had to give up on the river and head back over the mountains. On the drive back, we discussed the local rivers and their summer and winter runs. We talked about the Canadian waters and their monsters. The steelhead chatter ran ceaselessly. Never once did we discuss a silly little trout. When he dropped me off at my house, he had a scheming smile on his face.

"What's up?" I asked.

"Can I borrow one of your rods?"

"One of my steelhead rods?"

"Of course," he scoffed.

"What are you thinking?"

He didn't answer.

Three days later, I got a call from my mother. The steelhead he'd hooked and lost had caused my father to stop in at home only long enough to kiss her on the cheek and call in sick at work, before heading back to the Deschutes. While fishing on his own there, he'd hooked a few more fish, landing three. "What have you done to your father?" she asked. "He's possessed or something."

The damage was more extensive than either of us knew. Within six months, he'd retired. He bought his own steelheading gear and started fishing three days a week. Pretty soon, he was the guy I called when I wanted an update on the river.

Life provides few pleasures as sweet as swinging a traditional wet fly through a long run of holding water. The process of casting, swinging, casting lets you see the ospreys and eagles overhead, the otters and deer along the shores, the parr darting around your ankles. The classic swing provides a new view of the river, one that contains more than just the water and the fish, one that contains the ecosystem. Booming cast after cast quartering to the far shore, then feeling the line come under tension and begin the slow swing to the near shore, is steelheading in its finest form. And the fact that this technique is able to convince a steelhead every now and then is only an added bonus.

The technique in its general form was developed centuries ago in Europe and eventually made its way to the West Coast of the United States. Before A. H. E. Wood developed the greased-line presentation, anglers in Europe

A twelve-pound buck that took on the last swing of the day.

were presenting their silk lines and gaudy flies in the classic swinging form. They'd heave a cast from the heavy rod and follow the line's swing as it cut toward the near shore. In the Americas, Zane Grey fished the technique, as did General Mott, Clarence Gordon, Al Knudson, Roderick Haig-Brown, Bob Arnold, Trey Combs, and nearly everyone else important to the history of steelheading. The technique still is the most commonly used on nearly any big river with a solid run of steelhead. The swinging of wet flies *is* steelheading to many people.

And it's easy to understand why. There is a magical power about the presentation. When you step into a run, especially a named run on a famous river, and start fishing the classic swing, you become intimately connected to the great history of our sport. You're working the water just as generations of like-minded individuals have before you. Maybe you're even using one of the patterns developed on that river generations ago.

Swinging a wet fly hasn't become as ingrained and ritualized in trout fishing as it has in steelheading, even though the technique does take many trout. Many trout anglers never swing a wet fly; for some reason, the technique fell by the cultural wayside generations ago. But for steelheaders, the classic swing has taken a lofty seat

at the throne of the sport. Why is this? One explanation might be the treatment given the technique by some of steelheading's great authors and spokespersons. An entire generation of writers highlighted the benefits of the technique. People like Trey Combs and Lani Waller, in their efforts to draw needed attention to the sport and the fish during the seventies and eighties, showed the potential effectiveness of the technique. Moreover, their generation experienced a cultural renaissance, a reaffirming of steelheading's connection to the Atlantic salmon fishing of the late nineteenth and early twentieth centuries. Some modern anglers still shiver at the thought of trying something different.

Yet many modern steelheaders talk quietly about the limitations of the technique. Such conversations are often in hushed tones and in dark rooms, for many people seem to be insulted by the notion that there are other ways to catch a steelhead. But these conversations have become more commonplace. And it is easy to see why. Evidence suggests that the average steelhead today is more likely to take a pattern that is lifting from the bottom or dead drifting than it is to take a wet fly on the surface. Our rivers see so much more angling pressure than they did twenty years ago; the hot steelhead that so willingly strike a swinging fly learn their lesson fast these days. And those rivers dominated by hatchery runs just don't contain as many eager takers to begin with. Often the steelhead of the twenty-first century require you to try other techniques if you are to be consistently successful.

But the classic swing still offers specific advantages that will forever keep it in high demand on western rivers. First of all, the technique allows you to cover a tremendous amount of water quickly. With long casts, you can reach to the far bank and watch as your cast swings from shore to shore, covering all the water in between. This is an essential ingredient in those situations when you are fishing broad water. With the casts being measured by the amount of line off the reel, you can simply cast, swing, step, and cast again. Few techniques are as efficient. And swinging flies is strikingly simple. The lines and leaders required lack any of the complex-

ity of other presentations. A simple weight-forward line and a store-bought 9-foot leader are perfectly adequate. There are no complex knots to master and no extra devices, like split shot or indicators, on the line. The technique of swinging itself is simple. Any beginning angler can develop proficiency with the technique in a few trips to the river. Only time will teach the subtleties of the presentation, but the basics can be learned quickly. For these reasons, the classic swing will forever have utility on the West Coast's steelhead rivers.

The Water

Swinging with a floating line is best done in specific types of water, during specific circumstances. The advantage of the technique is that it can cover big water quickly. Long sections with a cobbled bottom—where a steelhead might be holding anywhere—are ideally covered with a swinging technique. In just a few minutes,

Swinging with a floating line is best done on broad water—such as riffles, runs, or tailouts—less than six feet deep.

you can search every lie in an entire run. Swinging doesn't entice every fish that sees the fly. Even under ideal conditions, the majority of steelhead will let a swung fly pass. The presentation is effective because it allows you to show the fly to lots of fish—any one of which might slam it. The most successful swingers use the technique only in water types that facilitate showing the fly to lots of fish, namely the broad water of many riffles, runs, and tailouts. Pocket water and some heavily structured riffles are not good locations for the swing, because you will be forced to work slowly through a section, limiting the number of fish that will see the fly.

Swinging with a floating line requires fish to leave their lies on the bottom and travel to the fly, so the technique is best fished in water less than six feet deep. Fish are sometimes caught in deeper water, but you are typically better off using a different technique in such places. The ideal water depth for the classic swing is two to four feet.

Besides depth, the speed of the water is an important consideration. Water that is too fast, although it might hold a fish, will pull the fly directly to the surface and cause it to drag on top. Rarely will a steelhead rise to slam a fly skipping over fast water. Also, water that is too slow to give the line a steady swing is rarely productive.

The temperature and clarity of the water are essential to the success of the swinging steelheader. When the water drops below the ideal temperature range, steelhead become less willing to move far to the fly. Swinging depends on active and aggressive fish; cold water suppresses such attributes. Also, the clarity of the water can have a major effect on the success of the classic swinging technique. When the water is very murky, steelhead can have a hard time seeing the fly. To counteract this problem, you can use a pattern with a bigger silhouette. There comes a point, however, when even the biggest of flies won't help.

The Logistics

Swinging with a floating line is a simple technique, maybe the most simple of the entire sport. Little is complicated about its application. But a lack of complication doesn't make the technique easy. Booming a long cast to a distant lie is never child's play, especially while standing in a roaring river.

Swinging is successful because it's systematic. You perform a cast, step, swing, cast rhythm that guarantees the fly will pass through every lie. This system is employed with several other techniques discussed in later chapters, with added complexities. Swinging with a floating line allows you to learn the system in its most basic, user-friendly form.

Kari Mullenmaster with a hen taken on the swing.
TOM CHRISTENSEN

After finding ideal swinging water, maybe a hundred-foot-long riffle of generally even speed and depth, you'll want to wade into the top of the riffle so that you're thirty feet upstream from the holding water closest to shore. Many steelhead hold close to shore, especially in the fall months; by wading out too far into the riffle, your fly will not be shown to these frequently willing fish. Often water well suited to swinging a fly has a seam between nearly still water along the shore and the faster riffling water away from shore. If your run has such a seam, try to position yourself directly upstream.

The next figure illustrates the technique. Strip off thirty feet of line and make an overhead cast that quarters downstream (A). Each cast will be longer. If you're a confident caster, you can use a reach cast, reaching the line farther out into the current. Immediately after the cast, mend using a line lift (B). This initial mend helps slow the fly's swing across the current, increasing the likelihood of a take. In some situations, the more grandiose line flip is useful to slow the fly, particularly if a fish is thought to be holding in a specific lie. The line flip will slow the fly's progress even more than the line lift, giving the fish more time to see it. But typically you're fine relying on the line lift.

As the fly swings, the rod is best kept parallel to the water's surface and pointed at the fly. If the fly begins to skip on top of the surface, you can move the rod in, meaning the rod points between the fly and the near shore (C). Moving the rod in inclines the fly to drop back below the surface. But typically this is not necessary. The rod can stay pointing at the fly. Doing so provides the best position for hooking a fish that strikes.

The current will eventually swing the line until it hangs directly downstream of your position. It is best to allow the fly to hang there for several seconds, as fish

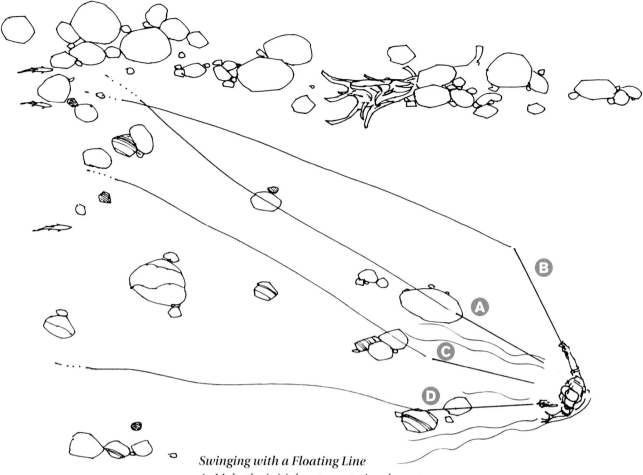

Swinging with a Floating Line

A. *Make the initial cast quartering downstream.*

B. *Immediately make a line lift mend, affecting as much line as possible.*

C. *If the fly skips on the surface, use an "in" rod position.*

D. *Let the line hang below, then give twitches before picking it up for another cast.*

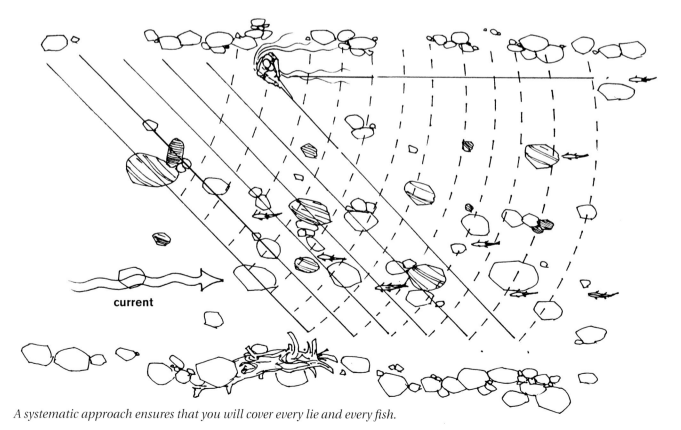

current

A systematic approach ensures that you will cover every lie and every fish.

often follow the fly and watch it before striking. If a few seconds pass and nothing takes, try twitching the fly for a couple more seconds (D). If still no fish takes, pick up the line for a fresh cast.

If you've decided the fish will likely have a two-foot strike zone that day, and hence the slots should be two feet wide, go ahead and peel two feet of fly line from the reel. Make another cast quartering downstream. Gradually lengthen your casts by the size of the strike zone, and you'll systematically cover every lie within reach. Once you've reached the limit of your casting range—or your casts threaten to land on the far shore—start using your feet to cover the water. Take a step downstream the size of the strike zone after each swing. In this manner, you'll be able to cover every lie for the length of the riffle (page 98).

The size of your mends will affect the time it takes your line to swing across the current. A few anglers claim the fly is best swung as slowly as possible, meaning big mends. The majority of steelheaders seem to feel otherwise, however. You want your fly to be shown to every lie in not only this riffle, but others downstream as well. Doing so will allow you to show your fly to the most fish possible, increasing the likelihood of a take. Generally, the ideal swinging speed then is just slightly slower than the current's speed. This allows the fish time to see the fly and strike, but also allows you to cover as much water as possible. Reserve those ultra-slow swings for specific places in the river where you're confident a fish is holding.

Rods, Lines, Leaders, and Flies

The swinging presentation requires little specialized tackle: a long rod, a floating line designed for distance casting, a flawless leader, and a simple fly. Nothing more.

Swinging with a floating line demands long casts and big mends. Being able to control your line while it swings is key to consistently taking fish. For these reasons, the swinging presentation is best done on a long rod. A 9-footer is the minimum for most rivers. A fast-action 10-footer is better. The rod needs to throw a heavy enough line to bust its way through summer winds, so few anglers use anything lighter than a 7-weight on big water. For small streams, a rod as small as a 4-weight can safely be used. On big water, no tool will be as effective as a Spey rod. Two-handers as long as 16 feet are commonly employed on the West's biggest rivers. And their advantages are obvious. Besides making long casts quick and easy, they have tremendous mending ability.

Fly lines with oversize heads and long running bellies make the ideal floating lines for swinging. They'll push the fly into even a stout headwind, helping you reach distant lies. And the long running belly will simplify long-range mends. Fly lines advertised as salmon and steelhead or distance lines typically have this ideal construction. Most floating Spey lines are already designed for the classic swing presentation. Select one that is known to cast well with your rod.

For several years, single-handed casters rushed out to buy shooting tapers, a line system consisting of a 30-foot section of thick fly line and a long section of level running line. A simple double haul would deliver the system to distant lies. With this easy technique, even novice casters could reach great distances with the line. On big waters, shooting tapers can be an advantage, especially if there is wind. Most anglers now prefer a more traditional line system for swinging, however. First, a shooting taper doesn't lend itself to the various mends necessary when fishing the swinging fly. The running line is the culprit here. It can't be tossed and flipped with the same ease as a more conventional fly line. And second, shooting tapers are rather clunky during the casting stroke. All pleasure normally associated with a smooth casting stroke is lost to the heavy taper's cumbersome loading of the rod and passage through the guides. For these reasons, shooting tapers have been falling out of favor with single-handed casters.

But Spey fishers who cast using the Skagit and Scandinavian styles have been picking up shooting taper systems with increasing frequency. The tapers can be cast farther than conventional lines, and the long Spey rod allows the running portion of the line to be controlled with ease.

The ideal leader for swinging with a floating line is simple: a knotless leader that is 9 to 12 feet long and tapered to 8- or 10-pound-test, depending on the conditions. Fluorocarbon is best because of its ability to stand up to abrasions. To save money, many anglers buy a conventional 9-foot leader and tie on a 2- to 3-foot section of fluorocarbon using a blood knot. A simple improved clinch knot is perfect for connecting the tippet to the fly.

Patterns for swinging are as plentiful as migrating smolts in April. It seems every steelheader has personally invented at least a dozen patterns, some more. But despite all these options, an angler excited about swinging flies need only carry a few in varying sizes and colors. Rarely will a fish refuse one pattern and hit another that isn't drastically different. For instance, a fish that refused a size 6 Max Canyon will rarely hit a size 6 Freight Train. For this reason, many guides carry only a few patterns, each drastically different from the others.

My own fly box contains three trusted patterns for swinging from a floating line. I'm one of those guys who

tend to fall in love with a pattern's look, tie a bunch, and experiment. If the pattern catches fish when others won't, it'll earn a slot in my box. Right now, only three patterns have earned permanent status. Each of these three fills a niche, consistently taking fish in certain conditions.

During normal conditions, when the water is clear, I trust the Beach Bum to move fish. Its dark body produces a sharp silhouette against the sky, and its bright tail catches the eye of holding fish. I've found it especially effective on steelhead that have spent a few weeks in fresh water, like those typical of many inland summer steelhead streams. I carry sizes 4 through 8, fishing the bigger patterns over heavier water or when the light is dim and the smaller patterns over thinner water or when the light is bright.

During especially low flows, when the steelhead are spooky, I fish a September Sunset. This low-water pattern has a drab coloration, one that fish rarely fear. I've found the fly especially effective on heavily pressured rivers where the steelhead have been turned off to bigger flies. Often this subtle fly is exactly what is needed to spark the fish's striking reflex. A size 8 covers nearly all situations.

And finally, for those times when the flows are high or fast, I carry a Strung-Out Politician. This pattern moves fish from a great distance. Moreover, its beaded eyes keep it riding low despite strong currents. It is particularly effective on steelhead that have recently entered fresh water. Some people speculate that these fresher fish are more responsive to patterns containing colors commonly seen on bait at sea. The Strung-Out Politician has a shrimp-pink rear section. I carry sizes 2 through 6 and select the bigger patterns during higher flows and low-light conditions.

You never know what is going to spark that steelhead into striking, but there are some general rules in the selection of any fly pattern for swinging. First of all, clear water, low water, or sunny conditions generally call for smaller flies and purple or drab colors. These patterns will show up clearly yet not run the risk of spooking a shy steelhead. Murky water, high water, or low-light conditions generally call for larger black or bright patterns. Visibility is diminished, and these larger flies will stand out more clearly. When the fish are fresh, bright patterns will draw more takes. When the fish have been in the river a while, dark patterns will be more effective. Slower water usually demands flies with more action. The softer currents won't move stiff materials, and therefore the fly won't receive as many strikes.

Facing page: An angler works his wet fly along the North Umpqua.

Beach Bum

Smeraglio's September Sunset

Strung-Out Politician

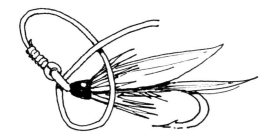

The Riffle Hitch

1. Attach the fly to the leader using an improved clinch knot, then fold a loop of line over the eye of the hook.

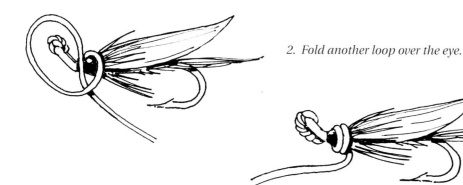

2. Fold another loop over the eye.

3. Position the leader securely on the head and pull tight.

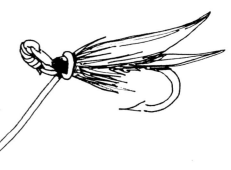

4. As the fly swings, the leader should be on the shore-side of the fly.

Variations

An alternative to attaching the fly to the leader with an improved clinch knot is to use a riffle hitch. The riffle hitch helps turn the fly out into the current, giving it a unique action. This also helps slow the fly's swing without excessive mending. On glassy water of ideal speed, the riffle hitch brings the fly into the surface film, creating an enticing wake.

The riffle hitch comes to us from the Canadian Atlantic salmon angling tradition. In a time when hooks used eyes made of fragile cord, a fly could be fished only for so long before that cord wore through. The frugal guides of eastern Canada invented the riffle hitch as a way of extending the life of their flies. They quickly realized that the riffling flies took more salmon than did the flies tied without the riffle hitch. Naturally, the riffle hitch found its way to the West Coast and into steelhead mouths.

Generally, most anglers find the riffle hitch to be of the greatest advantage when they're fishing slower and smoother water. It provides just enough action to the swinging fly to contradict the overall consistency of such water.

The disadvantage of the riffle hitch is that it can facilitate the fly's ascent to the surface. Depending on the water type and current speed, a riffle hitch can actually cause a fly jump on top of the water, dragging in a manner that is sometimes less prone to draw strikes. Another disadvantage is that the knot wears the tippet down by forcing it into a position it isn't designed to support. Many anglers find they need to cut the tippet and reattach the fly frequently when using the riffle hitch. But usually the advantages outweigh these minor disadvantages. Any angler who wants to use the classic swing over many different types of water should be versed in the riffle hitch's application.

Another variation to the rigging of the swinging fly is the addition of a stinger hook. Often steelhead, especially in warmer water, will strike short on the fly, meaning that the fish nips at the fly's tail rather than taking it whole. Such takes sometimes feel similar to the takes of trout. To combat the short-take problem, anglers attach a 1- to 2-inch section of heavy tippet material, typically something in the order of 12-pound-test. This small section is attached to the bend of the fly's hook via an improved clinch knot. Then with another improved clinch, a size 8 short-shanked, thin wire steelhead hook is attached. This hook rides behind the fly through the water and hooks those steelhead that strike the tail of the fly. Such stinger hooks are best kept barbless, as barbless hooks penetrate a steelhead's hard mouth better, and the stinger hook will undoubtedly pick up the occasional trout as well. A barbless hook will ensure that the fish can be released unharmed.

The stinger hook should never be bigger than the fly that is fishing it. And it should never be allowed to hang back more than three inches. Doing so can mean a complicated and possibly detrimental hookup on a steel-head that takes the fly wholeheartedly. Avoid using a stinger hook on rivers that contain smolts, as it will hook these juvenile steelhead as fast as it touches the river.

Hooking Takers

The ideal hook set on a steelhead is either in the center of the top jaw or in one of the corners where the upper and lower jaws meet. Such hookups increase the likelihood of a landed fish. As with all techniques, there are certain steps you can take to increase the likelihood of such hookups.

Usually, when a steelhead takes a fly that is swinging across the current, the fish strikes the fly and then turns. Ideally, the fish turns and heads downstream, which provides the perfect angle for a solid hook set. But often the fish turns and heads side-stream to its lie.

Many anglers new to steelheading, especially excellent trout fishers, instinctually raise the rod when a fish takes. This reaction happens without thought and likely stems from the impulse ingrained in us to raise the rod when the fish takes a dry fly. But this reaction is absolutely the wrong one in the world of swinging flies for

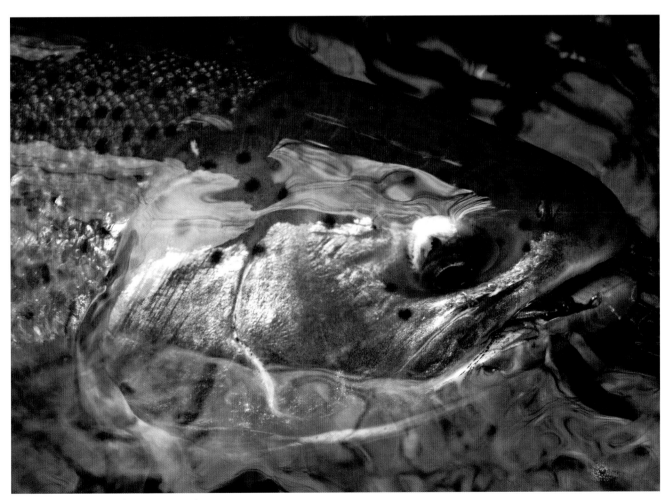

An eight-pound hen from a coastal stream.

steelhead. Such a quick tugging at the fly often pulls it from the fish's mouth before the fish has a chance to turn downstream. If the fish is still facing upstream when you set the hook, it is likely to come straight out of the fish's mouth or, if you are lucky, to be set in the flesh of the jaw. Either way, you are unlikely to land the fish. Bottom line: You're best off refusing the impulse to immediately raise the rod when a steelhead takes your swinging fly.

If you are fishing the fly properly, there is firm tension from the fly up the line. A tight line is a good line. You always want to be in contact with the fly. Because the rod is pointed down the line, you should feel little through the rod when the fly is taken. The jolt of the take will be felt directly in the line. Some anglers allow the line to feed directly from the reel out to the fly. In this situation, when the fly is taken, immediate resistance is delivered to the fly from the reel. If the fish took the fly from the side, the hook will find a firm home. But more often than not, the fish will take from behind and will be in the middle of its turn when the sudden resistance is delivered, and the resistance will pull the fly from the fish's mouth. Allowing the swinging line to have direct contact with the reel is almost as detrimental to a solid hookup as rapidly raising the rod at the take.

To solve this problem, you need only take one precaution when fishing a swinging fly: Hang a loop of line between the rod hand and the reel. Doing so will allow the fish to take the fly and turn downstream before the sudden resistance from the reel is delivered. Ideally, this loop will be a foot to a foot and a half long. Let the line hang, applying just enough pressure to keep the river's current from pulling it out. When a fish takes, the loop slips from your fingers on its own accord, giving the fish enough slack to turn in the current. Just as the fish has turned, the line comes tight on the reel, and the hook buries itself in the fish's jaw.

If the hook slips into the corner of the steelhead's mouth, the pressure applied by the reel will be sufficient for a solid hookup. But if the hook found its way to another, more bony section of the jaw, another set might be necessary. For this reason, once the line has come tight to the reel, the best practice is to raise the rod in a firm and steady motion. You shouldn't raise the rod in an erratic and jolting motion, as this will unduly strain the tippet. Rather, raise it consciously, firmly, and steadily. Because the fish will be taking the fly downstream of you, raise the rod up and toward the downstream shore. Creating this angle helps further ensure that the fly will find a solid placement in the fish's jaw.

CHAPTER 10

Swinging with a Sinking Line

A seam formed where the whitewater slid along the pool's green. An impossible seam to fish. The whitewater moved at blurring velocity, hell-bent on reaching the ocean by nightfall. The green water held motionless, content to spend eternity in a single pool. And the seam extended down—way down—fifteen feet or so below the surface. Despite the seam's obvious difficulty, it begged to be fished. The thing extended for seventy-five feet into the pool, collecting tired steelhead as they recovered strength. And something about the emerald color of the water, with sunken bubbles spinning like snowflakes caught in a windstorm, grabbed my angler's instinct by its scrawny throat.

Halfway down the pool, a massive rock projected from the water. A dozen battered logs hovered atop it, placed there by ancient floodwaters. The provocative seam coupled with these remnants of catastrophic deluge gave the place a palpable wildness—I thought, just for a second, I smelled the musky stink of a bear nearby.

This spot had a reputation with gear fishers for collecting big winter runs. But under normal water levels, it was inaccessible to the fly. A month of no rain had dropped the river to near record lows, and now the impossible seemed possible.

Under the green water, where the seam touched the bottom, something moved. I blocked the light with my hands, squinting for a better view. For a long moment, there was nothing. But then, near the bottom, a glimpse of polished chrome.

Mike, my client for the day, stood perplexed at the head of the pool, a 9-weight over his shoulder. He watched the water rushing by, the logs atop the rock. "I don't know where to start," he said.

The seam's depth demanded my longest and heaviest sink-tip, a homemade line spliced together from a massive shooting taper and an 11-weight floater. An old guide had suggested the dimensions: "Back when I started, we had to make our own," he had said. "Mine are still the best lines on the water. No factory knows the river like I know the river." By the way the line fished, I was inclined to agree. Mike delivered a competent cast into the rapids, hunching to full attention. He mended, then slack-tossed a pile of line into the drift. The line sank and sank and sank, then came tight below. After the fly hung in the seam for what felt like a minute, Mike stripped out another foot and a half and presented the fly again. This time the fly sank deeper.

"This one feels good," he said, tossing a smile over his shoulder. As the line straightened and swung toward the seam, it jarred taut. Mike slammed back on the rod, delivering an arm's worth into the mysterious depths. For a long moment, nothing happened. Mike stayed contorted, the rod stayed doubled, and the water stayed green. Then it came: a slow, heavy tug that stripped out

Above: Jim Larison swings a sink-tip through a deep winter run.

two feet of slack. And another. And another. Each came faster than the last, until Mike's rod bent to the cork and his reel squirted pulses of song. "Fish!" he said, his voice cracking like a thirteen-year-old's.

Then it stopped. The line held tight, but the pulsing rushes were gone. We wondered if the fish had traded places with a submerged log. If the head shakes had been nothing more than a communal hallucination. And then the pool erupted as if a bear had blasted into it. The fly line razored the water open as the fish ripped toward the tailout. Mike held the rod high, straining against the weight. The fish arced into the air—streaks of silver and red over the water. Upon landing, it thrashed the water white and finally darted to the depths once more. After a long bulldogging session and another blazing run, the hen came to shore. I tailed her as she came by, a wild winter fish of thirteen or fourteen pounds.

Mike waded in beside me, unpinning the fly. Without lifting her from the water, we traded positions, his hands slipping under mine. I backed away, giving them space.

He barely had to rock her back and forth before she bolted away.

Winter steelhead are the larger and more powerful of the two general types of steelhead. These fish spend more time at sea, enter the rivers when the water is running harder and faster, and spend only a short amount of time in the fresh water before spawning. These conditions conspire to make a race of superior strength and agility. The extra time at sea means the winter fish have consumed more food and usually gained more mass than their summer cousins. The faster rivers of winter mean only the strongest of fish make it upstream to the spawning water, a process of selection that produced long hereditary lines of powerful fish. And because the steelhead are entering the river as late as March and spawning shortly thereafter, any fish hooked could be days from the salt. For many steelheaders, winter's long nights are punctuated by glistening dreams of wet chrome.

Such dreams have delivered die-hard anglers to the river's edge for nearly a hundred years, despite all the

The reward for swinging a sink-tip on a rainy winter day: a mint seventeen-pound buck just days from the salt.

Pacific could throw: rain, snow, snowmelt due to warm rain, deep frost, heavy winds, landslides, mudslides, rockslides. The winter sorts anglers as a set of rapids sorts fish. During the cold and murky and high flows of winters past, steelheaders fished their flies the best they knew how—floating lines and heavy hooks swung through riffles, runs, and tailouts. Technology had yet to offer the kind assistance of plastics and graphites. And with the odds so stacked against them, most anglers rarely felt the tug of a fish, even while baitfishers across the river dragged out hogs requiring two hands to lift into the truck.

But then a beam of glimmering hope split the clouds: Fly lines started being weighted. By adding a lead core to an otherwise typical fly line, a fly could be swung close to the river bottom, down where the fish were more likely to take. These early lines made the casts clumsy and awkward, as the weighted section hinged at the connection with the regular fly line. The lines required as much ducking as they did chucking. And if the swinging line hit a rock, the rock would leave a bend in the line requiring straightening by the angler. These lines couldn't be mended; instead, the cast had to do the jobs of both delivering the fly and properly positioning the line for a good swing.

Early sinking lines didn't win many converts, but they did catch a few big and powerful winter steelhead for the die-hards that used them. It wasn't long before new lines came onto the market—lines weighted with more technologically advanced materials, lines that could actually be cast in the traditional sense of the word. With the success came the converts, and with the converts came a market that could support more determined innovation. New lines bloomed onto the market, each generation an improvement from the last. The sink-tips available today cast almost as effortlessly as floating lines. In fact, some actually cast better. And a variety of densities exist now, allowing you to pick the right line for a specific type of water.

Thanks to the ease of casting a modern sink-tip, winter steelheading is no longer the sole domain of the hard-core—although the quality lines didn't do anything to change the weather. Now you can comfortably fish a high and murky run and still have a realistic expectation of hooking fish. Moreover, with the popularity of sink-tips came anglers willing to experiment. The lines proved their utility not only on winter rivers, but on summer streams as well. A sink-tip allows you to fish nearly any riffle, run, or tailout normally inaccessible to a floating line.

The sink-tip is effective because it delivers your fly closer to the steelhead than a floating line. When the water is too deep or the strike zone of the steelhead too small, a sink-tip can be the only way of putting a swinging fly within striking range of a fish. The modern steelheader doesn't need sink-tips to consistently catch fish. But owning them and applying them correctly can make the essential difference.

The Water

Whereas other techniques are described in terms of "ideal conditions," the conditions that justify the sink-tip's use are hard to talk about in terms of "ideal." Sink-tips are employed because the fish won't respond consistently to a fly swung from a floating line. Their strike zones are too small in relation to the water in which they are holding. Though there are no "ideal conditions" for the sink-tip, there are conditions that warrant its use.

Sometimes steelhead have a strike zone small enough that they are unlikely to rise to the surface for a fly. Picture a winter steelie holding in a four-foot-deep run along the Sauk. The fish has a small strike zone and is willing to move only two feet vertically to take a fly. You can present a swinging fly from a floating line to this fish all day and never produce a strike—your fly will always be outside its strike zone. Enter the sinking line. On your first cast, the line plummets to the bottom, taking the fly with it. As the fly swings, it lifts off the bottom and hangs one foot over the steelhead's nose. Now the fly is within the fish's strike zone.

Sink-tips are best employed when a floating line can't put the fly within the strike zone of a steelhead. But because every steelhead is more likely to strike a fly presented nearby, aren't you always better off fishing a sink-tip with a swinging presentation?

A minority of anglers believe that, yes, you are better off using a sink-tip any time you want to swing. And they do, throwing the lines every day of the year, regardless of the conditions. But sink-tips have an extreme disadvantage: They cover most types of water more slowly than a floating line. After the initial cast with a sink-tip, the line requires a bit of complex mending and feeding to allow it to sink. After the swing, the line takes longer to get back in the air and redelivered. Effectively presenting a sink-tip is a slower process than effectively presenting a floater. Hence the majority of steelheaders choose to employ sink-tips only when the conditions demand it. Using a floating line whenever you can ensures that you'll be able to effectively cover as much water as possible, increasing your likelihood of a take.

Besides putting your fly deep in the water column, sink-tips have another advantage, one they share with other swinging presentations: They allow you to cover broad sweeps of river where a steelhead might be hold-

A sink-tip allows you to keep your fly close to the bottom—within the strike zone—over large swaths of water. Long, deep runs like this one on the North Umpqua make ideal sink-tip water.

ing anywhere. Many larger rivers are made up of extensive riffles and runs. On giant rivers, a run might be five hundred yards long. By swinging the water, you're able to show your fly to every lie in the run in the shortest amount of time possible. This advantage means sink-tips are best employed in riffles, runs, and tailouts where you need to search a lot of water to find holding fish.

But sink-tips offer another, lesser-known advantage. Often steelhead hold under extremely fast water like that found in rapids. The fish maybe holding there because of bright light, low levels of oxygen in the water, or intense angler pressure. They press their bodies against the stones and hold in the slow water there. Most techniques aren't suited to fishing such water. A weighted fly

allowed to dead drift, for instance, will be yanked downstream because of the drag applied by the faster water on the surface. A wet fly fished from a floating line will skip over the surface, its shape hidden from the fish by the copious bubbles produced by the fast water. Only a sink-tip is able to cut through the fast water, delivering the fly within sight of the fish.

The presentation used when fishing rapids with a sink-tip isn't the conventional swinging presentation discussed in detail below. Instead of covering broad sweeps of water in a single cast, the angler searching rapids hits small places likely to hold a resting fish. After locating midstream rocks, submerged ledges, and to some extent, cobbled bottoms, the angler can move upstream and hang the fly line and fly downstream into the lie. The technique can be deadly, especially on those days when little else is working.

The Logistics

Fishing a sink-tip is an art form, one built on a confounding paradox. An effective presentation requires the fly be near the bottom, but you are rarely able to see how deep the fly actually is. To consistently catch steelies on a sink-tip, you need to know the unknowable. Luckily, with a little practice, you'll develop a sixth sense.

There are two types of sink-tip presentations used over broad expanses of holding water. If the water is shallow, less than four feet deep, you fish the sink-tip as if it were a floating line. Simply cast, mend, and swing. As long as the fly is swinging through the strike zone, you're fishing it correctly. Typically, however, sink-tips are used to present flies to deeper water, requiring added line control techniques. The sink-tip presentation to deep water has three main parts: the cast, the sink, and the swing. Each of these three parts builds on skills learned while swinging a floating line.

To start, find a wide riffle or run that is four to six feet deep and moving at a walking clip. Position yourself at the upstream end, directly above the holding water closest to shore. As with swinging a floating line, you'll want the end of your swing to hang over good holding water.

Determining where to place the cast is the toughest part of the sink-tip presentation. If you simply cast where you would when swinging with a floating line, the sink-tip will come under immediate tension. If the tension is strong enough, the sink-tip won't sink more than a couple inches. To help get the line down in the water column, you must give it slack immediately after casting. As you give it slack, the line will dead drift downstream and drop through the water column. After the line has reached the desired depth, you can bring it under tension and allow it to swing. Determining where to place the cast in the first place is the most essential decision you'll make in the presentation.

While standing at the head of the riffle or run, identify the first slot you want to hit, and make sure you're at least quartering upstream from its location. As shown below, make an overhead cast that positions the line

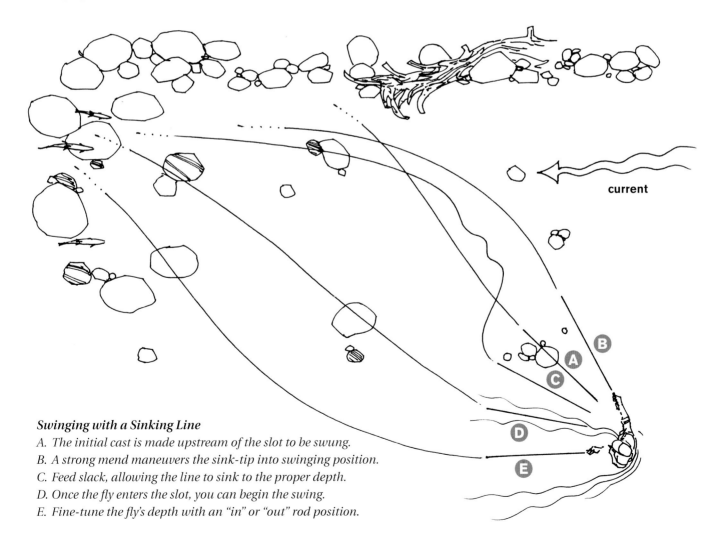

Swinging with a Sinking Line

A. *The initial cast is made upstream of the slot to be swung.*

B. *A strong mend maneuvers the sink-tip into swinging position.*

C. *Feed slack, allowing the line to sink to the proper depth.*

D. *Once the fly enters the slot, you can begin the swing.*

E. *Fine-tune the fly's depth with an "in" or "out" rod position.*

several feet upstream of that first slot (A). Until you have sound knowledge of how fast the sink-tip you're using sinks, the exact placement of the initial cast will take a little trial and error.

Immediately after the line lands, make a strong mend—either a line lift or line flip—repositioning the sink-tip into its swinging position (B). Executing this mend quickly is essential, as the sink-tip will drop through the surface tension quickly. The deeper it gets, the harder the line will be to reposition. The mend should place the sinking portion into its swinging position, meaning that the line should be straight and somewhere between quartering and eighthing downstream. If the sinking portion doesn't end up in swinging position, the tension applied by the current will be greater, causing the line to rise through the water column as it swings.

Once you have cast the line and repositioned it with a strong mend, you need to feed slack into the drift using a slack-feeding technique (C). Slack tosses usually are adequate, but depending on the water's unique characteristics, line flips or even stack mends might be necessary. The slack allows the line to plummet through the water column, placing the fly within striking distance of the steelhead. If you feed too much slack, the line will drop too far, and the fly will hang up on the stones. Worse, the sinking line itself can tangle and be sliced apart by the rocks. Fish sink-tips long enough and you'll eventually lose one. If you don't feed enough slack into the drift, the line won't sink deep enough, and the fly will pass over the fish's strike zone. Determining how much slack to feed takes time on the water and the willingness to lose a few flies.

Once you've fed the proper amount of slack, you can start swinging the line (D). To do this, pinch the line with the rod hand, bringing the full force of the current to bear on the line. As the fly swings, you can adjust the rod's position to help raise or lower the fly's depth. Often the riffle, run, or tailout you're plying isn't of uniform depth. Sometimes the water below you is shallower or deeper than the water where the swing began. The rod can help fine-tune the fly's depth. An "in" rod position, one pointing between the swinging fly and the near shore, reduces the current's tension on the fly line and helps sink the fly deeper. Conversely, an "out" rod position, one pointing between the swinging fly and the far shore, increases the current's tension on the fly line and helps raise the fly (E). Steelhead tend to prefer swung flies that are moving slower than the current speed. So while you're working to keep the fly near the stones, keep the fly swinging just slightly slower than the current.

Once you've completed the swing, you can either strip the line to you or, if fishing a single-handed rod, roll cast it onto the surface and pick it up with an overhead cast. The new cast should position the fly and line so as to fish the next slot downstream. As when swinging with a floating line, strip extra line from the reel until you reach a comfortable casting distance, then take steps downstream. In this manner, you'll cover every slot within a given section of water, increasing your odds of a hookup. To help sink the line further without feeding more slack, you can step into your casts, meaning you take your downstream step as you're feeding slack into the drift. Stepping into your casts will help you cover more water in less time.

Rods, Lines, Leaders, and Flies

Fishing sink-tips requires a serious rod. Though adequate lines are offered for rods as light as a 5-weight, most serious single-handed casters use 8- and 9-weights for their sink-tip fishing. Heavier rods offer super lifting power, a serious advantage when trying to raise a heavy line from deep water. They also allow you to apply more pressure to a big steelhead holding in a deep run. But beyond these advantages, the lines matched to 8- and 9-weights sink much faster than lines matched to lighter rods. A 7-weight rod is best matched to a sink-tip that weights 200 to 250 grains, a density allowing for a sink rate of 4.5 inches per second. But a 9-weight is best matched to a sink-tip that weighs 350 to 400 grains and will sink at 7.5 inches per second. With a heavier rod, you can use a faster-sinking line, allowing the fly to reach deep water and stay there despite heavy currents.

As with all swinging presentations, a long rod is invaluable when fishing sink-tips. The added length helps make powerful mends, the type capable of maneuvering a distant sink-tip. Also, longer rods are able to roll-cast sink-tips more effectively, allowing you to fish the technique in tight quarters. Spey rods are of tremendous benefit when fishing sink-tips. These rods are line-control machines, allowing you to precisely place sink-tips at great distance. And some lines made especially for Spey rods allow you to dredge the deepest big-water run with ease.

Just ten years ago, fishing sink-tips was an expensive prospect. Because the line used must match the water being fished, effectively fishing sink-tips requires you to own myriad lines. Ten years ago, this meant anglers had to invest in many lines and just as many spools on which to place them. In order to cover both big and small water, anglers needed to buy almost half a dozen lines and spools. Luckily, in the last decade, line manufacturers have made the prospect more cost-effective. Now you can buy just two lines and two spools and cover any type of water anywhere in steelhead country.

Whether fishing Spey or single-handed rods, the most useful line for the modern steelheader is the quad-tip, a single line that has four different heads. The main line is

Heavier rods allow faster-sinking lines to be cast. Moreover, they offer the requisite backbone to lift big fish through big water.
NATE KOENIGSKNECHT

a standard floater missing the majority of its head. On the end of the floating main line is a small loop for attaching one of the various heads. Most manufacturers offer these lines with a floating head, an intermediate head, a moderate-sinking head (type III), and a fast-sinking head (type VI). In less than a minute, you can swap one head for another. The floater and the intermediate offer the steelheader little utility, but the two sinking heads provide two different sink-tips on a single spool. Some manufacturers sell quad-tips with 10-foot heads, some with 15-footers, and others with 25-footers. The 15-foot heads are of the most use to steelheaders.

The 15-foot moderate-sinking head is ideally suited to riffles, runs, and tailouts of slow current speed. If the current's pace is slower than a comfortable walk and the water is less than six feet deep, the moderate-sinking head is likely the perfect fit. This head is also useful in shallow water with a faster current. If the water is less than four feet deep but moving faster than a walking pace, the moderate sinker might be ideal.

The 15-foot fast-sinking head is perfect for covering deeper riffles, runs, and tailouts of faster speed. If the water is more than four feet deep and moving faster than walking speed, the fast sinker is a good bet.

Fifteen-foot quad-tips will cover nearly all your sink-tip needs. But even the fastest-sinking head won't reach the strike zone in water more than ten feet deep. If your homewater has productive runs or tailouts deeper than that, you may want to invest in a couple quality sinking poly leaders, thin leaders dusted with tungsten to help them slice through the water. The fastest-sinking polys drop as fast a stone. Currently, they're available in 5- and 10-foot sections. By looping a poly leader to your sink-tip, you can present your fly to deeper water without buying an extra line and spool. But a word of caution: If you attach a poly leader that sinks more slowly than the sink-tip portion of the fly line, the line will belly underwater, resulting in two potentially major problems. The belly can be on the bottom without your knowledge, snagging rocks and limbs. It won't take long until the

Selecting the right line for the water is an essential part of consistently hooking steelhead on a sink-tip. This fish came from eight feet of water, striking only after the fly was put within a foot of the bottom.

sinking portion of the line is severed. Also, the belly can soak up the shock of a bump in certain situations, limiting your ability to hook fish. If you use a poly leader, be sure it sinks at least as fast as your sink-tip.

One disadvantage of a quad-tip line matched with a poly leader is that it doesn't cast as silky smooth as you might like. If you fish big rivers where long casts into the wind are frequently needed, a spool loaded with a floating running line might be a requirement. A running line is just thin fly line, about the same diameter as a 2-weight fly line. Once you loop in a shooting taper, the line

becomes easily castable. Shooting tapers come in various sink rates and can be matched to the water being fished. Unfortunately, the heavy shooting taper isn't easily mended with the running line. So instead of mending as you would with a quad-tip, your initial cast must place the shooting taper in the swinging position. Then you can feed slack as needed to sink the taper into position. As most anglers don't fish water big enough to justify a 30-foot shooting taper, and as quad-tips have proven their effectiveness, the popularity of shooting tapers has dwindled among single-handed casters in steelhead country.

Leaders for swinging sink-tips are simple. The overall length ranges from 2 to 4 feet, based on the performance of the swinging fly. If you have trouble keeping the fly off the stones—even after maintaining an "out" rod position and allowing less sink time—the leader can act as a fine-tuning device. A longer leader helps keep the fly higher in the water column. A shorter leader helps keep the fly closer to the bottom. Most steelheaders use a 10- or 12-pound-test tippet running from the line to the fly. Because the tippet will be near the stones continually, fluorocarbon is recommended. Its abrasion resistance will help ensure that a hooked fish becomes a landed fish.

The same flies used when swinging with a floating line can be fished with a sink-tip. The sink-tip is often swung in murky and cold water to fish with small strike zones, however, so you need to carry a few extra patterns to match the conditions.

Three patterns have earned permanent slots in my box for use with the sink-tip presentation in murky and cold water. One is the Cabero Leech in pink. This pattern has tremendous action in slow and fast water, attracting fish from a greater distance than a more rigid pattern. Because the fly doesn't sink much on its own, I often fish it in shallow sections of river. When tied with lead eyes instead of a bead, it can be made to ride hook-up for fishing especially snag-prone runs. I trust this pattern more than any other under typical sink-tip conditions. Depending on the situation, I fish either a size 2 or a 1/0.

For deep water, I trust a Fire Ball Leech with lead dumbbell eyes. The pattern plummets through the water column on its own and stays near the bottom in the deepest and fastest of runs. The fly rides hook-up, so it doesn't snag often. But when it does, I'm not shy about breaking it off—the pattern takes less than three minutes to tie. During the winter, I fish pink, as winter steelhead in my area seem most responsive to bright colors. During the summer, I trust the purple version, as it seems to spook less wary summer fish. I carry sizes 4, 2, and 1/0, matching the size to the conditions.

Finally, I carry a Double Articulated Leech tied with Krystal Flash. The dark color mixed with the Krystal

Cabero Leech

Fire Ball Leech (purple)

Fire Ball Leech (pink)

Double Articulated Leech

Flash, I believe, helps the fish see the fly in the murkiest of water. And the articulation gives the pattern a tremendous action in fast and slow water alike. The pattern's overall size makes it tough to cast but throws a mean silhouette once in the water. Steelhead often chase the pattern down and demolish it. When the water is on the verge of blowing out, this is my fly of choice. I carry a size 1/0.

Variations

Steelhead with small strike zones are often made curious by a large fly moving nearby, yet these fish won't be curious enough to strike. Anglers who have spotted a fine fish holding in a tailout, for instance, might see the steelhead leave its lie and follow the fly, only to turn away after closer inspection. Such refusals seem especially common with steelhead in cold water, conditions typically matched with a sink-tip presentation.

Many anglers attach a small pattern behind the larger one while fishing a sink-tip. Typically, a 3-foot section of 10- or 12-pound-test fluorocarbon is clinch-knotted to the bend in the main fly. This tippet is then connected with an improved clinch—or any other trusted knot—to the second fly. A popular pattern for such work is an unweighted Lifter tied on a size 6 short-shank hook. The fly has its own enticing action that often seduces tough fish. A hesitant steelhead will drop back from the main fly and sip up the trailer without a thought.

As with all trailing patterns, this technique shouldn't be used on rivers with wild steelhead, as the trailing pattern can wrap around the body of a fish that took the main fly. If the main fly pulls free, the trailer could foul-

hook the steelhead. Such an event is rare indeed, but the risk warrants leaving the trailer hook off on wild steelhead rivers.

Hooking Takers

As when swinging with a floating line, you're always wise to keep 1 to 1½ feet of line coiled behind the rod hand's pinch and the reel while swinging a sink-tip. When the steelhead takes, it will pinch the fly in its jaws and turn its head. As the fish does this, the loose coil of line will slip from your pinch. As the line comes tight against the drag of the reel, the hook will be pulled sharply into the corner of the steelie's mouth.

Sometime the take on the sink-tip is so subtle that the coiled line won't be tugged free. You might not know if you've just hooked a fish or a five-ton rock; the initial result is often the same on the line. As the line swings, tension begins to grow. The line stretches tight, and the rod flexes with the weight. Some steelhead will bolt at this moment. Others will sit tight. If the fly is lightly snagged on a rock or limb, slamming back on the rod will cause the fly to pop free and zip through the water—ruining the remainder of the swing. A new cast, sink, and swing will be needed to cover the slot. As swinging flies on a sink-tip

Facing page: On days like this one, when the water temperature was in the low thirties, attaching a small trailing fly to the larger pattern can produce strikes. Trailing flies should be avoided whenever wild steelhead are present, however.

line keeps your flies near the bottom, and such light snags are common, slamming back on the rod every time the fly hesitates will slow your pace tremendously. To maintain a steady fishing pace, you might avoid raising your rod when tension grows. Instead, try a solid strip set. By using your line hand to tug, you can usually pull the fly free from a light snag, keeping it in an adequate position for completing the swing. And if the light snag turns out to be the solid jaw of a fish, the strip set will help bury the hook.

Besides being heavy, sink-tips move awkwardly through the water. They add tremendous drag on a running fish, especially if that fish is moving cross-current from you. To compensate, you must adjust your drag appropriately when a fish takes. The sink-tip in the current adds a great deal of pressure to the fish; cranking a reel's drag down might overstress the tippet, resulting in a lost fish. Keep in mind that the steelhead is towing that heavy line through the current when adjusting your drag during the battle.

Sink-tips offer another problem once the fish is hooked. Because the line is near the bottom, it can easily wrap around rocks and submerged trees. By quickly raising the rod once you feel the fish and keeping a high rod position until the line climbs up through the water column, you can limit your chances of a tangle. Then as the fish dodges and runs, you'll be assured that your line is away from submerged debris. Later, when low rod pressure is needed to turn the fish, you can drop the rod without putting the line onto the stones.

CHAPTER 11

Greased-Line Presentation

teelheading's fly-fishing tradition has its genesis in the Atlantic salmon fishing practiced by the British upper crust. And nowhere is this lineage as transparent as it is with the greased-line presentation.

In the first days of the twentieth century, a single fisherman stumbled upon a discovery that would profoundly affect both Atlantic salmon fishing and, later, steelheading. A. H. E. Wood, a gentleman of the highest degree who, because of his social standing, managed to secure the Carinton beat on the England's Dee River, sat along the bank watching a pool of dour salmon. He'd fished all day without success and thought the day might be better spent musing than casting. And for a time he was content. But then he watched an Atlantic rise from its station along the bottom and take something in the surface film. Wood found this amusing and at first thought little of it. But then the fish rose again. And quickly a different fish rose in an identical manner.

At the time, fly fishing for salmon depended on the classic wet-fly swing. Anglers using silk lines that inherently sank made casts quartering downstream and allowed the fly to sink and swing. The theory guiding the practice said that salmon responded best to flies near the bottom of the river.

But these salmon were rising to the surface. And they weren't just rolling or splashing for their own amusement. These fish looked to be feeding in the surface film. Wood's mind turned. His line would never float, but trout anglers used a technique called dapping to take rising fish. This technique depended on the angler getting close to the fish and then dangling the fly from the rod's tip. Luckily, the pool Wood sat beside happened to have an eel weir with a wooden walkway connecting it to the bank. Wood made his way onto the walkway and dug through his fly box. As he did, the salmon continued to rise all around him. As fate would have it, Wood happened to have a White Moth Fly that might float. He connected the pattern to his catgut leader and dapped it over the pool. Immediately a fish rose to the surface and studied the fly but panicked when it saw Wood's looming figure upstream. The fisherman kneeled and presented the fly again. This time a different fish rose with another salmon in hot pursuit. Without pause, the fish swirled violently on the moth fly.

Wood nearly lost his marbles. A large salmon had just done the impossible. In his haste to hook the fish, he raised the rod skyward and upstream. The fly pulled free.

The same scenario continued for some time. Wood rose countless fish and missed them all. And just before he slid headfirst into the dark depths of insanity, he realized his mistake. By setting the hook upstream and with a high rod, he was actually pulling the fly out of the fish's open mouth. On his next cast, another salmon rose and inhaled the fly. This time he struck low and to the shore,

Above: The greased-line presentation has changed little in its migration from the Atlantic salmon streams of England to the steelhead streams of the Northwest.

hooking the fish solidly. It turned and bolted downstream. Wood kept pace, using his rod to keep the brute off-balance. After several minutes, he slid the fish onto the grassy shore.

Over the course of the day, after not hooking a single fish on traditional presentations, Wood landed six salmon. And his success got him thinking. Just maybe salmon could be risen to the surface even when they weren't rising readily on their own. But Wood's gear limited his ability to experiment. If he cast the fly, the line would sink it. He could experiment only on water that allowed him to use the dapping technique of trout fishers. Suddenly, a second epiphany hit Wood. He realized that his silk line might be made to float—if he greased it with animal fat.

On his next trip to the Dee, with a greased line strung on the rod, Wood fished a fly near the surface. He made casts quartering downstream that allowed the fly to be fished under a minimum of tension. And his efforts were rewarded with rising salmon. But again, he missed most of the fish that struck. Remembering the painful lessons of all those rising fish missed with an upstream striking motion, Wood had his third epiphany: He could mend the line so that it produced a small belly. When a fish took and he struck on the rod, this belly would pull the fly toward the shore rather than upstream and, in doing so, pull it into the corner of the fish's mouth. It was at this moment that the greased-line presentation, used by countless modern steelheaders, was born.

Wood refined the technique over the next several years and found that it took far more fish than the traditional presentations, even in cold and otherwise adverse conditions. After raising hundreds of salmon, he determined the best way to cast, fish, and strike with the greased line. Wood knew he had stumbled upon something big, so he kept extensive notes. His plan was to publish these notes in book form once he had the technique mastered. Unfortunately, Wood died before he could complete this task.

Several years later, his son passed these notes onto a fellow named Donald G. Rudd. Rudd put the notes together into a book and published it under the pseudonym Jock Scott. He called the book *Greased Line Fishing for Salmon: Compiled from the Fishing Papers of the late A. H. E. Wood, of Glassel.*

What followed was nearly eighty years of confusion and misunderstandings stemming from a single problem: Rudd was not nearly the fisherman Wood was, and he used his own interpretations and thoughts to help fill in the blanks in Wood's notes. In so doing, he caused nothing short of mind-bending paradoxes to emerge within the text. Anglers reading closely can't help but be flabbergasted by statements like "He often told me that he liked the fly to float down like a dead leaf. . . . When the cast is made and mended, and line floating delightfully without drag, you should lead it around by keeping the rod point in advance of it." Obviously, leading a fly can be done only when it is under pressure. And any angler knows that a fly under pressure is not dead drifting. This is only one example of the contradictions within the text that are more suited to Buddhist meditation than fishing instruction.

These contradictions and the confusion that followed created a crisis for those steelheaders concerned with fishing the technique as Wood fished it. Anglers spent hours reading the book, trying to figure out the minutiae of the greased-line presentation. And different anglers came up with different conclusions. Hence steelheading's canon contains numerous books with differing, and often contradictory, instructions. Some say the fly should be fished broadside and dead drifted. Others suggest that it should be fished with tension. Still others say it should be fished like the classic swing until the end of the drift, when the line is given a few shoreside mends.

The details of how Wood fished his technique are vital to fly-fishing historians, but not to the success of steelheaders. What is important to steelheaders is how modern steelhead guides have found that the technique fishes most effectively. This chapter provides exactly what you need to know to fish the guides' version of Wood's presentation.

The greased-line presentation has become a favorite of many of the world's finest steelheaders. It has a tremendous ability to provoke strikes and is immensely pleasurable to fish. It requires the utmost attention to details like line control and fly position, yet it doesn't depend on tricky gear. The greased line readily lends itself to fishing wet flies, dry flies, and even sink-tip lines. This diversity allows it to cover nearly any condition properly. And it can be fished immediately with the same gear you just used to fish the classic swing, allowing you to reapproach a section of water with a new technique without having to cut the tippet.

But the greased-line presentation's greatest attraction, in my opinion, is its ability to move steelhead from the invisible bottom to the visible surface. Many takes on the greased-line presentation—when fished on a floating line—occur within clear view of the angler. As the fly swims through the riffling current, the steelhead rises and takes in a flash. The next thing you know, the fish is hooked and headed for distant water. Few thrills, short of the steelhead's rise to the dry fly, can compare.

My first fish that rose to the greased-line presentation came along a Willamette tributary famous for its

A fall hen brought to the surface by a broadside fly.

wide runs of moderate speed. On one such section, known as the Riffle to End All Riffles, I found myself standing in knee-deep water. Below me for nearly a hundred yards was water from two to five feet deep with moderate current. Throughout the run sat boulders the size of pumpkins. I knew from experience that fish lay in front of, beside, and around these boulders. And I also knew that the steelhead often could be found in random places elsewhere in the run. I'd taken several fish over the course of a few seasons on this run, mostly on the classic swing, but generally the water hadn't been as good to me as it had to my friends.

I'd not fished the greased line much because of my confusion about its finer points. Every book seemed to give differing advice. Rather than dig through the contradictions, I stuck to my go-to presentations. But I knew that the greased line had a reputation for success. And that reputation watered my budding determination to master the technique. Eventually I devoted time to it, talking with better anglers than myself. With their help, I began to get a handle on how to fish the presentation. I'd been greased-lining on most trips for a month or so, but up until that day on the Riffle to End All Riffles, I hadn't moved a fish.

I now know why. It wasn't that I fished the technique incorrectly. Rather, I was forcing it on the wrong types of water. The greased line depends on precise types of water. Trying to force it on water that doesn't have the basic requirements is futile; the fly won't fish properly and will provoke a strike only if the luck gods are smiling upon you. And anglers are rarely so lucky. But on the Riffle to End All Riffles, I didn't need luck. As it turns out, the steelhead in this run just can't say no to a fly fished on the greased line.

I made short casts to be sure I presented the fly broadside and as slowly as possible. The fly swam beautifully, despite my tentative rod play. I'd cast, give a wobbly upstream mend, and the fly would fish itself. I'd stepped through a quarter of the run when a fish flashed on the fly. In my surprise, I jerked the rod to set the hook. And when I did, the fly pulled free from the water.

About three slots above where the fish was holding, I started anew. And on the third cast, the fish rose again. This time the hook found a firm home, and my reel sang with the pulsing runs of a feisty fish. The hen put me into my backing and then jumped, throwing silver spray against the afternoon light. A few small runs later, she docilely slid onto the shoreside pebbles. The hen went six pounds, bright for an upriver fish. The clipped adipose fin gave away her hatchery origin, and despite my barbecue's desire for flesh, I couldn't bring myself to kill her. The river had no native steelhead, and she'd rewarded my efforts with the greased line. That was enough for me. With a kick, she disappeared into the green current.

From that day on, I started fishing the Riffle to End All Riffles religiously. And the greased-line presentation has proven the most deadly approach to the water year in and year out. Its currents are the perfect speed, its lies are at the perfect depth, and the fish seem especially active when they hold there. Indicator tactics, the broadside rise, and even the classic swing don't move fish as readily in this water. And hence the run has produced in me an undying confidence for the greased-line presentation. I trust it anywhere the water willingly accepts it.

The Water

The greased-line presentation isn't all that hard if the water suits its use. In other types of water, however, it can be nothing but trouble. The technique requires certain traits from the river, and if those traits aren't there, you are better off using a different approach.

The most important requirement of greased-line water is an even current. The water needs to be moving at a generally consistent pace from shore to shore, meaning the distant water needs to be moving downstream as quickly as the close water, and there should be few swirling eddies. Some inequity in the current can be managed with precise line control, but at a certain point, the effort required for a proper presentation won't be worth the time it requires. Because of these requirements, the best greased-line water is usually a broad and even riffle or tailout. Luckily, such water is common on medium to large steelhead streams.

Once you've found such a section, you need to figure out whether the water is better fished with a floating line or a sink-tip. Making such a determination is easy.

Steelhead have predictable strike zones. Rarely, even in the best conditions, will a steelhead move vertically more than six feet for a fly. As steelhead hold along the bottom in riffles and tailouts, water deeper than six feet

The greased-line presentation can be incredibly effective—when applied to the right types of water. Broad riffles less than six feet deep are ideal places.

will rarely produce a fish to a fly presented near the surface. Trust the floating line in water with good visibility that is five feet deep or shallower and in the ideal temperature range. Such conditions abound during the summer months.

When the water is deeper than six feet, colder than the ideal temperature range, or off-color, a sink-tip line might be required to consistently move fish. Many rivers have plenty of runs ideally suited to the greased-line presentation that are between six and eight feet deep. Such water often holds big steelhead; it's worth a try.

The Logistics

Once you have found the right water, the work of covering it can begin. Fishing the greased line isn't as difficult as Rudd made it seem. It's simply the balancing of two

Because the greased-line presentation requires precise line control, you are usually better off making shorter casts.

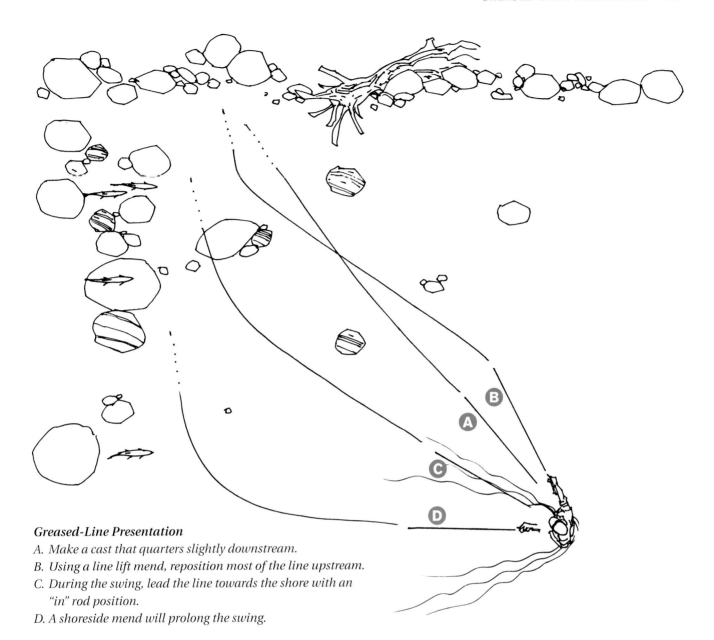

Greased-Line Presentation

A. *Make a cast that quarters slightly downstream.*

B. *Using a line lift mend, reposition most of the line upstream.*

C. *During the swing, lead the line towards the shore with an "in" rod position.*

D. *A shoreside mend will prolong the swing.*

contradictory desires. You want to keep the fly broadside to the fish and swinging as slowly as possible. As physics will have it, a fly kept broadside wants to swing fast; conversely, a fly staying parallel to the current wants to swing slowly. The proper greased-line presentation can be thought of as the ideal balance between staying broadside and swinging slowly. The presentation will be most successful when you're able to swing your broadside fly slower than the speed of the current.

Wade into the riffle, run, or tailout so that the first slot is quartering downstream. Make a slightly quartering downstream cast landing upstream of the first slot (see figure). This cast is more across than quartering (A). Immediately make an upstream line lift mend, moving all the line down to within five feet of the leader's connec-

tion with the fly line (B). A small belly will be formed. The mend serves two functions: It slows the swing of the fly over the surface of the water, and it enables the fly to stay perpendicular to the current. The mend is the most important part of the presentation. Luckily, you will know immediately if you've made the mend correctly by the action of the fly. If it is done correctly, the fly will fish well throughout the swing. If done incorrectly, the fly will fish too fast or won't stay broadside.

Once the mend has been completed, lead the fly with an "in" rod position, with the rod pointed between the fly line and the downstream bank (C). The lead works to keep the fly broadside to the current during the swing, and it also serves to aid in the hook set if a fish happens to take. You want the fly to swing as slowly as possible, so keep the rod as close to the line as possible—in other words, leading just slightly. A bigger lead will increase the speed of the fly's swing.

In order to diminish the amount of line in the water and hence the speed of the fly's swing, keep the rod high as it leads the line. Most anglers keep their rods between a 10:30 and 11:30 position.

As the fly swings toward your bank, it will eventually straighten out below. To increase the size of broadside swing—in other words, to increase the amount of water covered by the broadside fly—make a mend toward the near bank (D). This mend should come just before the fly turns parallel to the current. And once you've made the mend, you can keep the rod down near the water, as the need for the high rod is gone.

The fly will eventually straighten out and hang below you. Sometimes fish follow the fly and can be enticed to strike with a few twitches of the fly. Whether you twitch the fly or not, allow it to hang for at least five seconds, as sometimes a fish needs this time to make up its mind.

Make the next cast so as to cover the next slot of water, meaning either stripping more line from the reel or taking a step downstream.

Because of the precise line control demanded by the greased-line presentation, most anglers rarely fish a line longer than 70 feet when using either a single-handed or double-handed rod. Most anglers keep their presentations to about fifty or sixty feet. This works to your advantage not only for line control, but also for seeing the take of the fish, the most exciting part of the presentation.

The greased-line presentation with a sink-tip requires the same general fishing procedure, using the overhead cast slightly downstream, the upstream mend, and the leading of the rod as with the floating line. The upstream mend goes to within a foot of the sinking section in most water. You can then use the rod's position to help keep the fly off the bottom, as in the classic swing with sink-tips. More lead drops the fly in the water column; moving the rod out, ending the rod's lead, brings the fly up in the water. This latter move also brings the fly out of its broadside position, however, so use it only when necessary.

The sink-tip with the greased-line presentation is the modern equivalent of something fished by A. H. E. Wood. Wood would try an ungreased silk line when the water was cold and the air was colder than the water. He found

The greased-line presentation often brings feisty steelhead to the surface.

that during these conditions, the fly was best presented "on the stones." His silk lines sank naturally over their entire length. Imagine how hard it would be to control such a line! We've got it easy.

Rods, Lines, Leaders, and Flies

Like all steelheading techniques that depend on the proper control of a swinging fly, the ideal greased-line presentation is best achieved with a long rod. Most single-handed casters fish rods that are at least $9^{1}/_{2}$ feet long when greased-lining. One friend will fish nothing shorter than an 11-foot switch rod. Traditional Spey rods make ideal tools for the presentation, especially over big water. In fact, Wood himself used a Spey rod when developing the technique. These longer rods permit you to mend the line precisely and at great length. And of special importance to the greased-line presentation, these longer rods allow you to keep a long section of line actually out of the water. This is essential in the all-important task of slowing the fly's swing.

The greased-line presentation is tremendously versatile. It can be fished on the surface with floating lines or near the bottom with sink-tip lines. The floating line is the most common application. Because the presentation is best done at distances under seventy feet, you don't need a heavy rod to deliver the cast with a floating line. Fast-action rods as small as 6-weights are typically employed.

The same floating lines used with the classic swing work fine with the greased-line presentation. Some single-handed casters prefer long-bellied weight-forward lines. These cast well, and most important, they can be used for several other techniques, letting you remain quickly adaptable. Traditional Spey casters prefer a double-taper line, as it allows fast casting and easy mending.

The leader for greased-lining with a floater should be between 9 and 12 feet long and tapered down to 8- or 10-pound-test. Most anglers rely on 8-pound-test the majority of the time, especially when fishing in clear water to steelhead that average less than ten pounds. I often rely on the greased line during summer and fall, when the rivers are clear and the steelhead smaller. In these situations, 8-pound-test is the ideal leader. It won't put a fish down but still has enough backbone to turn a running summer fish. If I'm fishing a river that is known for steelhead over ten pounds, or when the water is off-color, I'll fish the 10-pound-test. It has the strength to fight even the biggest steelhead from a floating line, and it is supple enough to allow the fly to act naturally.

A fluorocarbon leader isn't necessary with the greased-line presentation when you're fishing near the surface.

The floating line keeps the leader far from the debris of the bottom. Standard monofilament will suffice.

The sink-tips used for the greased-line presentation are typically different from the sink-tips you would use if fishing the same water with the classic swing. When you're fishing the classic swing with a sinking line, the current applies a great deal of pressure on the line as a result of the fly's slow swing. Because of this added tension, you lift the sinking line in the classic swing.

With the greased-line presentation, the amount of tension on the line is substantially diminished because of the leading position of the rod. If you were to use the same sink-tip you used with the classic swing, the line would most likely drag over the rocks, snagging the fly. To combat this, most anglers employ a lighter-density line.

In addition to a lighter sink-tip, many anglers use a line with a shorter sinking section as well, allowing you to better control the fly's position and speed. My favorite line for most greased-line water is a 10-foot sinking head rated to 200 grains. This line delivers my flies near the bottom but manages to keep them from snagging excessively. By adjusting the amount of tension you keep on the line, you can fish water three to eight feet deep with this single line.

When fishing the greased line with a sink-tip, most anglers shorten the leader to between 4 and 6 feet. The longer the leader, the farther up in the water column the fly will fish. The shorter the leader, the lower the fly will fish. The leader can therefore be used to fine-tune the fly's depth. Since the fly will be near the bottom, a 10-pound-test fluorocarbon leader should be employed in clear water. A 12-pound-test fluorocarbon leader is best when the water is murky water and the fish are large.

Fly patterns for the greased-line presentation are as varied and plentiful as the technique's countless aficionados. Some of fly fishing's finest patterns were designed by steelheaders looking for the ideal greased-line fly. But as with the classic swing, having a large number of flies isn't a necessary component of success.

Two types of flies are commonly fished with the greased-line presentation: waking flies and wet flies. Waking flies are tied on light-wire hooks and usually contain elements that will help them float, such as deer hair. These patterns are fished in the surface film, where their progress across the river causes small wakes to form, hence their name. Most advocates of the greased-line presentation prefer these flies in calmer water, although they can be very productive in gently riffling water as well.

After extensive discussion with other anglers and years of experimentation, two waking patterns have

October Skating Caddis

Arctic Fox Purple Muddler

Motion Prawn (purple)

earned permanent slots in my box: the October Skating Caddis and the Arctic Fox Purple Muddler. Each fly is used for a different type of water; rarely do I fish both in the same run. The October Skating Caddis pattern is an excellent representation of an adult caddis. The fly's deer-hair wings and dubbed body keep it waking well despite current variations. It's the pattern I fish in water with a smooth or gently riffling surface. These types of water allow the fly to work to its full potential. I carry sizes 6 and 8, using the bigger size over deeper or slightly murky water. I've found the fly most effective when its body color is matched to the color of the dominant caddis found on river, usually orange, yellow, or drab green. As steelhead spend more time in the river system, many steelheaders feel that they become more likely to strike flies that at least generally represent the insects in the river.

The Arctic Fox Purple Muddler is a mystery to me. I'm not sure whether the pattern represents a caddis pattern, a wounded fish, or a jerky stick. What is certain is that the fly moves steelhead. I fish it in heavier water, riffles and runs with broken surfaces. The pattern floats very well and wakes in the surface film despite the river's best attempts to sink it. I first started fishing the pattern on small coastal streams during the summer months, when the steelhead hold under the river's fastest currents. The Muddler moved the fish from their lies with regularity, and it became a trusted companion. Since then, it has produced fish on many different rivers, especially the Deschutes. I carry sizes 8 to 4.

The other type of fly commonly fished from the greased line is the standard wet fly. In this presentation, the wet fly is designed to ride just below the surface and is likely successful because of its clearly visible silhouette. If done correctly, the presentation keeps the fly broadside to the fish, providing the fish an unparalleled view of the fly. For this reason, wet flies fished from the greased line typically have robust and attractive side views.

Two wet flies have earned permanent slots in my box: the Motion Prawn and Silvey's Spey. Both of these flies have broadside views characterized by full and active silhouettes. As these flies swim toward the bank high in the water column, their shape at once remains well defined and fluid. Steelhead can see the patterns from some distance, and as the fly approaches, the fish can't help but be drawn to its appealing action.

I fish the Motion Prawn the majority of the time. It fishes well in large and small sizes and over a wide range of conditions. Its silhouette can be seen even in off-color water, and I've observed steelhead come a great distance to strike it in clear water. I carry sizes 6, 2, and 2/0. I fish the bigger flies in murky or deep water and the smaller sizes in clear or shallow water. Because of the demands of the water and the moods of the fish, I tie the 2/0 with slightly more bulk around the body to increase the fly's visibility. I tie the smaller sizes with less bulk, as I use them when greater visibility isn't needed. The fly seems to work best in fast water, where the current can add tremendous action to the tail.

I use Silvey's Spey in slower water. When rivers are low or the light is bright, sometimes the Motion Prawn is just too much fly for the water. Steelhead can be put off by the big pattern. Silvey's Spey, however, casts a much smaller broadside view and rarely spooks fish. I fish the pattern in smaller sizes, mostly 8 and 6. The materials used in its construction give this pattern tremendous action under the water. The Spey hackle catches the current and flutters. This subtle action coupled with its small broadside view make the fly just deadly under the right circumstances.

Both the Motion Prawn and Silvey's Spey are commonly fished in purples and oranges. I carry both colors in my box, using orange when the fish are more recently arrived from the salt and purple when the fish have been inland for more time. The purple continues to fish well despite bright light on the water.

Variations

The most common variation to the rigging of the greased-line presentation is the addition of a riffle hitch. This causes the fly to twitch slightly within the current, increasing the chance of enticing a strike. The hitch is considered so effective that its use seems universal on many steelhead streams. See chapter 9 for rigging details.

Hooking Takers

The rising of a steelhead to the greased-line fly is a double-edged sword. The excitement causes the immediate delivery of the body's equivalent to twenty-four ounces of fine coffee. This sudden shot of go-juice can be enough to leave you shaking with pleasure on the bank. And the first few times it occurs, you are nearly guaranteed to pull the fly from the fish's mouth.

When the fish takes the fly, it does so most typically in a swirling motion, turning the fish either right or left. If the fish turns toward you—which seems to be all but guaranteed by Murphy's Law—and you come back on the rod, you will pull the fly directly out of the fish's mouth. If this unfortunate fate does happen to befall you, at least you can find comfort in knowing that Wood experienced the same suffering. And you can rest assured that the fish

Motion Prawn (orange)

Silvey's Spey (purple)

Silvey's Spey (orange)

will most likely take again if given a few minutes to forget about the experience. If the fish doesn't rise again, a smaller fly of the same design might be all that is needed to change its mind.

The proper striking motion on a fish raised to the greased-line fly is no motion at all. Simply continue to lead the fly as if no fish took. This will cause the current to apply a small amount of pressure on the fly, pulling it to the corner of the fish's jaw. As the fish pulls the other way, tension builds on the line, and the hook will find a secure home of its own accord. You will experience this as building tension followed by a series of strong head shakes. At this moment, you can give the fish a strong pull with the rod, guaranteeing the deep placement of the hook, and fight it as you would if you had hooked it by any other means. Most typically, the hooked fish will break upstream at unparalleled velocity, leaving a goofy smile on your face.

The best striking motion when a fish rises to a broadside fly is no striking motion at all. BRIAN MARZ

CHAPTER 12

Skating Drys

As a kid, I spent as many hours as possible in fly shops. They were physical structures that replicated the architecture of my mind. I spent hours wiggling rods, reading magazines, and soaking up conversations. I trusted that fly fishing's secrets could be absorbed via proximity.

What I loved most about fly shops—more than the gear and fish pictures—were the people they attracted. Men and women whose auras reeked of obsession. At the mere mention of a favorite river, they'd lick their lips and wallow hard. Their faces glowed red with sunburn, minus the harsh tan line where polarized glasses always sat. Their forearms bulged with strange muscles, veins pushed high by excessive casting. They spoke in a language at first incomprehensible: tippet this, adipose that. And in gleaming moments of ritualistic exuberance, they'd lean in and whisper their most cherished secrets: "Hit the pocket water at the two-and-a-half-mile mark. They're stacked in there thick as hell right now." Even at the indecisive age of twelve, I knew fly-shop people were my kind of people. And they must have seen a little fly shop blooming in me too, for they were always kind enough to save me a stool.

I learned of steelhead rising to skated flies from one especially passionate shop guy—a long-haired twenty-something named Matt who followed the Grateful Dead when the fish weren't in. It was a fall day, leaves fluttering by the open door. Shop people trickled in and out all day. A question or two of Matt, a few serious moments at

the fly bin, and they'd be off toward their favorite river. I envied the hell out of them—they had driver's licenses.

At around 4 P.M., as Matt and I discussed a recent trip he'd taken to a remote Washington river, an older man came into the shop. Matt beamed a wide smile and snapped his head toward the ceiling.

"Bill," he said.

"Matt," the man said back.

They moved through pleasantries with a handshake, both their arms rigid and veiny, and then skipped straight into more serious business.

"How'd it go?" Bill asked.

Matt knew exactly what he was asking about. "Awesome. You know the big orange rock in Miller's Run?"

"The one at the top or bottom?"

"Top. Rose them there every time we hit it," Matt said without a hint of gloating.

"You'd better have. That's the fail-safe slot. I brought something for you." Bill raised a VHS cassette. "Mike and I filmed this."

Matt fed the tape to the VCR just as a lanky customer walked in the front door. They shared nods, and the man took a viewing position behind us.

The film showed Bill, wearing a tweed cap and chest waders, making casts across the tailout of a pool. "You recognize the spot?" Bill asked.

"Of course," Matt said.

Above: Dawn patrol on the North Umpqua.

On the end of Bill's line danced a big, clunky fly. As the tension came tight, the fly threw wide wakes on the surface like a scaled-down motorboat.

"So, you know how the fish average on the small side there?"

"Four to six pounds," Matt said.

"Exactly. So that's what I thought I was fishing over."

On the video, Bill cast again. This time the fly landed farther out. Suddenly a bulge appeared near the fly, waking straight toward it. The motorboat disappeared into a swirling boil.

"That wasn't any six-pounder!" Matt said.

After a delay, Bill raised his rod and shouted back toward the camera. Water exploded in all directions, a serious fish slapping its wide tail like a beaver.

"I knew right then I was in trouble," Bill said.

The fish bolted upriver, Bill first stripping in line, then watching as the line zipped back out through his fingers. His little rod was already bent to the cork, yet the fish kept cranking up the violence of his head shakes. The cameraman shook trying to move into a better position, the camera's microphone picking up an expletive.

After a series of runs and several near beachings, Bill finally landed the fish, a buck with bright red gill plates and bold stripes down its sides. The beast looked forty inches long. Bill held it in his shaking hands, water pouring off the fish, orange sunlight sparkling in the drops. Then he lowered it back into the current, and with a massive tail stroke, the fish was gone.

We stood awed by what we'd just seen. Finally Bill severed the silence. "Anyway, thought you guys might get a kick out of that."

The skating dry fly has a powerful hold on the mind of any angler who has seen it work. The fly's wakes can't help but create a sense of heightened tension. A fish could rise at any moment, and as the fly swings, it's easy to be convinced that this is the cast. Some of us have spent entire weeks in this state of mind.

In the forefront of the angler's mind is the knowledge that any take, even a miss, will be dramatic. Steelhead don't just tenderly suck in a skating fly. They often take it in a gator rise, jaws open and chomping. "The Louisiana take," a friend calls it. "It'll make your knees clang together faster than a drum roll." The human body isn't built to sustain such blinding rushes of adrenaline.

It's no wonder that anglers miss most steelhead raised to the dry fly. Overwhelming doses of adrenaline limit our ability to perform; when those gaping jaws

During the fall, a skated dry fly can be the most successful tactic for taking steelhead. This five-pound buck took after a wet fly failed to bring a response.

emerge, the rush gets the best of our senses, and we yank the fly away with a sharply raised rod. Even the finest dry-fly fishers tug the fly away with embarrassing frequency. But angler error has a partner. Often steelhead themselves are so jazzed by the waking fly that they completely miss. Between stoked steelhead and spastic anglers, it's a wonder that steelhead are ever landed on the skated dry.

The dramatic rises of steelhead to the dry might be linked to the desperate response of the juvenile to insects fluttering over the surface. Likely, our skating dry fly taps into the most urgent of striking instincts, the high-speed rise to an egg-laying caddis.

Steelhead rivers breed huge numbers of caddis. Some of the same conditions that make a good steelhead stream make a good caddis stream: fertile water, cobbled bottom, fast riffles and runs. In most of steelhead country, a species of caddis hatches every day of the spring, summer, and fall. From the tiny black caddis to the bird-size October caddis, juvenile fish always have a species on which to gorge themselves. The bugs are nothing if not ubiquitous.

For all their diversity, caddis behavior is consistent. As trout anglers know, the insect spends its early life along the river bottom. Most species live in small structures of pebbles or sticks built around their larval bodies. When ready to hatch, the larva form morphs into the pupa form, and the insect either floats or crawls to the surface. Quickly the pupa morphs into the adult, and the mature insect flutters away to streamside rocks or vegetation. If a juvenile steelhead is quick on the draw, it may catch the pupa as it morphs into the adult. But any hesitation in the fish's response will result in a missed bug.

After the adults mate, the female caddis comes back to the water to deliver her eggs. Some species drop their eggs from high in the air; others dive underwater and swim to the bottom; and still others skim over the river's surface, depositing eggs here and there. The caddis that skim the surface appear frequently on most steelhead streams, and the juvenile fish await their appearance. But the adult caddis often proves difficult to take. The feisty bug moves quickly over the surface, and a fish that hesitates will end up going hungry. Successful juvenile steelhead attack adult caddis flies with abandon. Often steelheaders see these young feeding fish on the river; their splashy rises give them away. Sometimes an especially eager juvenile will rocket into the air after a caddis, completing a somersault or two.

Such constant feeding activity, of premium importance in the life of a preimmigrant steelhead, surely informs the adult fish's behavior once back from the salt. Steelhead strike from an instinctual reaction to certain stimuli. As the adult fish sees a caddis skimming over the surface, the years spent urgently attacking such insects as a juvenile prompt it to react. Not every steelhead's striking reflex will be prompted, but if you find the right fish at the right time, the steelhead will rise just as it did as a preimmigrant.

It's no wonder that steelhead miss our skated flies so often. Hitting a caddisfly as it lays its eggs on the surface takes incredible precision. The insect is rapidly skimming, and the water underneath is rushing by. If the steelhead is a fraction of an inch off here or there, it'll miss completely. While at sea, steelhead don't need to be precise. Film footage of steelhead and salmon feeding in the salt shows that the fish often move through schools of baitfish, striking and hitting as many little fish as possible. Their goal seems to be to wound them. Once a fish has passed through the school, it turns around and eats those fish it wounded. The steelhead likely brings the sloppy habits of such feeding behavior back into the fresh water. Moreover, there is little evolutionary pressure for a returning steelhead to be an efficient feeder. Successfully ingesting caddis will do little to secure a place on the spawning grounds. Even if the steelhead managed to swallow every insect within striking range, the caloric intake wouldn't be enough to help the fish maintain its weight. In fact, the steelhead would likely use more calories feeding than it would gain from capturing insects. Steelhead rivers just aren't fertile enough to support such big fish. The steelhead's job is to get upstream and spawn, not take up a feeding position and put on weight. Striking at a skating fly is simply an instinctual response, one prone to be done haphazardly. Just think about it: A successful take on a skimming caddis is hard enough for a resident trout whose life depends on it.

Hit or miss, the steelhead's rise to a skating dry fly is a glorious phenomenon, one that every serious steelheader needs to experience. Unfortunately, not every steelhead is a willing participant.

The skated dry fly requires fish with a large strike zone, a trait unlikely to be found on heavily pressured rivers. Steelhead grow dour when exposed too often to lures, lines, and flies. In river sections visited by many anglers, steelhead travel to secure holding lies and shrink the size of their strike zones. Any fish that doesn't is quickly removed from the river. Presentations that place the fly near the remaining steelhead, especially dead drift presentations, are more likely to move the fish. The dry fly depends on steelhead with a large strike zone, so it is best employed on lightly pressured waters.

Some races of steelhead are more prone to rising to a dry fly than others. *Gairdneri* steelhead are known for their love of the dry fly, maybe because their natal streams

contain such healthy caddis populations. Steelhead from the Deschutes to the Methow viciously chase skated drys. In fact, skated drys often move these fish when the water temperatures suggest that nothing but flies near the bottom will be effective. Some *irideus* populations are known for their proclivity for the skated dry. The North Umpqua supports a strong dry-fly tradition, the summer fish eager to rise once the sun is off the water. Several rivers in British Columbia, the Skeena drainage included, have populations of willing risers. Steelhead in western Oregon and western Washington are generally considered more stubborn. Fish can still be raised, but you're usually better off using a swung wet fly.

Dry-fly enthusiasts adamantly agree that wild steelhead, those fish raised naturally in their natal streams, are much more likely to rise to a dry fly than steelhead of hatchery stock. Wild steelhead spend two to four years feeding as juveniles on the insect populations of the river. Hatchery steelhead spend that time within the cement walls of an oversize fish tank, feeding on pellets of ground protein. The behavioral difference between the two types of fish—especially in response to the dry fly—is logical enough: The impulse to chase down a skating caddis is more practiced in the wild fish.

The largest steelhead ever known to be raised, hooked, and landed on a dry fly was a British Columbia fish over thirty pounds. Despite this, the skated dry fly has a reputation for raising the smaller fish in a river. This trend follows the dry everywhere it goes, from California to Alaska. If a river typically produces steelhead in the six- to ten-pound range, the dry fly will most likely raise those six-pound fish. This phenomenon has intrigued anglers since the presentation's first application on steelhead rivers. As with other facets of steelhead behavior, speculation produces comforting potential explanations.

Trout are a territorial fish. When they spread through a section of water, the biggest trout always gets the best lies. If a ten-inch trout is holding in the prime seam—a seam that offers protection, rest, and a steady supply of food—and a fifteen-inch trout wants the seam, the larger fish chases smaller one out. Certainly, as a parr and later a smolt, juvenile steelhead play this dominance game. When adult steelhead reenter their natal river, they once again live by the game's rules—just to a more limited extent. When steelhead densities are high enough, as they often are in the fall, the fish begin competing for the prime lies, the bigger fish in a section taking the better holding lies. The best holding lie is one that offers a steelhead complete protection from the

Facing page: Streams with healthy wild steelhead populations are the best places for skating dry flies.

outside world, well-oxygenated water, and respite from the current. In many rivers, this ideal holding water comes in the form of deeper runs. As the skated dry fly is best fished in shallow water, it makes sense that usually the smaller fish—the fish relegated to the shallow water—will be inclined to rise.

Another possible explanation for the propensity of the dry fly to take smaller steelhead might lie in a different facet of steelhead behavior. Most steelheaders who have been lucky enough to hook big steelhead admit that the biggest fish are rarely the best fighters. These big fish are prone to bulldogging an angler, making short runs to deep and fast currents, and rarely launching themselves airborne. These big fish seem prone to conserving their energy, even when fighting for their lives. Smaller fish, on the other hand, are often the most dramatic fighters, running and jumping and exhausting themselves quickly. These smaller fish are prone to expending energy without regard to conservation. The reasons for this difference are mysterious. Maybe it has something to do with the physical difficulty of quickly moving such a massive body through the water. Maybe it has something to do with the different metabolic rates of the different-size fish. Who knows? But the behavioral difference between large and small fish when hooked might explain why smaller fish are more likely to rise for the dry fly.

A final explanation that many Northwest guides posit involves the relative ages of the fish. A big steelhead is likely to have spent more time at sea than a smaller fish. A twenty-eight-inch steelhead typically has spent two years in the salt, but a twenty-three-inch steelhead likely has spent just one. Possibly these younger fish are more influenced by their freshwater lives than the older fish. A steelhead returned from one year in the salt might be more inclined to fall back on his parr behaviors—including eagerly chasing down skimming caddis adults—than a steelhead that spent two years in the salt.

A conclusive explanation for the phenomenon is unlikely to emerge, guaranteeing us a perennial point for debate at the fly shop.

The Water

The skated dry-fly presentation is most effective on rivers with minimal angling pressure. Steelhead that are relaxed and comfortable in their holding lies are the fish most likely to feel brazen enough to shatter the surface with a rise. The general conditions on the river also need to facilitate large strike zones. A rise to the surface requires the fish move a great distance, in some cases many feet. Provoking such a response is much easier if the water is in prime shape.

Of utmost importance to the skating angler is water temperature. Steelhead, being cold-blooded, are made lethargic by cold water. Icy conditions slow a fish's metabolism and hence shrink its strike zone. With a thermometer, make sure the water temperature falls into the ideal range for your area.

The amount of light on the water affects how willing steelhead will be to approach the surface. If the sun is blazing down, save the skated dry until the afternoon. On some rivers, steelhead will become responsive once the sun reaches afternoon angles, even if the light is still on the water. But on most rivers the steelhead won't become consistently interested until the light is off the water. Heavy cloud cover is usually enough light protection to make steelhead comfortable. If your homewater's valley is socked in, odds are you'll be able to fish the skater all day.

As summer steelhead spend more time in fresh water, their striking reflexes become more troutlike in nature, peaking sometime in the fall. Because the skated dry fly requires a fish in tune with its freshwater instincts, September and October are typically the best months for skating drys in the majority of steelhead country. When you are first learning the technique, the consistent success of the fall months can really speed up the process.

Certain types of water will provide the most consistent success. The skated dry fly is best fished over water that is two to six feet deep. Skating over water that is less than two feet deep can result in spooked fish. And skating over water that is more than six feet deep will rarely persuade a fish to move all the way to the surface. Because a relatively smooth surface is required for a skating dry fly to perform properly, most fast water will not suffice. Rather, the prudent angler will fish water that is of medium current, the type of water typically found at tailouts. By far, tailouts account for the majority of fish raised to skating dry flies.

The Logistics

The skated dry fly can be presented in two different ways. The more common method is similar to the classic swing presentation. The other, the preferred technique of most ardent skaters, is similar to the greased-line presentation.

The classic swing-style presentation of the skating dry fly is easily performed by any angler proficient in fishing wet flies. Much of the technique is the same, with one major exception: The skated fly requires a great deal of detail work to keep it fishing properly, work that is superfluous with the wet fly. In this way, skating adds a new challenge to the classic swing.

Because of the attention to detail required, casts are rarely longer than seventy feet when fishing the skating fly. Long casts make the task of controlling the skate difficult. Casts under twenty feet are also tough to control properly, as the line won't allow the kind of belly needed to maintain the swing.

To start, find a smooth tailout three to six feet deep, and wade in until you're forty feet upstream from the first slot to be fished. As shown on page 134, make a forty-foot cast quartering downstream (A). As soon as the cast is made, complete a large line lift mend toward the far bank, properly positioning the fly line for the swing (B). The best mend allows the fly to skate as slowly as possible over the slot. Steelhead that refuse a fast-moving dry fly can sometimes be convinced by one that moves more slowly.

As the fly swings, it will occasionally drop under the surface tension. To maintain the perfect skate, you can move the rod out from the swing (C). An "out" rod position points between the fly and the far shore and hence increases the current's pressure on the fly line. If the problem isn't corrected, try raising the fly rod slightly to further increase the speed of the fly's swing. If the pattern still won't skate properly, a quick line flip downstream—to produce a larger belly—will usually solve the problem. Once the pattern completes its swing, strip it in, dry it with false casts, and reposition it in a new slot.

Because any steelhead willing to take the fly will inherently be a feisty fish, and as the skating pattern is visible for a great distance, the slot size will be comparatively large when fishing the skated fly. Most anglers fish slots between two and four feet wide with the skated fly. Such large slots allow you to fish the technique quickly, covering a great deal of water. The more river you cover, the more likely you'll find a willing fish.

The other technique for presenting a skated fly is a variation of the greased-line presentation, the preferred method of most skated-fly aficionados. This technique allows the fly to act in three different manners during the swing. The result is a fly that shows many sides of itself during one presentation, increasing the likelihood of a rise.

Position yourself forty feet upstream from the first slot to be fished. Instead of booming a cast all the way to that first slot, make a cast directly across the current (page 135). Ideally, the fly will land in line with the far end of the slot to be fished (A), thirty feet or so from the angler's position. On each subsequent cast, the fly can be placed two feet further out, allowing the fly to be shown to more water.

Using a large line flip, mend the entire line—minus three to five feet near the connection point with the

Facing page: Steelhead become increasingly interested in surface presentations once the sun is off the water.

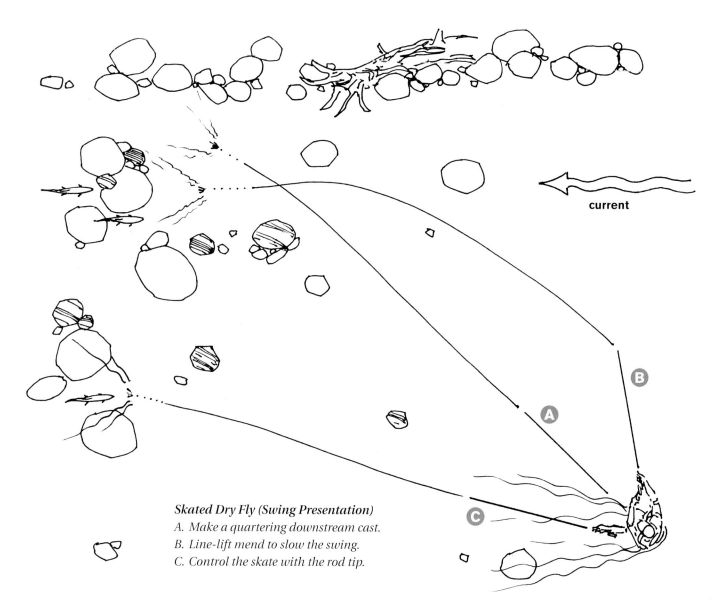

current

Skated Dry Fly (Swing Presentation)
A. Make a quartering downstream cast.
B. Line-lift mend to slow the swing.
C. Control the skate with the rod tip.

leader—upstream (B). The mend creates a small belly near the fly and lays the majority of the line into position for a near dead drift of the fly.

Feed line tosses to allow the fly to drift downstream (C). Each toss should be strong enough to twitch the fly slightly. Steelhead lying on the bottom will see the twitching fly—an enticing vision—and occasionally rise for the take.

As the fly reaches the first slot, bring the line under tension from the rod, and the fly will begin to skate (D). The majority of takes induced by this technique come at the precise moment the swing begins. Not surprisingly, it is this moment that most matches the natural movements of the egg-laying caddis. With the swinging presentation, you control the fly's swing to be as slow as possible; with the greased-line presentation, you swing the fly as slowly as possible while maintaining its broadside position in the current. As the line swings, keep the

rod in to lead the fly toward the bank. If the fly dips under the surface, you can use the same techniques as for the swinging presentation to pop it back onto the surface. If a simple "out" rod position doesn't solve the problem, a quick raise of the rod usually will.

This technique is especially deadly because it allows the fly to be presented dead drifting, twitching, and skating, all on a single cast. In this way, you can show the steelhead in a section of river three different options, any one of which might spark the strike reflex.

Rods, Lines, Leaders, and Flies

Skating dry flies requires little in the way of tackle. In fact, in most situations, you can use the same rod, line, and leader as for swinging with a floater or greased-lining a wet fly.

The ideal single-handed rod for this presentation is a long 7- or 8-weight. Six-weight rods work fine but have more trouble turning over the big, wind-resistant flies often used when skating. On the other end, a rod as heavy as a 9-weight will needlessly tire the casting arm. But 7- and 8-weights handle the work ideally. As with all swinging presentations, the longer the better. 10- and even 11-foot single-handed rods provide the most control over a distant fly. Some anglers favor light Spey rods on bigger water, as they allow longer casts and more precise control of the skating pattern. Most Spey anglers prefer rods designed for traditional casting techniques when fishing drys.

The same salmon-steelhead or distance fly line used for the swinging or greased-line presentation will handle the skated dry fly ideally. The more massive head offered by these lines will turn over the bulkiest of dry flies, even

into a stiff wind. As precise mending is required, the long running belly of the line will prove invaluable. For Spey rods, the same double-taper line used in the swing will suffice, but make sure to buy one that has been proven to cast well with your rod model.

A 9- to 12-foot leader is ideal for fishing the skating dry. If the fish are overly spooky or are holding in thin water, use the longer leader. Most skaters trust tapered leaders, as the knots found on a knotted leader will throw their own wakes when on the surface. A leader tapered to 8-pound-test allows plenty of sensitivity while still providing the strength for turning a heavy fish.

The archetypal steelhead skating pattern has its genesis in the Atlantic salmon tradition. Atlantic salmon

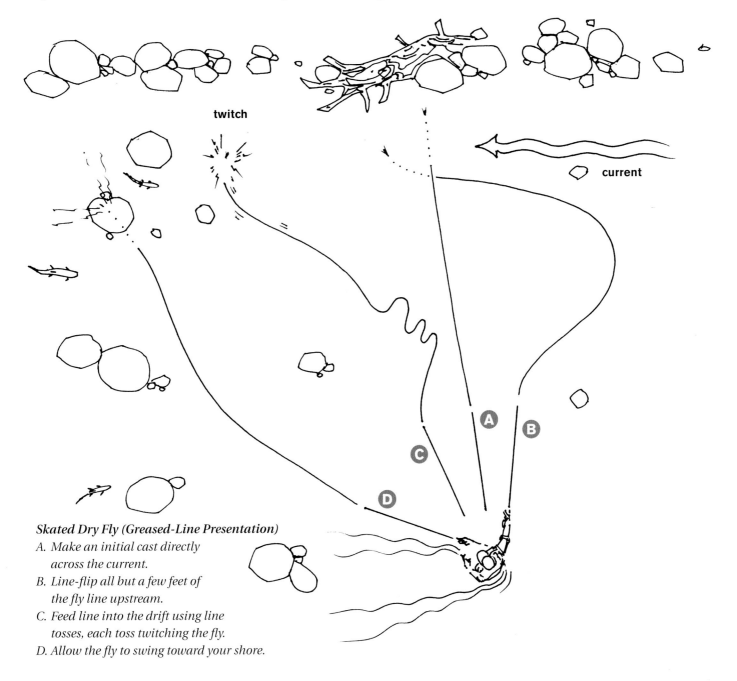

Skated Dry Fly (Greased-Line Presentation)
A. *Make an initial cast directly across the current.*
B. *Line-flip all but a few feet of the fly line upstream.*
C. *Feed line into the drift using line tosses, each toss twitching the fly.*
D. *Allow the fly to swing toward your shore.*

A ten-pound buck from a small summer stream.
TOM CHRISTENSEN

have been pursued with skating techniques for decades, and several generations of innovation have produced a series of patterns known as Bombers. The Bomber typically is tied with a calf-hair tail, a spun moose-hair body, and a strong calf-hair wing that points at a forty-five-degree angle forward. The wing catches the meniscus and helps keep the fly above the water line. The pattern quickly found its way to West Coast streams, much to the delight of summer steelheaders. The Bomber has taken steelhead for almost two generations of anglers, but ever-innovative fly tiers have worked to improve the pattern. Bombers are famous for tipping sideways in the current and riding under the surface tension—a fate made more likely when fished at typical steelhead distances.

While filming 3M's Pacific Steelhead Series with John Fabian, Lani Waller designed a new generation of skating patterns that would eventually be called the Waller Waker. In the low dusk light typical of skating conditions, the Bomber was hard to see on film. Waller sat down at the vise, aiming to make a more visible skater, and ended up creating the quintessential steelhead skating pattern. The Waller Waker employs a tail and ungulate fur body similar to the Bomber's, but instead of a single wing, the Waker has a spilt wing. The double wing stabilizes the fly, keeping it upright as it swings across the river. And to help the fly stay afloat in the most challenging of currents, Waller added a stiff throat of moose hair at a forty-five-degree angle backward. The result is a pattern that not only stays visible in low light, but also can't help but skate.

Recently, another generation of skating patterns emerged, flies employing highly buoyant foam. The result is the most efficient skating patterns ever designed. Most of the recipes call for foam to be angled off the top

front of the fly, actually pulling the pattern onto the surface. Some of the patterns even wobble as they skate, throwing deadly vibrating wakes. Foam is such a buoyant material that some patterns don't even demand floatant to stay afloat. The flies are so effective that many skating buffs fish nothing else. Foam patterns like Nate Koenigsknecht's Weapon of Mass Deception (WMD) that incorporate the colors of local caddis species have become the gold standard on many Northwest streams.

My skating box contains two patterns: the Waller Waker and the WMD. With these two patterns, I'm able to fish all skating water, from flat, gravylike tailouts to bumpier runs. The Waller Waker's thick body and beefy wings make it ideal for provoking steelhead in bumpy or deeper water—places where spooking a steelhead isn't likely. The WMD's smaller profile makes it perfect for thinner or smoother water, where fish might be more sensitive. For each pattern, I carry sizes 8 and 6. If a

The Waller Waker

Weapon of Mass Deception

Few sights in the angling world are as mesmerizing as a fly skating over prime holding water.

steelhead rises to the bigger pattern, misses, and won't return for another take, switching to the smaller fly can often persuade the fish to rise again. And if the more subtle pattern fails, switching to a small wet fly can also do the trick. I treat the Waller Waker in advance of the trip with Goop, so as to stiffen the wing and help the fly stay afloat. Then, by applying more floatant on the stream, I can be assured that the fly will skate as long as possible. To help limit the number of fly changes, I also carry a drying agent in powder form. When either fly gets soaked and has trouble fishing properly, I simply give it a few false casts and place it the drying agent. The pattern instantly regains its skating ability.

Variations

Employing a riffle hitch with a skating pattern generally increases its performance. The fly will ride higher in surface film, wake more visibly, and even twitch slightly: all traits that will bring more steelhead to the surface. In slow water, the riffle hitch is a necessity. In fast water, the current might not allow its use. Experiment and use the hitch if it helps the fly skate more enticingly.

Because of the tremendous wakes produced by the skating dry fly, the presentation gets lots of attention in the river. Steelhead frequently are intrigued by the commotion and rise up to the skater without hitting it. They'll slip up behind it, eyeing it from nearby, then disappear back into the depths. Some may even bump the fly with their nose before returning to their lies. The curiosity of these fish can be exploited by the savvy angler.

Many steelhead that are hesitant to hit the skater will be enthused enough by its presence to hit other patterns. The skating pattern seems to awaken a steelhead's striking reflex. Some anglers carry an extra rod rigged with a floating line and a swinging pattern. When they see a steelhead rise and refuse the dry, or if a fish repeatedly misses the skater, they'll quickly deliver a cast with the wet fly. Often the curious fish—so hesitant to break the surface—will readily slam the swinging wet.

Other anglers go a step further and attach a wet fly to the skater. Often steelhead rise and peek at the skater while remaining invisible to the angler. By always fishing a wet from the dry, you can pick up those more elusive fish. Plus, a skater–wet fly combo seems to encourage more fish to rise in the first place, likely because of the provocative action of two patterns moving in tandem. Attaching the wet fly is easy. Tie the dry fly to the leader as usual, with either a riffle hitch or improved clinch. On the bend of its hook, attach another section of leader. A thirty-six-inch section of 3X is ideal. The wet fly should be slightly smaller than the dry fly to keep from dragging the skater under the surface. I prefer a lightly dressed fly in size 8, either a Copper Top or a Spawning Purple Peril. The dry will do the attracting of the distant steelhead, so the wet fly can be smaller than normal and still induce strikes.

As with any trailing hook system, this rigging shouldn't be risked on wild steelhead. The possibility exists that a steelhead will strike the dry, become hooked, and twist the trailing leader around its body during the fight. If the dry comes unpinned, the trailing wet fly could foul-hook the fish. Such unfortunate events are exceedingly rare—but so are healthy runs of wild steelhead.

Hooking Takers

Though steelhead frequently miss skated drys as they enthusiastically rise, occasionally they're on target. But just because the fish performs correctly doesn't mean you will.

Hooking a steelhead risen to the skated dry is one of the most challenging acts of our sport. Every impulse in your body tells you to raise the rod and set the hook when a steelhead hits your skating fly. But immediately striking all but guarantees a missed fish. When a steelhead rises to the skated fly, it rarely places its mouth around the pattern. Instead, it usually flushes water through its gills and pulls the fly into its mouth. If you raise the rod when the fish rises, nine times out of ten you'll tug the fly directly out of the fish's open mouth.

Instead of immediately striking when a fish rises, you're better off remaining motionless. Doing so allows the pattern to slide into the steelhead's mouth. Once the fish chomps down and turns, the line will come tight on the rod. At that moment, raising the rod will drive the hook's point home. To further increase the odds of a good hookup, you can hold a coil of line in the rod hand, as done with other swinging presentations. A foot to a foot and a half of line will act as a leash, allowing the fish to turn completely on the fly before you deliver tension. The leash helps ensure that the hook buries into the corner of the jaw.

Not raising the rod on the take also has another benefit. A steelhead that misses the skated fly completely, having never felt the point of the hook, will often hit the pattern again. By letting the fly continue to swing, the fish may turn and take it immediately—if you're lucky, with more accuracy this time.

A guide I know insists the best way to consistently hook steelhead that rise to the skated dry is to actually throw slack at them as they take. He insists that feeding a couple feet of slack into the line allows the fly to slide more easily into the fish's mouth. He explained his theory as we fished an autumn river, the setting sun throwing long shadows over his swinging line. Only a few moments went by before a determined little chromer rose for his Waller Waker. Instantly, the rod arced toward the sky, and a pile of line landed at his feet. "You didn't see that," he said.

CHAPTER 13

The Broadside Rise

The striking responses of steelhead are ingrained during the long parr phase of the fish's life. Steelhead spend one to three years as parr, feeding voraciously on the insects of their natal stream. They see mayflies drifting downstream, caddis laying eggs on the surface, and stoneflies crawling over rocks. The fast river environment requires parr to respond quickly; those that hesitate starve.

Most steelhead streams have vibrant caddis and mayfly populations. The riffling shallows that create ideal habitat for 5- to 8-inch fish also create ideal habitat for many juvenile insects. Several common species of fast-water caddis and mayflies hatch from their larval and nymph forms in a similar manner: The insects collect air bubbles from the surrounding water, causing them to rise toward the surface. Trout anglers call the rising caddis pupae and the rising mayflies emergers. Anyone who has spent a few years chasing trout with a fly rod knows the importance of these two forms. In the early stages of a hatch, trout often exclusively select pupa and emerger forms, turning a contemptuous eye to the best-tied dry flies.

Steelhead parr spend a great portion of their spring, summer, and fall months feeding on mayfly and caddis species that are rising from the bottom to the top. Such behavior ingrains in them an immediate response to the rising motion, a response that often is still intact when they reenter their natal streams as adults.

The broadside rise presents a fly in precisely this rising motion. An upstream cast followed by a dead drift allows the fly to sink low in the water column. Then as the fly moves downstream of you and comes under tension, it turns broadside and rises toward the surface. The rising motion has an extraordinary ability to spark the dormant striking reflex in a resting steelhead, often convincing steelhead that have refused several other presentations. And the broadside position of the fly casts a larger silhouette, enticing steelhead from distant lies.

Steelheaders realized long ago that a fly moving from the bottom to the top could take fish. Before lead was frequently attached to hooks, anglers tied sparse patterns on heavy wire and made long upstream casts on slack lines. The flies would slowly sink to the bottom and could be brought to the surface with a little tension. The advent of weighted beads and eyes, as well as thinner and stronger leaders, helped anglers reach deeper and faster water. Besides opening up more fishable water to the technique, these modern innovations allowed the broadside rise to be fished with more speed, enabling an angler to cover more water quickly.

Today, as anglers find themselves casting to dour fish more and more often, the broadside rise has become increasingly popular. On rivers swarmed by hordes of other anglers, where every fish has seen two or three different swung flies by breakfast time, the broadside rise has an ability to tap into the deepest instincts of the fish

Above: An angler sinks his weighted fly into a deep slot known to hold steelhead. The broadside rise is deadly year-round.

and produce a violent take when nothing else has. With this fresh enthusiasm for the presentation has come a fresh wave of technical innovation. Modern anglers present the broadside rise differently than past generations, developing ways to maximize the time the fly spends rising. These innovations have made the technique even deadlier than before.

A few seasons ago, I found myself drifting a fork of Oregon's Willamette River, searching for winter steelhead. Before becoming a nearly featureless river twisting its way through a flat valley edged by endless grass fields, the Willamette roars down steep mountains and slides into long riffling sections. The river's winter fish are wild, sort of. No steelhead existed in this particular fork of the river before game managers arrived on the scene, according to Oregon's Fish and Wildlife Department. For half a dozen years in the 1950s, the department stocked smolts in the river below a recently completed barrier dam. When money ran thin, the efforts of the state managers were directed to other streams with more "recreational potential." In the years since, the offspring of the original smolts have bred naturally in the stream without further intrusion from game managers. Generations of Willamette steelhead hatched from the gravel, sur-

vived as parr, smolted, and returned upriver as adults. The unique conditions of the river—the long migration and high flows—have selected for certain traits in the fish, most notably size. Willamette winter steelhead can be big fish.

But the size of the fish is only one of the river's attractions. The other has less to do with a bending fly rod and more to do with cocktail party novelty. Feral steelhead are a rarity. Countless examples exist of wild stocks being genetically degraded by the intrusion of hatchery fish, but there are few instances of hatchery fish beginning the slow process of genetic improvement. With each passing generation, the feral steelhead become a better fit for their environment, closer to what would naturally exist in the river. Rarely does an angler get a front-row seat to the creation of a new stock of fish.

Usually, any plans to fish the river are thwarted by heavy rains and snowmelt during the best months. Most days the river looks more like a rice paddy than a steelhead stream. But occasionally the clouds part, the arctic air slides over the valley, and the water drops into shape. And when this happens, boats get hitched.

Brian, a friend with a serious chromer addiction, called to say the river would be in shape the next day, so

Few steelhead can resist the temptation of a fly lifting from the bottom.

long as the rain didn't rush onshore during the night. The river hadn't been fishable for a month, and once the headwater snow started melting in another couple weeks, it would be blown for the rest of the season. It was now or never.

We started early the next day, sliding the boat down a steep bank below the same barrier dam where the original smolts had been stocked fifty years prior. Already a quilt of clouds sat over the western sky. "Let's push straight down to the Producer," he said, checking the knots in his leader while I oared. "If we've only got a couple hours, might as well spend them there." The Producer had earned its name over the years. It was a long run, a roll cast wide, that for inexplicable reasons collected winter steelhead en masse. Water that appeared to us to be identical, runs just up- and downstream of the Producer, had rarely given fish. In the past few seasons, we'd come to see the Producer as the river's barometer. If it didn't offer a fish, we probably wouldn't find one anywhere.

Half a mile into the float, the river braided into channels, and a yellow sign stood on an island: Danger Ahead. Impassable Routes. Stay Right. We went left, and Brian took the oars. Around the first corner, a logjam spanned the river. Gray old trees hung over the river's surface, hundreds of trees piled on top of one another. At first glance, it was an impassable route for sure. But in years past, Brian had perfected a route. He oared toward an especially big log, and I climbed onto it, the bowline securely in my hand. Brian kept the boat from drifting with the current into the main mass of the jam, while I walked down the log, pulling the boat behind. In one place, I had to lean into the rope, and the boat barely squeezed through the gap. "Textbook," Brian said.

Once we were through, the channel made one turn, and the Producer lay before us. We anchored the boat and climbed ashore.

"Thirty-nine," Brian said, shaking dry his thermometer. "Small slots."

We both looked at the rods in the boat. In the years past, indicator tactics had taken the majority of the Producer's steelhead. But it made little sense for us both to fish the same tactic.

"You take the indicator rod," Brian said, grabbing the sink-tip rod and checking the point of the hook on his fingernail.

"Then you go first," I insisted.

When the sun finally burst over the Cascades, casting orange light on the naked trees overhead, Brian had already worked half of the Producer's length. I rubbed my hands to warm them and started in above. About a quarter way through the run, the yellow indicator dove. When I came back, the rod bowed, then rose, then bowed again. Before I could think better of it, I yelled, "Fish!" and then was forced to retract the statement as the limb my fly had snagged broke free from the bottom.

"A real hog," Brian said, before going back to fishing.

An hour later, we'd worked through the run, and neither of us had felt a steelhead. The clouds completely obscured the Coast Range now. The rain would be on us in no time, and the river would turn to mud. I poured a cup of coffee, content with the day.

But Brian wasn't so easily pleased. "One more time," he said. He sorted through the rods along the gunwale.

"Going to give it something new?"

"Broadside rise."

"Isn't the water a little cold for that?" I blew the steam off my coffee.

He shook his head. "You never know." He looked out over the run. "There have to be fish there."

Though steelhead could come from anywhere in the Producer, three specific lies had given the majority of the fish. The first one was a trough in the center of the flow. Fifteen feet farther downstream, a big rock collected fish in the wake behind it. And near the tailout, along the far bank, a trough behind a submerged log frequently held fish.

Brian worked the fly through the first spot, breaking the area into micro slots of a few inches and putting the fly through each. But nothing took. He moved downstream a few feet and started again. He made a tuck cast quartering upstream, then a large mend, and after the fly had dead drifted into position, he brought gentle tension onto the line. Underwater, the fly would be rising slowly toward the surface.

Before I saw the arc in the rod, I heard Brian yell, "Fish!" He reeled in his slack, the rod firmly bent, and calmly backstepped onto shore.

I met him there on the beach. "Are you sure it's not a big stick?"

He smiled, then leaned into his rod, and a steelhead swirled on the surface—a big steelhead.

The fish, suddenly realizing the seriousness of its predicament, broke into a sprint downstream, the neon fly line struggling to keep up. Brian trotted after it, his rod high, his eyes on his feet. When the fish should have stopped, should have turned to rest in the Producer's tailout, it didn't.

"Oh, so that's how you want to play," Brian said.

The steelhead was in the big pool downstream—within thirty feet of another logjam. We ran down the bank, Brian spooling his backing onto the reel as he went.

The broadside rise is most effective when specific lies are targeted. Here the fly is allowed to sink before being brought under tension near a tailout boulder.

"I'm going to get downstream of him," he said. "Between the fish and the logjam." It was a radical approach. From that angle, he'd have no leverage if the fish went for the logs. But on the other hand, if the fish was as strong as we both suspected, it might work directly against any pressure applied by the rod.

Once downstream of the holding steelhead, Brian put the fighting butt on his hip and leaned into the fish. Immediately, just as he'd suspected, the steelhead fought against the pressure, upstream and away from the logjam. For a moment, it looked as if the fish might go all the way back through the rapids and into the Producer. But the current proved too much. Brian rushed back to the shore. After several minutes of bulldogging in the deep water, the buck came close, and I tailed the fish on the sandy beach.

"Dang!" Brian said, laying his rod on the stones and extracting a cloth tape measure from his pocket. While I revived the fish in the current, he taped the length and girth. "Thirty-four by . . ." He worked quickly, mumbling to the fish as he did. "Eighteen."

Just then, while the morning sun slanted in from the east, the Pacific rain arrived from the west, and the fish disappeared into the current. Three hours later, the river was blown.

The Water

The very attribute that makes the broadside rise so deadly—the fly's rising motion off the bottom—limits the technique's ability to cover water. The rising motion can't be sustained over long sections of river, making the broadside rise ineffective as a general searching tactic.

Whereas swinging or dead drifting allow you to cover huge slots on a single cast, the broadside rise limits you to small portions of river. For this reason, the technique is best fished to specific lies, defined places where you think a fish is likely holding.

Once you've developed a relationship with a specific section of your homewater, you'll recognize certain holding lies as hot spots. A few midstream boulders in a tailout, for instance, might consistently produce fish. The broadside rise is best fished to these specific places. The rising motion of the fly can be slowed, however, allowing you to present it to a slightly larger area. Though the broadside rise will never be able to cover an entire riffle, you can readily present it to an especially fishy twenty-foot section. If you fish your homewater often, odds are you'll eventually locate areas where the fish consistently concentrate.

Unlike most steelhead presentations, the broadside rise isn't dependent on precise current conditions. Swinging tactics, for instance, depend on even currents for the fly to perform properly. Indicator tactics depend on currents moving roughly the same speed on top as they are on the bottom. The broadside rise, on the other hand, fishes equally well in all sorts of currents, from deep runs to broken pocket water. The presentation even fishes the swirling water of a canyon pool effectively.

Though the broadside rise can readily be applied to any current type, it has trouble fishing water much deeper than ten feet. The fly is held aloft by the floating fly line. A long leader helps the pattern reach deep lies, but most single-handed rods are capable of fishing leaders fourteen feet or less only when a weighted fly is attached at the end. A fourteen-foot leader allows the fly to sink to about ten feet or so, before the pressures of the current catch up with it. Spey rods can allow the fly to get a little deeper, but not more than a couple feet. The minimum effective depth is also limited. Rarely are fish that are holding in less than two feet of water convinced by the presentation. Such shallow water doesn't give the fly adequate room to work its magic; the rising motion barely starts before it's over.

Another advantage of the broadside rise is the presentation's ability to fish both clear and murky water with equal success. Steelhead are rarely spooked by the rising motion of the fly, even while holding in gin flows of a summer stream. The motion is a natural one in the river, one that the fish likely sees every day. It will either respond with a strike or choose to ignore the fly. When the water is murky, a simple adjustment of the fly, bumping up to a larger size, helps steelhead see the pattern despite the decreased visibility.

The Logistics

The two variations of the broadside pull allow you to match the situation. The fast rise variation is best presented to precise holding areas—a rock or trough—where you suspect a fish to be holding. Steelhead typically respond with more vigor to a fly rising rapidly than to one rising slowly.

To fish the fast-rise variation, locate a specific holding lie and position yourself twenty feet to the side and thirty feet upstream. Midstream boulders suspected of holding fish are ideal places, as they often disturb the surface, helping you know when to begin the rising portion of the presentation.

Strip out sixty feet of line, and make a tuck cast directly across the current, as shown on the next page, placing the fly so that if it were allowed to dead drift unabated, it would pass about a foot or so to the far side of the lie (A). As with all tuck casts, the line should land directly on top of the fly, allowing the fly to sink unhindered by drag. An effective tuck cast is essential for dropping the pattern to the stones along the bottom. If a tuck cast isn't possible, try a roll cast followed by a stack mend that deposits the leader on top of the fly.

Once you've made the cast, make an upstream line flip mend, producing roughly a ninety-degree angle two to four feet up the line from the leader (B). The amount of line in this belly will affect how fast the fly rises. In faster currents, make a smaller belly. In slower currents, make a larger belly.

Upon completion of the mend, feed line using slack tosses, allowing the fly—and its belly—to dead drift downstream (C). If the fly's dead drift is interrupted at any point, the fly will rise off the bottom, and no amount of slack will get it back down. Often, steelhead strike as the fly dead drifts. Stay alert and strike if the line hesitates.

Just before the fly reaches the steelhead's lie, stop feeding line, allowing the fly to come under direct tension. Immediately, the sunk fly will turn broadside to the current and rise to the surface (D).

If no fish takes, allow the fly to swing toward shore (E). Fish often notice the fly's rising motion and become curious enough to follow, finally striking as it slows near shore. As with a swinging presentation, allow the fly to hang below you for several seconds before picking it up for another presentation.

Whereas the fast rise is used to cover very specific lies, the slow rise is used over more general ones. With proper mending, the fly will gradually ascend toward the surface, showing the tantalizing action to more area. The slow-rise presentation (page 145) is conducted in much the same manner as the fast rise. You make the same

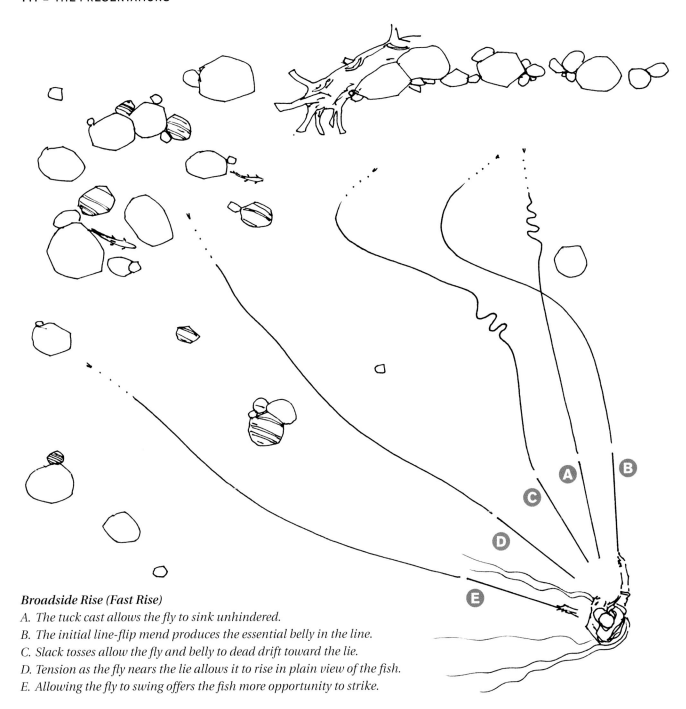

Broadside Rise (Fast Rise)
A. *The tuck cast allows the fly to sink unhindered.*
B. *The initial line-flip mend produces the essential belly in the line.*
C. *Slack tosses allow the fly and belly to dead drift toward the lie.*
D. *Tension as the fly nears the lie allows it to rise in plain view of the fish.*
E. *Allowing the fly to swing offers the fish more opportunity to strike.*

tuck cast across the current, positioning the fly on the far side of the slot to be fished (A).

As with the fast-rise presentation, you use a line flip mend, but producing a larger belly. Instead of a two- to four-foot belly, create a five- to ten-footer (B). This longer belly allows the rising motion to be extended over a longer section of water.

As the fly and belly move downstream, toss slack to allow a dead drift (C). The dead drift assists the fly in reaching the bottom and helps properly place the line for the fly's coming rise.

In the fast-rise presentation, tension comes on suddenly, causing the fly to rise from the bottom quickly. In the slow-rise presentation, tension is applied gently, causing the fly to rise from the bottom slowly. Applying the proper amount of tension is tricky. To be successful, slack line must enter the drift—just more slowly than the current desires. Allow the current to pull slack into the drift, but control the rate with your rod hand's pinch on the line (D). If done correctly, the fly will rise through the water column slowly. The rate at which slack is fed can be adjusted to either increase or decrease the rate of the rising motion.

Once the fly finishes its rise, allow the line to swing toward shore (E). As with the fast rise, curious fish often leave their lies and follow the pattern, striking only when it nears shore.

Since both the fast and slow rises are fished with identical tackle, you can adjust your presentation instantly. Fish a fast rise to a specific midstream boulder, a slow rise over the cobbled bottom downstream, and a fast rise to the next midstream boulder. By adjusting the presentation accordingly, you can thoroughly present the fly to a section of water in a short amount of time.

Rods, Lines, Leaders, and Flies

The broadside rise is as simple in its tackle requirements as it is complex in its presentation. All you need is a trusted rod, standard line, tapered leader, and sinking fly.

Any single-handed rod used for swinging with a floating line will be perfectly matched to the broadside rise. Most anglers prefer a 7- or 8-weight that is 9 to 10 feet long.

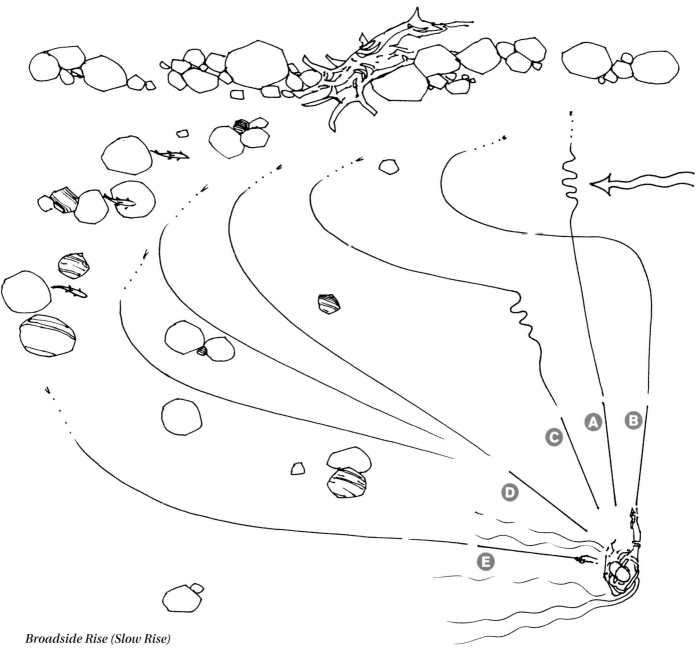

Broadside Rise (Slow Rise)

A. *A tuck cast helps put the fly on the bottom.*

B. *A line-flip mend produces a larger belly than is used with the fast rise.*

C. *Slack tosses allow the fly and belly to dead drift toward the lies.*

D. *By gently applying tension, slowing the rate at which slack enters the drift, you can extend the rising motion.*

E. *Fish often follow the fly and strike when it nears shore.*

The broadside rise requires little in the way of tackle. The same setup used when swinging a wet fly with a floating line will suffice.

The same floating line used for swinging a fly will perfectly present the broadside rise. Most single-handed casters prefer weight-forward lines designed for distance casting. The long bellies of such lines aid the precise mending required by the presentation.

A leader tapered down to 10-pound-test easily handles the broadside rise presentation. It allows the fly to sink quickly, can free snagged flies, and can handle tough steelhead. A leader much bigger than 12-pound-test hinders the rate at which the fly can sink, and for that reason, you should avoid using it if possible. Fluorocarbon is always a good idea because of its abrasion-resistant qualities.

The leader needs to be long enough to allow the fly to reach the bottom. A general rule of thumb is to use a leader that is at least one and a half times the depth of the water to be fished. If the water is six feet deep, the leader should be at least 9 feet long (6 × 1.5 = 9). If the water is eight feet deep, the leader should be at least 12 feet long. Thanks to the triangle effect, referring to the fact that water along the cobbled bottom moves more slowly than water at the top, the sunk fly will drift at a slower rate than the floating fly line. If a leader is used that equals the depth of the water, the fly will not stay as deep as needed. A 9- to 10-foot fly rod has a hard time handling a leader longer than 14 feet when a weighted fly is attached at the business end. This fact limits the single-hand caster to water that is about ten feet deep.

To help the fly sink, it's best to use an open clinch, or any other trusted open knot, between the tippet and fly. When free of drag, a weighted fly slices down through the water column. This sinking motion is slowed by the surface area of the fly. If you use a fly with weight near the head and employ an open knot (as shown on page 147), the fly is free to turn facedown as it sinks, doubling the rate at which it plummets.

To fish properly, the fly used with the broadside rise needs to employ barbell eyes up front. The eyes allow the pattern to sink headfirst and reach the bottom as quickly as possible. They also cause the hook

The Open Clinch Knot

1. *Make an overhand knot in the tippet, but keep it loose.*

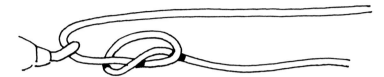

2. *Feed the tippet through the hook's eye.*

3. *As with a clinch knot, wrap the tag end around the tippet five times. Then feed the tag end through the overhand knot.*

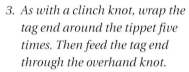

4. *Pull tight.*

shank to rise up, keeping the fly from snagging the bottom continually.

My box contains two flies for the broadside rise. My favorite pattern for summer rivers is the Hot Shot. The pattern's long tail flutters enticingly in the current as the fly rises. I carry sizes 6, 4, and 2, adjusting the fly's size to the clarity of the water and the amount of overhead light. My favorite winter pattern is a pink Thunderhead MOAL in sizes 4, 2, and 1/0. The bright colors of the pattern pull winter fish from a long distance, and the supple rabbit fur provides plenty of action in the slower runs frequented by these big fish. To help the fly reach the deepest lies, I tie it with a large tungsten bead.

Variations

A riffle hitch tied behind the head of the fly can be used to help keep the pattern broadside as it rises. The hitch turns the fly slightly, giving any steelhead nearby a better view of the pattern. The disadvantage of the riffle hitch is that it wears a leader out faster. If you use one, test the leader's strength often.

When employing the broadside rise on a river whose run consists of hatchery steelhead, many anglers add a small egg pattern behind the main fly. As the weighted fly rises, the egg comes up behind it, making an easy target for a steelhead too shy to follow the main fly. The trailing egg is best attached with a 36-inch section of 10-pound-test from the bend of the main fly's hook. A size 6 or 8

Hot Shot

Thunderhead MOAL (pink)

The strike to a broadside rise typically is violent and swift, requiring little more than a sharp lift of the rod. This 11-pound hatchery hen took a Lifter trailed behind a Hot Shot.

Lifter or other egg pattern tied on a short-shanked hook can be attached at the end of the 36 inches. This variation is especially deadly in the fall, when steelhead are used to seeing salmon eggs drifting downstream.

Hooking Takers

When the fly is rising from the bottom, your rod is best kept parallel to the river and pointed in the fly's general direction. If you're fishing the slow rise, odds are good you'll have slack waiting to be fed into the presentation. At the strike, if you allow the fish to pull that slack through the guides, you will most certainly lose it before the hook can find a secure home. To help lower the odds of this unfortunate occurrence, many anglers use the line hand to feed small controlled sections of slack toward the rod hand's pinch on the fly line. If a fish takes, it will come up against the firm resistance offered by the line hand's grip on the line.

Steelhead usually rise from the bottom and strike the fly violently, sometimes nearly yanking the rod from your hand. Because of the broadside position of the fly, the hook usually finds the solid corner of the fish's mouth on its own. Once a fish takes, you can raise the rod to ensure that the hook finds a deep and firm placement. The most effective striking motion is a steady one toward the downstream shore.

If no steelhead takes as the fly rises from the bottom and the pattern begins swinging across the current, you should take the same precautions as when swinging flies from a floating line. A loop of line about 1 to 1½ feet long is best left dangling between the reel and the rod hand's pinch on the fly line. This loop will give the fish time to turn in the current after the take, before the reel's tension buries the hook in its mouth. If no loop is employed, the immediate tension of the reel will frequently tug the fly free of the steelhead's mouth.

CHAPTER 14

Dead Drifting Drys

few years ago, I heard a rumor about a backroad—we'll call it FS 212—that led to a remote stream, one that is usually made inaccessible by a logging company's gate on the main access road. The rumor came to me from a friend who had heard from a reliable source that summer steelhead were stacked up in this spot. "Supposedly they're nose to tail through the canyon section. Nobody is fishing it because nobody knows about 212."

Small summer steelhead streams are few and far between south of the Canadian border. The few wild runs that do exist usually contain a couple hundred fish at best, hardly a fishable population. But for years I'd heard of this particular stream's boomer summer run. Everyone knew a person who knew a person who'd secured a key to the logging company's gate and fished the stream. After my friend drew a map of FS 212, I canceled my plans for the next day and packed a lunch.

Small summer steelhead streams are famous for their dry-fly fishing. The thin water and wary fish often make other presentations impossible. But a dead drifted dry fly is so unobtrusive it can be laid before a holding steelhead without raising the chromer's alarms. I loaded the 6-weight and my dry-fly box into the truck.

Dawn comes early in July, and mileage is hard to predict on twisting backroads, so I didn't make it to the river until the sun was nearly cresting the ridge. But what I saw put a smile on my face. White boulders protruded from the river like the bleached spinal cord of an enormous

dinosaur. Tea-colored water slid between the stones, racing through the occasional set of rapids. Steelhead could be holding anywhere. I parked the truck at a wide spot in the road.

Having never fished the little stream before, I decided to walk the bank looking for holding fish. In this way, I'd get a look at a lot of water, saving my casting for those moments when I knew a fish was present.

In most places, the water was three or four feet deep and clear enough to see the bottom. The shaded bank offered a camouflaged route to stalk upstream, checking the tailouts and the seams along the rapids, any place a resting fish might be holding. Ten minutes into my walk, I stumbled upon a bear track left a few days before in a patch of wet sand.

An hour later, just as I thought I'd been sent on a wild goose chase, a steelhead finally appeared in a tailout. The back half of its body was in a sliver of sunlight, the front half in the shade. Even from the bank, its adipose fin was plainly obvious. Five or six pounds, no more. A tree limb hung down near the water's surface only two or three feet upstream from the holding fish. My cast, if I could get one there, would have to land several feet upstream of the limb and drift back down toward the steel-

Above: On many small summer steelhead streams, a dead-drifted dry fly is the only presentation that won't send steelhead fleeing for the nearest rapids. Here Mary Ann Dozer drifts a dry fly over prime water.

head. But there was a bigger problem. Currents swirled near the fish, making a drag-free cast nearly impossible from my angle. In shallow water, steelhead are usually as spooked by a dragging dry fly as resident trout are, especially in the heat of the summer months, so I knew I'd need to change my casting angle.

Delicate presentations aren't my forte—maybe that's why I took to steelheading in the first place. If it is possible to spook a fish, I usually do. And when it seems nothing short of a grenade could spook a fish, I can usually figure out some way. So I didn't have much confidence as I crawled upstream of the steelhead, hid beside an especially big rock, and delivered my first cast.

The fly landed upstream of the limb and began drifting. I could see the fish through the glare on the water, finning lazily. As the fly neared, its fins went rigid, its eyes locked on the little Steelhead Bee. But when I should have mended, I didn't, and the fly rushed toward the eddy that possessed the leader. To my horror, the steelhead bolted upstream, past me and into the rapids at the head of the run. Gone.

Of course. I should have expected nothing else. I bit the dry fly off and tied on a Vitamin D. A small tuft of yarn attached along the leader completed the rig. The rapids readily accepted indicator tactics. I tried to reassure myself: At least one fish held under those bubbles. But then the same five- or six-pound steelhead drifted out of the rapids, within ten feet of me, and returned to its original lie in the tailout. Less than a minute later, the dry fly was back on.

The cast landed in the same place as before, except this time I tossed slack into the leader and mended early. The steelhead didn't seem to notice the fly this time as it neared the limb. But suddenly the fish rose in a rush and swallowed a mouthful of surface. I struck immediately, my fly evacuating the fish's still-open mouth and alighting in a Douglas fir fifteen feet up the back.

While the steelheader in me knew I should be pleased enough with the rise, I wasn't. Missing such a clean take was unacceptable, ridiculous even. Before striking, I hadn't given the fish enough time to close its mouth, let alone turn back toward its lie. A tyro's move.

With a shake of the rod, the fly came free. After a quick burr check of the leader, the fly was back in the river, drifting toward the steelhead still holding under the limb. This time the fish was more cautious. It rose from the bottom, pausing an inch below the fly, and gave the pattern a serious cross-eyed examination. Just before both the fly and the steelhead drifted out of the tailout and into the rapids below, the fish took—and again my fly shot out of its still-open mouth. Except this time, it landed in a tangle in the fir behind me.

Somehow, none of this spooked the steelhead. It casually swam back to the same lie in the tailout, pushing its nose up against a watermelon-size rock.

The tippet snapped with a rifle's report, leaving the limb swaying back and forth as if a gust of wind had hit it. I attached another fly, a smaller Steelhead Bee. If the fish wouldn't rise again—or worse, did rise and I missed it for a third time—it would be a long, hard drive home.

What happened next happened fast. As the fly passed under the overhanging limb, the fish lifted from the bottom and took it in a mad swirl. This time I didn't strike right away—I think I said, "God save the queen," or something to that effect. When the rod finally came up, firm head shakes bent it to the cork. I jumped to my feet and leaned into the rod. And the fish all at once sparked to life and leaped straight into the air.

Steelhead are known for their jumps, specially when hooked in shallow water. A friend from Florida calls them "Northwest tarpon." Instead of leaping headlong into the mangroves, my fish did the Northwest equivalent. The steelhead went straight up into the overhanging limb, snapping the tippet at its connection with the fly. A second later, the fly line lay at my feet, and the surprised steelhead vanished—for good—into the rapids at the head of the pool.

But that was enough for me.

Roderick Haig-Brown enjoyed little more than fishing summer and fall streams with a dead-drifting dry fly. He wrote much about it, even inventing the standard pattern for the activity. His *Fisherman's Summer* and *Fisherman's Fall* are still the two definitive texts on the subject.

The dead-drifted dry fly intrigued Haig-Brown for many reasons. On an intellectual level, the technique matches the nature of the steelhead more closely than any other. Steelhead spend their first few years as a trout might, feeding on insects, and their adult years as a salmon might, feeding on baitfish and crustaceans. On returning to their natal stream, steelhead are confronted by these two identities. For Haig-Brown, fishing a dry fly on tackle designed for big fish allowed him to match the two paradoxical identities of his quarry.

But abstract ideas rarely put a fish on the beach. Haig-Brown believed that the dead-drifted dry was more than intellectually satisfying: It led to a screaming reel and a sore arm. And the more time he spent fishing the dry, the more he came to trust it. "I am more than ever convinced that dry-fly fishing, under summer and fall conditions, is the most effective fly-fishing method, as well as the most attractive," he wrote. Few who have watched a summer steelhead refuse a wet fly, only to slam a dead-drifted dry, would disagree.

Dead-drifted drys are most successful on wild steelhead in small summer streams. Unfortunately, such streams are the most susceptible to habitat degradation, and few still exist today.

Yet the dead-drifted dry fly is the least employed presentation on today's steelhead streams. Sure, every technique has its die-hard users, those people who refuse any other approach on moral or aesthetic grounds. But survey steelheaders and you'll find that most don't even bother to carry a dead-drifting dry-fly pattern.

The lack of popular appeal for the dead-drifted dry fly might have more to do with the modern steelhead than the modern steelheader. Today's fish aren't what they were in Haig-Brown's time. Most steelheaders spend their summer months casting over fish of hatchery origins. A parr raised in a hatchery tank is trained via daily repetition to watch for feed pellets, not for adult insects. When the hatchery fish returns to spawn, the instinct to chase adult insects won't be as vividly ingrained as with a wild fish. And most rivers with healthy wild summer runs are big, and big water doesn't fish a dead-drifted fly very well.

Loss of ideal habitat might be another reason anglers have moved away from dead-drifting drys. As Haig-Brown and the anglers that followed in his footsteps discovered, the dead-drifted dry fly is most productive on smaller rivers with lower flows. Such water condenses the fish into smaller areas, helping the angler locate them. And the low flows make the fish hyperaware of their surroundings. When a dry fly lands overhead, they'll take notice. But such small streams with healthy runs of steelhead become fewer and fewer each year. Most of us are forced to fish big water in the summer months, rivers whose brute size helped insulate their fish from the marauding hands of greedy humans. The small summer streams of Haig-Brown's time are nearly gone; they proved too delicate to survive our rough treatment.

With the loss of wild stocks on small summer streams, the dry fly has taken a backseat to other presentations. Current fly-fishing publications, always attuned to the ebb of public opinion, give the dead-drifted dry fly less page space. Anglers new to the sport are more likely to see a dozen articles on nymphing and swinging than they are to see an article on dry flies. So the cycle spins, moving popular steelheading culture farther and farther away from the dead-drifted dry fly. Which is too bad.

Though the dry fly might not have wide utility as a searching pattern on big rivers, it certainly is useful. In fact, there are days in the low water of late summer and early fall when nothing is effective but a dead-drifted dry. The utility of the presentation might be limited, but it can't be denied. Besides, little in steelheading brings the tender pleasure of casting a dry fly upstream over thin water. When you're standing knee-deep in a sloshing riffle, August's heat drifting upstream, casting a dry fly seems the only fitting way to chase steelhead.

The Water

Though big-river steelhead can certainly be enticed to take dead-drifted dry flies, the technique is most consistently successful on smaller rivers. In small water, steelhead can't help but notice the pattern drifting by—they're tuned in to every disturbance within sight. Small water also offers the advantage of revealing its fish. Frequently while you're moving up a small steelhead stream, fish will be visible under riffles or in tailouts. By targeting specific fish, your success rate with the dead-drifted dry will go up drastically. The ideal section of water contains bursts of fast water followed by longer slow areas. Most low-water steelhead congregate in the fast water and the tailouts.

If a stream is frequented by other anglers, the fish will be harder to convince with a dry fly. Dead drifting a dry fly really does require unpressured steelhead. Many popular rivers that have fishable runs of summer fish have long expanses high in the drainage that are rarely visited by anglers. Explore these with your dry-fly rod. The harder it is to reach the water, the better.

Besides targeting small streams for the majority of your dead-drifting dry-fly presentations, selecting rivers with wild steelhead will increase the likelihood of finding takers. Wild steelhead are more likely to possess the spunk required to rise. The most likely steelhead to take a dry fly is a wild *gairdneri*. These fish spend their parr years in caddis-rich streams and develop a proclivity for the dry fly. Many of their natal streams also flow small in the late summer and fall, offering ideal conditions. The upper Columbia drainage offers many perfect dry-fly streams—most of which need more riverkeepers if they are to stay perfect dry-fly streams for much longer.

The dead-drifted dry fly depends on the optimum water conditions. Make sure the water temperature falls into the ideal range for the steelhead in your area. Also, the technique is most effective when the water is gin clear. A little murk can drastically reduce your odds of success. As with the skating dry-fly presentation, sunlight on the water usually will keep steelhead down. Waiting until the sun dips behind the hills will increase the chances of an eager fish hitting the surface.

The more remote the stream, the more likely you are to raise a steelhead to your dry fly.

Most anglers fish two types of water with the dead-drifted dry: faster riffling water and slower smooth water. Each type is treated differently.

In the summer months, when the water is clear, low, and warm, the dry fly searches fast water efficiently. For this type of fishing, find likely looking water and give each slot two or three casts. You're looking for moving water that is less than four feet deep. Ideally, the water will be between two and three feet deep. Pocket water, riffles, and thin rapids are all likely places. While you're searching, keep an eye out for holding steelhead. If you spot one, repeatedly show it the dry. Sometimes several casts are needed to wake a fish from its slumber.

The other water type frequently probed with a dry fly is slow water like that found in tailouts. Tailouts move quickly during higher water, but during the low water of summer and fall, they often hover nearly still. In unpressured areas at dawn and dusk, these tailouts often hold resting steelhead. Under such water conditions, you're better off spotting holding fish before casting. Once you sight a holding fish, try your smallest pattern first. If the fish doesn't take, try the next size up. Fish holding in slow water will be ultra-alert; one overhasty presentation and the fish will spook for the headwaters.

Pools, especially ones in canyon sections of river, offer the summer angler another place to look for steelhead. Fish often hold in such places, sometimes in schools that cruise like overfed lake rainbows. In rivers with spring chinook, the springers often monopolize the pools during the summer months, forcing the steelhead into the nearby riffles and runs. But once the salmon move into the riffles and runs to spawn, usually in September, they force many steelhead into the recently vacated pools. Though not every steelhead stream will have pools that collect fish, those that do can offer some epic fishing. The steelhead often compete for the recently landed dry fly, taking in violent swirls. Moreover, once you find a pool that collects rising steelhead, mark the date on your calendar. Odds are good you'll be able to find fish acting similarly next year.

As when casting to tailout steelhead, start with your smallest fly first. Place it in the path of the cruisers and hold on. If no fish takes, lift the line only after the school is out of spooking distance, for once they're spooked, they'll probably not return.

The Logistics

Dead drifting a steelhead dry fly is the same skill mastered by thousands of trout fishers each year. The same principles apply to presenting the fly to steelhead as with trout. The ideal presentation produces a fly that drifts as if it were not attached to any line.

Find an even riffle about two to three feet deep and at least twenty feet wide. Wade in quartering downstream from your target slot. Make a quartering upstream cast, as shown in the next figure, placing the fly on the top edge of the slot (A). As the fly drifts downstream, strip in any slack, keeping a nearly tight line between you and the fly. If you don't strip in line fast enough, a belly will form downstream that will drag the fly. If you strip in line too fast, your stripping motion will drag the fly. The goal is to maintain the fly's dead drift for as long as possible.

As the fly nears your position in the riffle, make an upstream line flip, placing the fly line upstream of the fly (B). Then with slack tosses, feed line into the drift (C).

To increase the chance of a hookup when presenting the dry fly downstream of your position, keep a curve in the line near the fly. If the rod is raised, the curve should drive the point of the hook toward the bank rather than directly upstream. Doing so will increase the likelihood of the hook burying in the corner of the steelhead's jaw.

Twisting currents or sharp seams are common in the faster water ideal for dead drifting drys. You can fish around such currents by using reach casts and mending as the situation requires. Use your line-control skills learned while trout fishing to maintain a dead drift.

Rods, Lines, Leaders, and Flies

Steelhead, like their resident rainbow brethren, need delicate presentations to be convinced by a dry fly. For this work, a standard 8-weight steelhead rod is too much gun. The heavy rod isn't needed to drive long casts into the wind, as most dead-drifting dry-fly presentations are done at short range. And an 8-weight line makes a serious disturbance on the water. For these reasons, many dry-fly anglers choose 5- and 6-weight rods. One of my favorite steelhead dry-fly rods is a stout 4-weight. Whatever rod you decide to use needs to have a robust butt section for turning heavy fish and a delicate tip for protecting light tippets.

As you'll be controlling drifting fly line, a long rod will be helpful. Its extra length will allow you to precisely mend and feed the line, maintaining the dead drift. Spey rods are overkill with the dead-drifted dry fly, however. Their extra length is better suited to swinging presentations, and their heavy line will make delicate presentations all but impossible. The advantage offered by Spey rods—casting length and long-distance line control—aren't needed when fishing a dead-drifted dry.

Fly lines for dead drifting differ from those used in other presentations. Most tactics in steelheading benefit from shooting long casts to distant slots. The lines used match those requirements: They load the rod at a distance and shoot beautifully. But dead drifting drys is

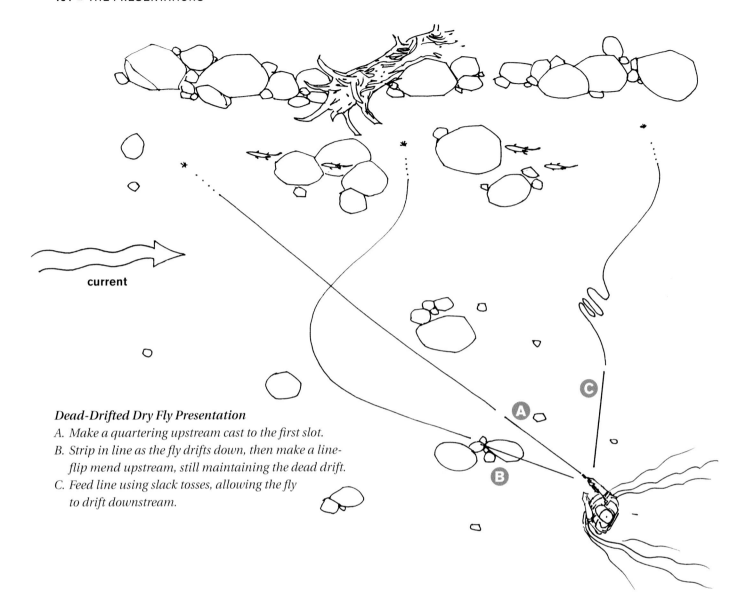

current

Dead-Drifted Dry Fly Presentation
A. *Make a quartering upstream cast to the first slot.*
B. *Strip in line as the fly drifts down, then make a line-flip mend upstream, still maintaining the dead drift.*
C. *Feed line using slack tosses, allowing the fly to drift downstream.*

close-up work, best matched by a line that quickly loads the rod. Most dry-fly anglers stick with a general-purpose weight-forward or double-taper fly line. The line can't boom casts to the far shore, but it can delicately place a fly anywhere from fifteen to forty-five feet from the angler. I like to overmatch the line to the rod when fishing drys. For instance, on my 4-weight rod, I'll cast a 5-weight line. Overmatching the line to the rod ensures that the rod will load early during the very short casts often demanded by small-stream conditions.

The best leader for dead drifting a dry through fast water is 9 feet and knotless, tapered down to 8-pound-test. Such a leader allows you to stay in direct contact with the fly at all times but keeps the line out of the fish's vision. When fishing smooth water with a dry fly, however, leader selection becomes more tricky.

Generally, steelhead aren't leader shy. The wrong fly in a steelhead's face might send it swimming for cover, but a fat leader won't. But the conditions that make a dry fly successful also put steelhead on red alert. A fat leader over thin water often sends a steelhead to the protection of the nearest rapids. At best, an overly large leader will simply cause the steelhead to refuse the pattern. About ten years ago, in a canyon pool, I located a pod of cruising steelhead. As the fish entered casting range, I placed my fly a foot in front of the first fish. It refused, as did every other fish in the school. For an hour, every cast was refused. I changed flies over and over. Even tried swimming a wet fly. Nothing worked. Then I tangled my leader in the tree, forcing me to cut it free. My pockets contained no more steelhead leaders, just a few trout versions. I tied on a 12-footer tapered down to 5X and attached the same dry fly I'd been casting before. As the school approached, the fly landed without a ripple. The lead fish swiped its tail and took in a high-speed rise, obviously trying to get the fly before any other fish did. Now I always present drys over smooth water with a 10-foot fluorocarbon leader tapered down to 4X or about 6 pounds.

Small flies rarely move steelhead holding in faster water. To get a fast-water fish intrigued by a dry fly, the pattern needs to be larger than those typically fished for resident trout. Trout strike at the hatching insect that will provide the highest number of calories for the least number of calories burned—a behavior that leads them to take certain insects even though the river is filled with bugs. To be successful, anglers need to match the hatch. But steelhead strike at insects for completely different reasons. They're not feeding to put on weight. Unlike trout, steelhead earned their livelihood at sea. They strike out of an instinctual reflex. A highly visible dry fly—one that stands out from the crowd—is much more likely to spark that reflex than one that blends in. Big flies are a good way to ensure that your pattern will be noticed by holding fish. The lone exception to the big-fly rule comes when steelhead are holding in thin, clear water. A big fly landing nearby might spark the wrong reflex in the fish—the bolting reflex. For this reason, the dry-fly angler needs to carry patterns to cover both situations: big flies for fast, broken water and small flies for slow, smooth water.

My fly box contains two dead-drifting dry-fly patterns, one for faster water and one for slower water. My go-to fast-water pattern is Haig-Brown's classic, the Steelhead Bee. The fly looks similar to the common Humpy trout fly and stays afloat in splashing water. The

Steelhead Bee

Chromer Caddis

The steelhead dry-fly technique is identical to the one used when fishing trout streams.

recipe calls for red fox squirrel as a tail and wing material. Besides helping the fly float, the oversize squirrel tail and wings make the pattern highly visible from below. Like Haig-Brown, I've found sizes 6 and 8 to be the most effective. If the water is shallow, I'll go with the 8. If it is deeper, I'll go with the 6. I like to use as much fly as I can get away with.

Tremendous pleasure can be found while fishing this pattern in bouncing summer riffles. When a steelhead rises to the pattern, often taking in the classic nosefirst rise of a large trout, the instant stoke sets a fire that is sure to burn for at least a week. And if a fish doesn't take, at least you have the acute pleasure of knowing you're fishing just as Haig-Brown did half a century before.

My pattern for slower water is the Chromer Caddis, a dry that sits lower in the meniscus, a trait that makes a fly look more like an insect and less like a piece of moss or lichen from a riverside tree. The fly rarely spooks a holding fish, even in very low and clear water conditions. I carry the pattern all summer and fall and try it first when I spot a steelhead lying in shallow slow water. Carrying sizes 8 and 10 allow me to match the fly to the situation. If I think the fish will allow the size 8, I'll use it. Otherwise, I stick with the 10.

Before fishing either the Steelhead Bee or Chromer Caddis, a strong dose of floatant is required. Either pattern won't float for long if the stuff isn't applied when the materials are still dry. Also, making sure the barb is nipped off will help keep trout from hooking themselves. When one takes a barbless fly, a few seconds of slack is usually all that's required to free the hook.

Variations

Many anglers searching fast water with a dead-drifted dry fly also attach a sinking steelhead pattern as a dropper from the bend in the hook. A slightly weighted size 8

Steelhead take the dead-drifting dry fly differently than trout, requiring a different kind of hook set.

Vitamin D is a good choice. Attach the pattern from a 36-inch section of 8-pound-test tippet. When the dry fly lands, the sinking pattern plummets toward the bottom. Some steelhead awakened by the dry fly, but not enthused adequately to strike, will take the sunk pattern. If the dry fly hesitates or ducks underwater, strike as you would when a fish takes a nymph below an indicator. The technique provides double the confidence, as each cast presents two different techniques.

As with any trailing-hook variation, the technique shouldn't be used on streams where wild steelhead are present, as the dropper fly might snag a fish that took the dry. But employing the dropper is a great way to improve the success rate of the dead-drifted dry fly on rivers composed of hatchery runs.

Hooking Takers

Hooking a steelhead that has graced you with a rise is the most challenging aspect of the dry-fly presentation. Nothing seems more unnatural than not striking a fish that has just swallowed your floating fly. But this is exactly what you must do.

Steelhead seem to take a dry fly differently than trout. Trout hit a fly and swallow it instantly. Steelhead often miss the fly, and when they do hit it, they often lip the fly instead of attempting to swallow it. Roderick Haig-Brown had an explanation for the difference between how a steelhead and a resident rainbow take a dry fly. From *Fisherman's Fall:* "The sea-run fish is like a ball player at the first batting practice of the season, liable to be quite a bit off his timing; and to make matters worse, he is not normally a hungry player." Though steelhead are inclined to miss or tentatively take a pattern, there are strategies you can employ that increase the likelihood of a firm hook set.

When a steelhead rises to a dry, if you set the hook immediately, the fly will usually come free. Often the fly comes back without any resistance, almost as if the fish had never touched it. Sometimes you will feel a slight hesitation. But if you hesitate for a moment after the fish rises, just long enough to say, "I raised a steelhead!" a fish is more likely to be attached when the rod is finally raised.

Besides the timing of the hook set, its direction is also important. If the fish takes upstream of you, you can strike at any angle and have a good chance of putting the hook into solid mass. But if the fish is across from you or downstream, the hook set must be done at an angle that pulls the fly into the meat of the fish's mouth. For instance, if you cast to a steelhead that is across the current, and the fish rises in the classic head-to-tail rise, you are best off striking toward the downstream shore. Such an angle is most likely to result in a solid hookup. In general, anytime a steelhead rises, strike so that you pull the fly toward the fish's tail.

To increase the chances of a solid hook set on a fish downstream of your position, allow a small belly of line to form as the fly passes. When the fish rises and you raise the rod toward the downstream shore, it will pull the hook toward the joint in the fish's jaw.

If you raise a fish and cleanly miss it, odds are it will rise again. Another cast to the water a few seconds later will usually do the trick. If not, rest the water for a few minutes and try again. If the fish still won't rise again, trying a new presentation technique will often convince it. When a steelhead rises and feels the hook, odds are it won't be interested for a while. But resting the water for ten minutes or so often gives the fish adequate time to forget about the experience.

Whether your hook finds a home or not, there is immense joy to be found in raising a steelhead to a dead-drifted dry. An gray-haired gentleman that frequented a fly shop where I worked summed it up nicely: "I'd trade five fish hooked and landed below an indicator for one raised and missed on a dry."

CHAPTER 15

Indicator Tactics

Few steelheading techniques are as consistently successful as flies dead drifted below an indicator. The technique appeals to both dour fish unwilling to leave their lies and aggressive fish eager to chase down an enticing morsel. To both wild and hatchery fish. It takes steelhead when the water shimmers with winter ice and when the summer sun threatens to melt your fly line. In high and low water. On pressured and unpressured rivers. Day in and day out, indicator tactics put steelhead on the beach.

And the technique entices anglers as well. A drifting indicator, bouncing over prime holding water, slices deep into the what-if section of the brain and punches buttons with little regard for the psyche of the brain's owner. The anticipation of watching the indicator, knowing that at any minute it could disappear, provides immeasurable pleasure. In a way, that floating piece of foam or yarn is a window into the deep. It's a visible connection to the invisible. The first time a bright indicator slips under the mirrored surface and you come back to feel the throbs of a chromer, fanaticism is guaranteed to pump like adrenaline through your veins. You'll be content to spend hours poised and ready as the indicator drifts through other prime slots.

Yet steelheading culture has been slow to bestow the presentation with the kind of grandiose respect it gives swinging presentations. For generations, anglers have balked at the use of indicator tactics on the steelhead stream. Why would anglers cast clunky indicators when they could double-haul gorgeous flies to distant lies? The answer was that the clunky indicator helped the angler pin into fish unwilling to move to the double-hauled pattern. But the skeptics weren't satisfied. Their resistance increased. An indicator, made grotesque by its subtle similarity to the bluegill bobber of dirty farm ponds, only disgraces the silver beauty of a clean-water steelhead. But does a sink-tip line, which dredges the bottom with the grace of a downrigger and absorbs the fight of the fish, do any better?

The resistance to indicator tactics is completely predictable, as is the resulting rift that developed between steelheaders. In fact, the entire history of the nymphing presentation, all the way back to its English chalkstream debut, is the story of exactly such a rift.

The Itchen, a glassy river snaking it way through the English countryside south of London, has long attracted anglers to its fertile chalkstream flows. More than 150 generations of Itchen trout have refused the finest presentations from some of the sport's finest anglers. Of course, a few chunky trout were duped over the years and found themselves baked and sliding down the gullet of some lucky chap. Frederick Maurice Halford was one such chap, an Englishman who prided himself on his ability to take the toughest Itchen trout. His secret? The

Above: Indicator tactics appeal equally to hatchery and wild steelhead and often take fish when nothing else will. Here, an egg pattern is worked through a cold winter trough.

dry fly. His success with dry flies ballooned his head with downright cocky blood. Halford told any angler he met that the *only* way to take chalkstream trout was with a dry fly. His confidence led to a series of books on the subject, the first being *Floating Flies and How to Dress Them,* published in 1886. Soon word of Halford's success spread, and within a few years his techniques were commonly employed on nearly all English chalkstreams.

But Halford wasn't satisfied. In his mind, the dry fly wasn't only the most effective presentation strategy, it was the only presentation capable of matching the grace of chalkstream trout. Halford argued that only a dry fly had adequate moral integrity to sit in a proper Englishman's fly box, and that only the practice of casting a dry fly deserved the prestigious label of fly fishing. Through his characteristically pedantic manner, Halford emerged as the original and quintessential dry-fly snob. His arguments must have been convincing, because soon not only English chalkstreams, but nearly all trout water in the English empire, became the sole domain of dry-fly exclusivists.

Enter George Edward MacKenzie Skues, another frequenter of the Itchen's flows. G. E. M. Skues didn't follow Halford's rules and made his reasons public in the book *Minor Tactics of the Chalk Stream,* published in 1910. Trout, Skues argued, fed on dry flies for only a small part of the time. When a feeding fish refused a dry fly, it could frequently be persuaded to devour a sunken fly dead drifted under the surface. The most effective approach to the stream would incorporate both dry-fly fishing and Skues's sunken-fly technique. In the years to follow, Skues's technique would spread the world over and eventually be called nymph fishing, the precursor to steelheading's indicator tactics. But at the time, his approach fell on deaf—or timid—ears. But Halford had heard Skues. The sound of the dry-fly master furiously pacing laps in his study may have echoed through the English countryside.

Halford responded with a text called *The Dry-Fly Man's Handbook,* published in 1913. In it, Halford vehemently opposed the use of a nymph, for predictable reasons. A proper sport would never depend on a sunken fly to take a fish as glorious as a trout. Such blasphemy as a sunken fly shouldn't be allowed anywhere near a trout stream. With the publication of the tyrannical book, Halford revealed himself as a doctrinaire, ignoring tactical innovation and rigidly holding to increasingly obsolete dogma.

His readers responded accordingly. After the publication of *The Dry-Fly Man's Handbook,* public support for an exclusively dry-fly approach to trout streams waned. By the 1930s, Skues's position had won out; an approach to the river employing both the dry fly and the nymph was the most logical. Trout didn't always take a dry fly, after all, and there was no sense in limiting the number of fish caught for matters of style that few people understood.

The conflict over the nymph quickly found its way across the Atlantic. Both Halford and Skues corresponded with the father of American fly fishing, Theodore Gordon. Gordon, who resided along New York's Neversink, would come to embody both the conflict and its resolution.

American anglers at the time fished only wet flies swung downstream. Gordon broke the standard presentation paradigm. Instead of swinging his wet flies, he tried casting them upstream. And to his amazement, trout took the patterns in the moments they remained in the surface film. Knowing about the English greats, Gordon wrote to Halford, who passed along a collection of dry flies. Immediately Gordon found success with the floating patterns, and following in the Halford tradition, he started fishing them nearly exclusively.

But Gordon quickly realized the flaw with the Halford dry-fly pattern. The flies were tied sparsely, designed to float on the glassy currents of the Itchen and other English chalkstreams. The Neversink was a fast river, splashing and tossing its way down a steep valley. In order for a fly to be successful there, it needed to withstand the constant dousing of a speedy river. So Gordon sat at his vise to develop a dry fly suited to American waters. This pattern, Gordon realized, needed stiff hackle to keep it high and dry above the surface film. But stiff hackles weren't available in the United States. So Gordon sent a letter over the Atlantic to—ironically—G. E. M. Skues. Skues sent over a pile of capes, and with them Gordon invented the first American dry fly, the Quill Gordon.

Armed with his new dry flies, Gordon easily could have maintained a Halford-esque devotion to the patterns, fishing them and nothing else. But on the Neversink, the fish often stopped rising during the middle of the day. A dry fly, even one so fine as the Quill Gordon, couldn't take fish constantly from dawn to dusk. So Gordon turned to the theories of Skues for guidance. He started fishing his dry flies when the trout were willing. When they weren't, he'd fish wet flies cast upstream and allowed to dead drift deep. If that didn't work, Gordon would try the standard American approach, swinging wet flies downstream of his position. In this manner, Gordon became the first well-rounded American trout fisher. He'd learned from the English debate between Halford and Skues. He innovated, adjusting his presentations and flies to the demands of American trout. And other New World anglers took notice.

Gordon died of tuberculosis in 1915, but his approach to fishing American trout streams didn't. The modern American trout fisher follows in his footsteps by

An individual steelhead is more likely to take a dead-drifted fly than a swinging or rising pattern. The problem is getting your dead-drifting fly near the fish.

carrying a vestload of tackle, enabling near infinite adjustment of presentation. With all these tools and a detailed knowledge of the habits of the fish, modern trout fishers are streamside innovators, adjusting the minutiae of their presentations until they synchronize with the feeding behavior of the quarry.

Steelheading's lineage doesn't contain a character like G. E. M. Skues or Theodore Gordon. Our sport has been passed down from generation to generation with only minor adjustments. Steelheading's history had its most profound shake-up when Jim Teeny suggested attaching a split shot to the leader and casting to sighted fish. But because of the limitations of Teeny's approach—spotting fish consistently isn't feasible on most Northwest rivers—it failed to steer mainstream steelheading practice. So the commonly employed presentations—and the overall approach to the steelhead river—have changed little, despite two hundred years of technical advancement, a completely new continent, and a drastically different quarry.

That is, until very recent history. The long lineage of steelheading and the equally long lineage of trout fishing

are colliding on modern steelhead streams. More and more trout fishers are leaping to steelhead, bringing their approach to the river in tow. This approach, based on the Skues-Gordon school of streamside innovation, is in direct opposition to the traditional steelheading approach. Instead of coming to the river and stubbornly swinging a wet fly, these trout-trained steelheaders appear streamside like a medical doctor appears bedside. They look at the symptoms—water clarity, temperature, race of steelhead, and so on—and determine which of their tactics will be the most successful. If one doesn't work, they try another. If swinging doesn't work, they try indicator tactics. They innovate. And their diligent effort pays off. Simply put, the trout-fishing approach to the steelhead stream produces more fish—steelhead are rainbows, after all.

Thus steelheading is experiencing a sea change. Most modern steelheaders have come to the same conclusion the Brits did in the early twentieth century: In the end, we'll catch more fish if we adjust our presentations to the moods of our quarry. After all, we're anglers before we're dogmatists.

The Water

One reason indicator tactics are so successful is that they can be applied to nearly any river at any time. By making adjustments to the basic presentation, indicator tactics allow flies to fish pocket water, twisting eddies, deep tailouts, fast rapids, riffles, runs, pools, and anything in between. No other steelheading presentation is as versatile. Because so little is required on the fish's part—the interested steelhead need only open its mouth to take the fly—the presentation is effective when the strike zone is large or small. As indicator tactics depend on dead-drifting flies, the presentation is less likely to spook fish made nervous by excessive angling pressure. The presentation is readily applied to nearly any steelheading situation.

Nymphing, as practiced by most trout anglers, drastically limits the size of the coverable slot. You make a quartering upstream cast and allow the fly and indicator to drift downstream on their own accord. As the rig passes you, you make an upstream mend, allowing the fly and indicator to continue their natural course past you. At the end of the slack, you strip in the line and make another cast. Because indicators are wind-resistant, the effective casting range is necessarily small. Nymphing in this manner, you can cover only nearby slots, and just forty or fifty feet of that slot at a time. Steelheaders use this form of indicator tactics frequently, referring to it as precision nymphing. Precision nymphing effectively covers small slots, like those commonly found in pocket water or on small streams. The fly can be fished quickly and effectively, allowing each slot to receive a presentation with minimal time lost in between casts. As the fly can be placed with remarkable accuracy, most sighted steelhead are covered using precision nymphing. But because the flies spend little time in the water, precision nymphing isn't an effective way to

Dave Dozer uses precision nymphing to cover a small slot on a thin October run.

fish big water, where the steelhead could be holding anywhere. And because the flies have a limited amount of time to sink, the tactic isn't effective for fishing water more than six feet deep.

On big or deep water, steelheaders rely on a tactic called downstream nymphing. On wide riffles, runs, or tailouts—water where steelheaders spend a lot of time—precision nymphing moves too slowly to consistently find fish. Traditionally, such big water was the sole domain of swinging presentations, as they allowed long slots to be covered on a single cast. But innovative steelheaders sold on the potential effectiveness of dead-drifted flies developed their own variation of nymphing, one that allows long slots to be covered on each cast. And because the fly spends plenty of time in the water, it can be fished into deep runs. Downstream nymphing al-

lows you to cover big riffles, runs, and tailouts nearly as fast as swinging presentations.

By applying precision and downstream nymphing at the correct times, you can quickly present dead-drifting flies to entire sections of river, showing your patterns to as many fish as possible.

Though indicator tactics readily take fish throughout the year, the presentation does have its limitations. The indicator used for steelheading is large. Its silhouette on the surface can spook fish holding in thin water, limiting the presentation's effectiveness on smaller rivers in late summer and early fall. The indicator also causes complications when casting long leaders. Long leaders have trouble turning over the weighted flies and wind-resistant indicators. Most casters using single-handed rods can't control a leader much longer than 12 feet, limiting the

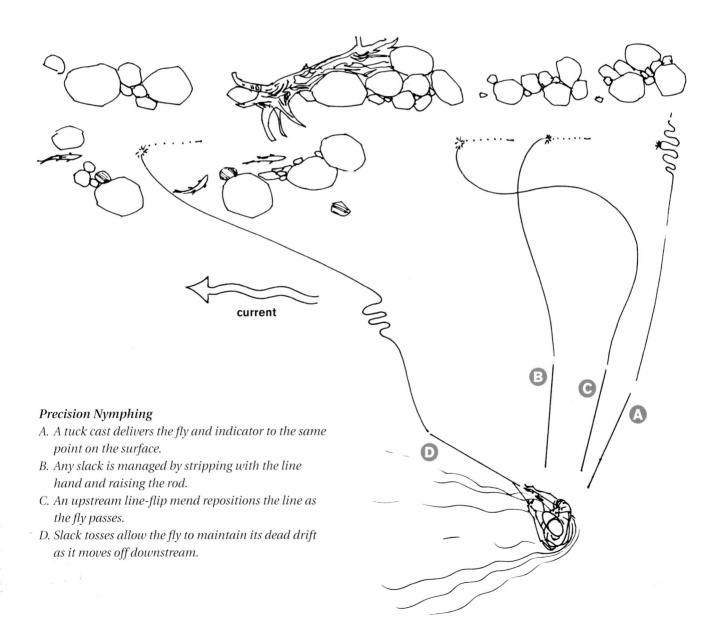

current

Precision Nymphing

A. *A tuck cast delivers the fly and indicator to the same point on the surface.*

B. *Any slack is managed by stripping with the line hand and raising the rod.*

C. *An upstream line-flip mend repositions the line as the fly passes.*

D. *Slack tosses allow the fly to maintain its dead drift as it moves off downstream.*

To help recover the long lengths of fly line typically fed into the drift when using the downstream nymphing technique, many anglers prefer to use a two-handed retrieve.

effective depth of the presentation to nine or ten feet. Some prime winter steelheading lies are just too deep for indicator tactics.

Also, on very large steelhead streams, indicator tactics might not be as effective as swinging tactics for searching broad water. The indicator can't be cast across the current very far, so the presentation can cover slots only relatively close to shore, whereas a shooting taper can deliver a wet fly some distance out from shore. But on small to medium-large steelhead streams, indicator tactics remain remarkably versatile.

The Logistics

In both precision and downstream nymphing, the fly is most effective when dead drifted six to twelve inches off the bottom. Both presentations seek to suspend the fly directly beneath the indicator, meaning that if the water is four feet deep, the indicator is best attached three and

a half feet up from the fly. When unsure of the depth, most anglers adjust the height of the indicator in six-inch increments. If the fly drags, the indicator is lowered down the leader. If the fly doesn't drag, the indicator is raised up the leader until the ideal balance is found.

Precision nymphing is the most familiar form of the presentation. To fish it, find a section on your homewater where the holding water is limited, such as a small run or a section of pocket water. Position yourself twenty feet from the first slot, across the current and slightly upstream.

Strip out forty feet of slack and make a tuck cast, as shown on page 162, positioning the flies at the upstream edge of the slot to be fished (A). An effective tuck cast is essential for dropping the fly to the bottom as quickly as possible. But it also positions the indicator on top of the fly, limiting any potential drag and ensuring that any take will be promptly displayed in the indicator's behavior. On some smaller streams, a backcast might not be

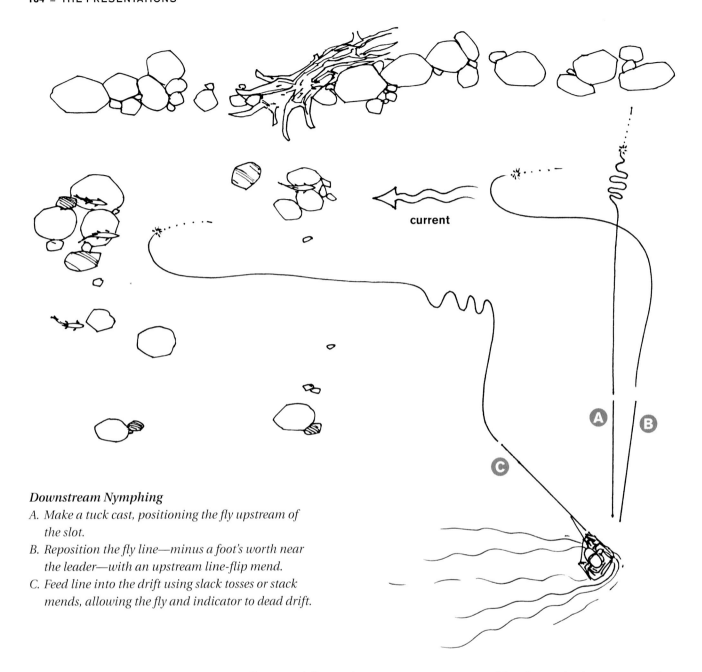

Downstream Nymphing

A. *Make a tuck cast, positioning the fly upstream of the slot.*

B. *Reposition the fly line—minus a foot's worth near the leader—with an upstream line-flip mend.*

C. *Feed line into the drift using slack tosses or stack mends, allowing the fly and indicator to dead drift.*

possible. In such cases, you can use a roll cast to deliver the fly and a second roll cast to lift the indicator and set it back atop the fly.

As the fly and indicator drift downstream, pick up the slack by stripping in line with the line hand and raising the rod (B). If you don't control the slack properly, a belly will form downstream of your position, and the fly will immediately begin to drag, limiting the likelihood of a take.

Just before the fly and indicator pass your position, make an upstream line-flip mend (C). This mend positions the fly line so that the indicator and fly can continue drifting downstream drag-free. By using slack tosses, you can feed line into the drift, lengthening the amount of water covered (D).

Downstream nymphing is used when you need to cover long sections of water quickly. With a little practice, you can easily achieve hundred-foot drifts, effectively presenting your fly through huge swaths of fishy water.

Find a section on your homewater where a steelhead might be holding anywhere. Riffles, runs, and tailouts are typically ideal places. Instead of presenting your fly to a precise area, you'll be searching the whole area.

Wade into the water at the top of the section, directly across the current from the top of the first slot to be fished. Position yourself fifteen feet from the nearest slot. After stripping out as much fly line as you'll need to cover the length of the slot—big water often requires all your fly line—make a tuck cast to the head of the first slot (A), as shown above. The tuck cast will deliver the fly, leader, and indicator to the same point on the surface, allowing the fly to reach the bottom as quickly as possible. A bungled cast will bungle the entire drift.

Make a line-flip mend upstream, repositioning the line for a drag-free drift (B). The best mend will affect the entire fly line except for a one-foot section near the connection with the leader. Leaving a curve in the line helps pull the fly sideways into the steelhead's mouth, should a strike come.

As the indicator and fly move downstream, feed line into the drift with slack tosses (C). Feed the line at the same pace as the current moves to avoid excessive slack separating you from the fly; too much slack will make a proper hook set nearly impossible. If the slot you're fishing is too far away for effective slack tosses, stack mends that feed line may be more appropriate.

Once you've covered the entire slot or fed out the entire fly line, strip in the line and make a new cast to the next slot. In this manner, you can cover an entire section of water quickly, with the fly spending as much time as possible fishing effectively. To help speed up the retrieval of all the fly line after the completion of the drift, some anglers employ a two-handed retrieve. Simply tuck the rod under your arm and pull line in with both hands. Some anglers also employ stripping baskets to help manage the slack.

Besides allowing the speedy coverage of large sections of water, downstream nymphing also lets you fish crowded waters without interfering with swinging anglers. On many popular steelhead streams, anglers wait their turns at the top of a riffle or run, watching as the anglers before them ply the water. Usually these steelheaders are swinging flies and don't appreciate the slow pace typical of precision nymphing. By nymphing downstream, you'll be able to cover the water quickly and effectively, without unduly slowing the progress of your fellow chrome addicts.

Rods, Lines, Leaders, and Flies

The ideal rod for nymphing is a long 8-weight with a fast action. The length allows precise line control, of essential value when stack mending to a distant indicator. The long rod also allows you to set the hook decisively on a far-off take, picking up a tremendous amount of line in a single striking motion. The 8-weight line turns over a heavily weighted fly and indicator despite heavy winds and distance. A heavier rod will do the same, but with added wear and tear on your hand, elbow, and shoulder. We're not getting any younger.

More and more anglers are using their Spey rods for increasing the effectiveness of indicator tactics. Most anglers in my area prefer rods designed for Skagit casting,

as the moderately fast action can send tight mends out over fast water. Spey rods are especially popular on medium-size rivers where broken currents require long lengths of line to be held off the water.

Arguably, switch rods are the most effective tool for indicator tactics. These lightweight two-handed rods allow all the same benefits of a normal Spey—increased casting distance and precision line handling—without the increased bulk. You can make a single-handed overhead cast to deliver the fly and indicator, then use both hands to power stack mends into a long-distant drift. I find them most helpful on winter rivers when high water demands heavy flies and bulky indicators. But because of their utility year-round, I wouldn't be surprised if switch rods are the standard tool for indicator tactics twenty years from now.

Indicator tactics with a single-handed rod are one kind of presentation that depends on a moderate to fast action. A slow stick can still get the job done, but a fast one allows for more exact line control and hence a better presentation of the fly. To effectively control the drift, frequent mends and feeds are necessary, often when fast water divides the angler and fly. A fast-action will place coils of slack precisely where they are needed. Also, the fast-action produces a faster line speed during casting, allowing the indicator and fly to be turned over at distance.

The long-bellied lines designed for distance casting, often labeled as steelhead or salmon tapers, cast an indicator and fly well from a single-handed rod. The long, heavy head isn't bossed around by the bulky indicator; it moves the indicator with authority. The long, thin belly makes distant mends and feeds quick and easy, not interfering with the drift of the fly. Some anglers swear by general-purpose lines for nymphing, relying on the trout tapers in their heavier sizes. These lines feel more like those we've grown up on, casting best at short distances. They don't handle as well at a distance, however. If you're employing indicator tactics on small rivers only, a general-purpose line might be the appropriate option. If you're likely to fish big water, give the distance line a try.

Successful nymphing depends on a leader matched to the demands of the presentation. The leader's dimensions make all the difference when casting a heavy fly and indicator, and as the fly will be near the bottom, it's likely to take serious abuse from rocks and submerged debris. Flippantly selecting a nymphing leader will likely result in enough wind knots and break-offs to make you pull out your hair.

Weighted flies resist our best casting efforts. The fly will never pass on an opportunity—no matter where you are in the casting stroke—to fall like a shot put to the water. A stiff leader can help the fly turn over properly.

Yarn or puff ball indicators are favored by many steelheaders because of their buoyancy. Also, the tip of the indicator points toward the drifting fly, allowing the angler to keep closer tabs on the pattern's drift.

Most steelheaders build their nymphing leaders from a knotless leader tapered down to 12-pound-test in the winter and 10-pound-test in the summer. Fluorocarbon is ideal because it resists the kinking forced on it by the connection with the indicator, and it stands up to the abuse applied by the bottom's debris. In shallow water, the overall length of the leader is best between 8 and 9 feet. In mid-depth water, the overall length can be closer to 11. And in deep water, the overall length is best between 12 and 13. A 13-foot leader allows a fly to be presented down to about 9 or 10 feet effectively, although the distance between the fly and indicator will make the cast difficult.

Hordes of indicator models flood the fishing market these days, the vast majority having little utility for steelheading. In trout fishing, the indicator is typically used to detect strikes. The fly sinks and dead drifts, but the indicator generally isn't required to suspend the fly. In steelheading, the indicator is responsible not only for detecting strikes, but also for suspending the fly off the bottom.

Three traits are important to keep in mind when selecting an indicator: floatability, minimal bulk, and visibility. Ideally, any indicator should be able to float the heaviest flies with ease. And it should be able to keep floating the fly throughout several hours of fishing, despite the best dunkings the river can toss it. Many indicators fail this first test. They simply follow the fly toward the bottom. Of those that pass the test, many are excessively bulky, too bulky to cast well. Excessive bulk increases wind resistance during the casting stroke, limiting your effective distance. Bulk also causes the indicator, when brought under tension in the river, to make a large disturbance on the water. If the fly snags a nearby rock and the indicator makes a big wake through the water, fish can be spooked. Some foam indicators will actually make an audible pop when brought under tension, alerting every chromer within casting distance of your presence. Try to find an indicator that will float the fly, cast well, and make a minimal disturbance in the water.

I prefer soft, puff ball indicators. Made from synthetic materials, they float well when applied with floatant, cast effortlessly, and are quiet through the water. Moreover, puff balls are highly responsive to the movement of the fly. If the fly drags along the bottom, the puff ball will twitch in the surface film. If a stray current pushes the fly out of the slot, the indicator will tip to one side. By fishing puff balls, or any other responsive indicators, you can tell a great deal about the progress of your drifting fly.

To help keep yarn indicators afloat, try treating them the night before with your favorite floatant. Squeeze some floatant onto the yarn, and brush it in with an old comb. The comb will fluff out the fibers, helping the yarn stay high and dry through an entire day of fishing.

Once you've settled on an effective indicator model, next comes color selection. Most indicator aficionados I know carry three colors: yellow, black, and mottled brown. Yellow is the go-to color, being used about 90 percent of the time. Yellow remains visible through even the fastest whitewater, not blending into the bubbling rapids like white does. And it stands out at distance. A yellow spot remains visible at the far end of a long riffle. When the sun casts a silver glaze over the water, as is common in the evenings, a black indicator actually shows up better than the yellow. Black casts a rigid silhouette, differentiating itself clearly from the metallic appearance of the water. On summer rivers, when the water is low and clear and the fish spook easily, the mottled brown indicator is the best choice. It looks like a drifting leaf and is much less likely to send the fish swimming for deeper waters as it floats by.

Fly selection for indicator tactics is simple. While many midwestern chromeheads—who also rely on indicator tactics—carry boxes of flies ranging in size from 6 to 16, those of us fishing West Coast rivers need carry only a small collection. Our steelhead are nuts. Their time in the salt water, feeding on baitfish and crustaceans, stirred up

Here, a winter steelheader uses a low profile and precision nymphing to target a known hot spot.

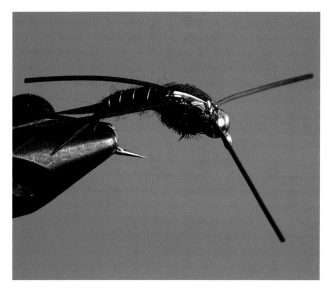

3-D Flashback Nymph

Dr. Evil (from A. P. Spy Series)

Bottom Licker Nymph

their striking reflexes to Pacific-size proportions. Most West Coast nymphers carry just a few patterns.

Flies for indicator tactics come in two types: point flies and droppers. Point flies are heavy. They're weighted to slice through the water column quickly, positioning the fly within the strike zone of the steelhead. Droppers are small, unweighted patterns that tag along for the ride. Either type of fly will take fish.

Some anglers don't weight their flies at all, preferring to attach split shot to their leaders. A weightless fly is more inclined to drift six inches off the bottom—in the prime striking area—whereas the split shot drags along the bottom. But split shot has a tendency to find the cracks along the boulder bottoms of most Northwest streams. And once snagged, they frequently can't be freed. Split shot also weakens the leader where it is attached. The more casting you do, the weaker the leader gets. Moreover, lead split shot are an environmental hazard that has been shown to be detrimental to the health of the river and the animals that depend on it.

Weighting the fly instead of the leader has several advantages. First, a weighted fly is in more direct contact with the indicator, which allows the indicator to signal a strike faster. The sooner the indicator ducks, the faster you can set the hook. And the faster you set the hook, the more likely you are to feel a fish on the other end. Also, a fly's weight can help it perform. For instance, flies like the Rock Hopper are made to twitch up and down in the current by the frontally placed weight. And bead eyes mounted on the top side of the shank can keep flies riding hook-up, helping keep them from snagging debris along the bottom.

In the summer, I carry three different point flies: the 3-D Flashback Nymph in black, the Dr. Evil from Matt Vander Heide's A. P. Spy Series, and the Bottom Licker. Each pattern is applied to a different situation.

The 3-D Flashback is a highly realistic pattern. It convinces steelhead made dour by angling pressure, low summer flows, or bright light. The pattern seems to work better the longer the fish have been in fresh water. A tungsten bead helps sink the fly quickly. All mine are tied on size 8 hooks, although I tie some with smaller bodies, roughly the dimensions of the size 10 version. I find the hookup-to-landing ratio on steelhead to plummet once I start using hooks smaller than number 8. For this reason, instead of using a smaller hook, I'll simply tie a smaller version of the pattern on a size 8 hook.

The Dr. Evil is a brilliantly designed pattern. At once, it looks reminiscent of a stonefly and an egg pattern. The fly's success likely grows from this dual persona. The pattern is most effective in riffles, where the current is able to give life to the rubber legs. I trust it on small and big rivers alike, and from the first days of the run to the last. Simply put, the Dr. Evil moves steelhead. I prefer to tie mine with a tungsten bead to help sink it. Also, wraps of lead under the dubbing will help the pattern get deeper. Unfortunately, the maximum effective depth for the Dr. Evil is around five feet. Although it can reach deeper lies, the bulky pattern sinks too slowly—no matter how much weight is attached—to effectively cover those lies.

For deep summer work, I pull out the Bottom Licker. One strategically placed tungsten cone, tied in at the eye of the hook, and a thin marabou body cause the pattern to sink headfirst. When given slack, the fly will plummet into slots ten feet deep. Once down, the pattern's marabou flutters tantalizingly as the indicator bounces over surface ripples, moving fish from a great distance. I carry a size 2.

Favorite summer dropper patterns vary as much as the anglers fishing them. But in every chromehead's box sit several rows of egg patterns. The classic egg pattern is the Glo-Bug. The fly is quickly tied, and it consistently—day in and day out—convinces fish. But I find that the fly sinks unnecessarily slowly, limiting the amount of water that can be covered on a single cast, so instead of Glo-Bugs, I carry Easy Eggs. These patterns use less material to create the same round-egg effect and hence sink more quickly. Plus, as their name suggests, these flies are ridiculously easy to tie. A wrap of dubbing around the shank and you're done. I carry sizes 4 through 8, both regular and low-water versions.

Besides egg patterns, every summer angler needs a few caddis patterns tied to represent the bigger species in the area. I trust the Steelhead October Pupa in size 8. This pattern often convinces tough steelhead, like those that experience regular angling pressure. When trying to reach deep lies, you can add a tungsten bead, helping both the point fly and dropper reach the bottom faster.

In the winter, fly selection is much easier. Steelheaders tend to be searching big water for eager fish. Such work requires readily visible flies with the ability to spark the striking reflex from a great distance. Both point and dropper patterns tend to be bigger and brighter to increase their visibility.

Besides the Bottom Licker, which proves valuable in both summer and winter, I also carry the Rock Hopper. Like the Bottom Licker, the Rock Hopper is constructed out of marabou with a frontally placed weight to help it sink. But the Rock Hopper uses lead eyes that allow the pattern to ride hook-up, limiting the number of snags. Also, the pattern can be made much bigger than the Bottom Licker for use when the river looks more like hot chocolate than a steelhead stream.

In addition to big Easy Eggs, the murkier flows of winter call for flashier dropper patterns. My favorites in-

Easy Egg

Steelhead October Pupa (with tungsten bead)

Rock Hopper (pink)

Beadhead Lifter (pink)

clude the Lifter, as the flashy body and bright tail make it visible for a great distance. Moreover, the supple veil tied in near the head gives it a gentle action in the slow water typical of winter runs. The Lifter is a deadly winter pattern. For reaching especially deep lies, the Lifter can be tied with a tungsten bead, or to help the pattern stay snag-free, lead eyes can be incorporated.

Summer or winter, there are a few essential traits of any dropper pattern. An effective dropper shouldn't significantly interfere with the sink rate of the point fly. Some patterns are too bulky to move through the water efficiently. They'll actually keep your flies off the bottom and out of the strike zone of the fish. Some rubber patterns, egg globs specifically, present another problem: They twist in the current while being brought back ashore. A twisted dropper can turn your leader into a bird's nest faster than a stiff back wind.

Variations

The standard approach to both precise and downstream nymphing calls for a dropper fly. Most steelheaders rarely nymph without one. By rigging the flies properly, a dropper can be used without increasing the risk of foul-hooking a fish.

In order to keep both flies near the bottom and to help wild fish stay safe, not to mention cutting down on wind knots and complicated reriggings, most steelheaders attach the dropper from the bend in the point fly's hook. Connect 6 to 8 inches of fluorocarbon tippet material, rated to 12-pound-test in winter and 10-pound-test in summer, with an improved clinch knot to the

To ensure the safety of wild steelhead when using a two-fly rig, it is vital that the dropper pattern be between six and eight inches from the point fly. This thirty-six inch winter buck took in six feet of water.

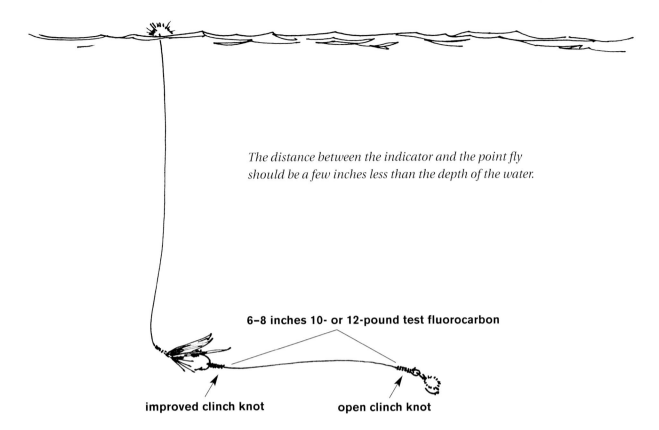

The distance between the indicator and the point fly should be a few inches less than the depth of the water.

6–8 inches 10- or 12-pound test fluorocarbon

improved clinch knot

open clinch knot

point fly. Then, using an open clinch knot, connect the dropper to the end of the short tippet section. If you use less than 6 inches, the dropper will follow too closely to the point fly. If you use more than 8 inches, the dropper will tangle in the leader as the point fly sinks. Moreover, the dropper might foul-hook a fish that struck the point fly. The system is quick to rig and deadly to fish.

Besides using a dropper pattern, another common variation is often employed in both nymphing presentations. An open clinch knot connecting the tippet to the point fly allows the fly to hinge freely. The loose connection allows the fly to sink headfirst, reducing the fly's drag through the water. The open clinch helps the fly reach the bottom as fast as possible.

Often you're actually better off fishing one fly instead of two. One point fly can usually be made to sink faster than a two-fly combo, even when both flies are weighted. When anglers want to fish very deep lies or need to penetrate an especially fast current, they often use a single fly.

Hooking Takers

When a trout sees an interesting fly dead drifting downstream, it often leaves its lie and floats with the pattern, giving it a proper examination before striking. Its take affects the indicator in a subtle manner—a small twitch here, a sideways shuffle there. Hence trout guides often tell their clients to strike immediately on the slightest unnatural motion.

Steelhead, however, aren't given to proper examinations of flies before striking. When they take, they either slide over and bite down or viciously rush out and slam the fly. Either way, the effect on the indicator is hardly subtle. Typically, the indicator will dart under the surface with certainty. Most strikes will be indistinguishable from a solid snag. Whether the fly is stuck in a robust log or a fish's jaw will become clear only as you raise the rod. Some strikes will be unmistakable, the indicator lashing through the water as it tries to keep up with a moving chromer. Sometimes a steelhead will strike as the fly sinks, the violence of the take dispersing through the leader, and the indicator registering nothing. Such takes usually appear to the angler as an aquatic flash at mid-depth. Anytime you see a flash, even if the indicator doesn't duck, come back on the rod with confidence—your best fish of the season might be attached.

Coming back on the rod isn't as simple as it sounds. When employing indicator tactics, the striking motion needs to be not only decisive, but also tailored to the specific location of the fly.

Precision nymphing requires you to stay alert. If a steelhead strikes while the indicator and fly are upstream of your position, the rod is best raised downstream, pulling the fly toward the solid meat of the fish's mouth. If the indicator and fly are across the current or downstream from your position, the rod is best raised toward the downstream shore. The direction of the striking mo-

This seven-pound buck rushed through two rapids, a down tree, and a submerged bush before coming to the beach. A firm hook-set made the landing possible. To ensure the hook finds a solid home after the take, raise your rod as if lifting a bowling ball off the bottom.

tion is essential. Raising the rod upstream while the indicator and fly dead drift below you, for instance, will cause the fly to be pulled directly out of the fish's eager mouth. Besides the directional characteristics of the striking motion, you also need to pay attention to the force you deliver into the strike. A tender strike, like that delivered to a taking trout, will allow the fly to lightly pin the chromer—certainly alerting it to the fly's fallacious nature—but won't bury the hook deep enough to last the duration of the battle. Whether or not you're sure it was a fish that made your indicator dive, pull back on the rod in a rigid and powerful motion. Imagine that the fly has pinned a bowling ball and you need to lift it to the surface immediately. A tender motion won't do the job; neither will a backcasting motion. You need to deliver some serious lifting power if that hook is to find a firm home.

Downstream nymphing adds a new wrinkle: slack. The fly will be downstream of your position, so when it ducks, you'll want to raise the rod to the downstream shore. The line will be loose between you and the indicator, however. Simply raising the rod usually won't pick up enough of the slack to deliver the hook firmly. Besides striking the rod toward the downstream shore, the line hand also needs to strike, helping pull as much slack as possible.

Despite the new wrinkle added by downstream nymphing, the technique does offer a serious advantage: Statistically, more steelhead hooked while nymphing downstream make it to the shore. In stage B of the presentation, when you deliver an upstream mend via a line flip, a small curve is produced in the line above the indicator. Upon striking, this curve helps pull the hook toward the corner of the steelhead's mouth. It also helps capture the current's drag, increasing the magnitude of the striking motion's power. Once the hook is set, the distance between you and the downstream indicator—sometimes as much as one hundred feet—protects the light tippet from the chromer's vicious head shakes. Each time the fish's body flexes against the resistance, the fly line stretches.

No matter which indicator tactic you're using, once the fish is hooked, you'll want to get any slack on the reel as quickly as possible. While nymphing, an angler often holds a dozen feet or more of loose line in the hand. When a pissed chromer breaks for waters unknown, that slack can go airborne in its rush to get through the guides, wrapping itself around a rod butt, reel seat, or worse.

This past winter, as a warm rain turned my homewater emerald, my indicator vanished into the depths. I raised the rod solidly and felt the pounding head shakes of a good fish. The buck immediately came to the surface, thrashing his silver sides in clear view. Against my better judgment, I struggled ashore before reeling in the slack—maybe I was afraid of going for a swim with a fish like that. Anyway, the fish turned and bolted, lifting the tangle of fly line into the wet air and, in a stunning display of Murphy's Law, laid coils of it around my neck. Near the middle of the pool, the line came tight, burning a smooth circle in my flesh and prematurely freeing the fish.

CHAPTER 16

The Deep-Water Dead Drift

A Radical Fly-Rod Technique

The winter steelheader's fate, in those weeks when the rivers flow high from rains that only Noah could appreciate, is akin to a sorry fellow from Greek mythology named Sisyphus.

Unlike most ardent chromeheads, Sisyphus did not live a good life. Instead, he used his cunning to trick travelers for his own material gain, once even tricking the god of death, Thanatos. For his crimes, Sisyphus was sentenced to eternal punishment.

To this day, so the myth goes, Sisyphus is pushing a rock up some steep mountain. Such vein-popping labor might be nice, might even be a fruitful way to spend eternity, if Sisyphus got to gaze upon his rock sitting atop a mountain at the end of the day. But the gods won't allow him such fulfillment. The moment Sisyphus delivers the rock to the summit, the gods give it a little push and laugh like schoolyard bullies as it tumbles back to the bottom. Thus Sisyphus must begin the work again, never coming nearer to completion.

The task of persuading a steelhead to move to a fly is hard enough in perfect conditions. When the water swells with winter rain, keeping even the strongest casters from placing flies in the strike zone, the task feels Sisyphean. Few blame the angler who hangs up the ol' fly rod to await fairer times.

But what if there were another option, one that would consistently hook high-water steelhead and didn't require giving up the pleasures offered by a fly rod? Oh, but there is such an option—although it might raise an eyebrow or two at the fly shop.

Fly fishing depends on a weighted line to move a weightless terminal end, in other words the fly. The ten-and-two casting motion we've all come to love relies on such design. Modern anglers push the boundaries by using weighted flies, but the line companies compensate by producing slightly heavier fly lines, still allowing the flies to be turned over by a traditional casting motion. Conventional fishing employs a different system. A heavy terminal end, the weight, pulls the light line from the reel. A simple heave—nearly the same heave used by a six-year-old targeting bluegill or a sixty-year-old targeting chinook—delivers the hook to a distant lie.

Fly fishing's dependence on the weighted line and weightless terminal end limits its ability to get deep. The weighted line is hard to control in the twisting currents of a deep river. To consistently access water more than

Above: The deep water dead drift, though far from graceful, keeps chromeheads on the water long after the levels are normally considered blown out.

ten feet deep is all but impossible on most fast steelhead streams. But a conventional rig isn't hindered in the same manner. The weighted terminal end darts through the water column, towing the weightless line down with it. The terminal end can then spend plenty of time in the strike zone of the steelhead, despite the river's heaviest currents. Hence flooded winter steelhead streams are sometimes considered the sole domain of anglers chunking bait. Or at least, they were.

A few seasons ago, a group of Northwest steelheaders with a bent toward the radical refused to retreat from winter's deluge. For this gang of subversives, the allure of the big winter fish proved too much for romantic notions of tradition. Over a few beers, they racked their brains for a presentation that could consistently punch a fly through ten or fifteen feet of water and deposit it in the strike zone. The system needed to get the fly down fast and keep it there. Sink-tips wouldn't work. The currents in such deep water wouldn't allow for consistent swings. The slinky systems used by midwesterners were out; they covered water too slowly for big West Coast rivers. Then what? The answer they came up with would blur the lines between fly and conventional fishing.

The deep-water dead drift, as they called it, combines the effective line control offered by a fly rod with the access to sunken lies offered by a heavily weighted terminal end. A floating running line is connected to a 12- to 15-foot section of level 10-pound-test monofilament. A sliding indicator is fed up the monofilament, its exact placement on the line controlled by a thread stop. At the end is a Popsicle tied up on a weighted body—in other words, a jig. The running line won't deliver the indicator and jig—the line's mass isn't sufficient to turn over the heavy terminal end—so a normal fly-casting motion is out of the question. Instead, the running line is coiled at the feet and the rod swung in an underhand motion. The weighted terminal end sails toward the target slot, towing out the running line. Once the system is in the water, you can strip, mend, and feed the running line as you might a normal fly line while using indicator tactics. When the indicator ducks, the rod comes back and the fish fights as if it had been hooked on a traditional fly-fishing presentation.

Few would argue that the system fits any definition of fly fishing. But the system requires all the current reading and line-tending skills of fly fishing's most challenging presentations. And what it lacks in romance and grace, it surely makes up for in the numbers of fish duped.

The very first test trip to the flooded river, the deep-water dead drift plucked a chrome hen from twelve feet of water. After some refinements to the specifics of the rigging—adjusting the type of running line, indicator,

and monofilament—the effectiveness of the presentation only increased. Casts went farther. Drifts got longer. And big fish started being consistently hooked and landed from deep winter runs.

To say that I was initially hesitant to try the deep-water dead drift would be an utter lie. Of course, I wasn't stoked about heaving a heavy terminal end or using my fly rod in manner blasphemous to many fly fishers. But the only prospect I was less stoked about was sitting on my couch as thick fish pulsed their way up my homewater. Too many winters, I'd hung up the equipment for weeks on end and gone stir-crazy as endless rain firehosed the land. Fishing books would get me by for a week or two, fishing catalogs for a few more days, but then the withdrawal shakes would start, my mind twisting like a rainbow with whirling disease. I'm not too proud to admit that the deep-water dead drift appeared as the spring sun must to an Inuit.

So I headed out as torrential rains soaked the logging road along my homewater, turning the normally rock hard surface into gelatinous mud. The tires tossed a spray of clumps skyward, some of which landed on the cab with irregular thuds. In the pull-off near a popular pool, a baitfisher lugged a hog of a hatchery buck toward his truck. He waved with his rod, and I slowed so as not to spray him with road sludge.

I pushed farther into the mountains, the road climbing away from the river, until finally the road and the river parted ways permanently. There I parked, hiding the truck up an overgrown skid road, grabbed the rods, and cut through the woods toward my homewater section.

Despite the rain, the river's upper sections flowed turquoise green instead of the mocha brown I'd expected. Largely unlogged headwaters ensured that the sediment stayed on land and out of the water. But the green flows climbed high along the banks, burying the runs and tailouts under an extra four feet of twisting currents. I'd never bothered to visit the river during such massive flows. At the first tailout, a bouldery section above a narrow set of rapids, my trusted lies were gone, buried under a blanket of churning water. I swallowed hard and moved upstream. At the next tailout, a wide cobble-bottomed spot where eager fish frequently held on cloudy days, the river slid like green gravy into the rapids below, much too fast to hold a fish. I rubbed my neck, the icy rain slipping down my back. Before hiking out, I decided to try one more spot, the Canyon Run. At normal winter flows, the lies sat under the weight of nine or ten watery feet. Today they'd be under thirteen or fourteen.

A fifteen-minute hike around the bend spit me out at the Canyon Run. The midstream boulder in the tailout, a trusted spot, was blown out, as was the upper riffle that dumped into the run. But the meaty section, the deep middle belly of the run, still flowed at the right current speed. For a moment I wondered whether I could nymph it—toss a Rock Hopper and a Lifter into the top, stack-mend it down, and feed line into the drift. The contorting green currents and river's expanded girth convinced me such thoughts were but idle fantasy.

The Canyon Run collects chromers partly because of its unique bottom structure. A long ledge extends through the center of the run, parallel to the current's flow. Steelhead could press against that ledge and find easy respite. The fast water overhead brought a serious dose of oxygen and gave ample protection from predators, inclining the fish to strike.

I stood at the head of the run, and a simple toss of my rod placed the rig a dozen feet or so upstream of the trench. I figured mending the jig to such depths would be laborious, maybe even impossible. But as the pattern hit the water, its own inertia punched it through the water column, forcing the indicator up the leader until it came tight against the thread stop at the thirteen-foot mark. In less time than it took to make a stack mend, the jig reached the strike zone. Surprised, I fed line into the drift using line tosses and watched as the indicator bobbed its way through the entirety of the run.

As the jig had never dragged the bottom, I raised the thread stop six inches. On the next cast, the indicator again floated evenly through the run. So I raised the thread stop one more time. Now the jig would be fourteen feet down—the thread stop only six inches away from the running line. A quick toss, a series of stack mends, and steady line tosses put the pattern down. The indicator danced on the currents with the loose-hipped rhythm of hula dancer, a spellbinding image in that cold rain. And then it was gone. For a moment I hesitated, questioning reality. A sober stare corroborated that the indicator was indeed missing, and without losing another second, I came back on the rod. The rod forked to the stripping guide with the chunky head shakes of a fish.

Instinct took over: Zip in the slack, guide it on the spool with a pinkie finger, slosh onto the bank, all the time maintaining even tension. The fish held its ground, the line humming against the current. Again I questioned reality. Were those really head shakes? Or maybe the flexing of a submerged limb? The odds of this being a fish . . . As if on cue, the fish turned in the

An eight-pound fish hooked in fourteen feet of water on the deep-water dead drift.

current and bolted downstream, the reel singing in rhythmic unison with the bucking of the rod. Just when I thought the fish would stay deep, it burst sidelong into the air and came down in a splashing rush, throwing diamonds of water into the air. I spun the reel and ran up the bank, trying to eat slack as the fish rushed toward me. It jumped again, straight toward the clouds this time, contouring its silver sides as it flipped end over end. Stunned upon landing, the fish paused for a moment to reassess the situation. I bent the rod toward the stones and leaned into it. The pressure convinced the fish that its volatile reaction was indeed warranted, and it finned first toward the far shore, but the rod's pressure was too much. It changed direction, diving toward the safety of the trench from which it'd come. But again the rod held it. Within moments, the bright eight-pound hen turned on her passive side and came within tailing distance. At the rod's release of tension, the jig fell free, leaving the fish newly invigorated. Her tail pulsed once, but I held on just to make sure. When she kicked again, I let her go into the green flows, watching her swim back into the deep water.

A year before, I'd have spent such an afternoon staring out my rain-glazed window, wondering how many gorgeous fish slipped upstream, wondering how long it would be before I could fish again, wondering how long I could stand wondering. The deep-water dead drift put an end to all that.

The Water

The deep-water dead drift, like swinging with a sink-tip, is a presentation dependent on tough conditions. The presentation's lack of romance limits its use for most anglers until the water conditions are so heinous no other presentation could be effective. Steelhead remain active despite high water. In fact, winter steelhead often display their most aggressive tendencies in such conditions. When more traditional fly-rod tactics are no longer feasible, the deep-water dead drift can provide unparalleled access to otherwise buried lies.

Like indicator tactics, the deep-water dead drift is highly versatile, allowing you to cover nearly any water type. The presentation easily covers pocket water, rapids, riffles, runs, tailouts, and even pools. In fact, since it uses a

The deep-water dead drift is best reserved for those days when the water is too high for traditional fly-fishing tactics.

lightweight running line and isn't as dependent on perfect stack mends to put the pattern down deep, the deep-water dead drift makes covering water even more efficient than indicator tactics.

Though the presentation can be used anywhere, it is of greatest value in the deep runs frequented by big winter steelhead. Increased water volume raises the average speed of a river; more water needs to move through the same narrow channel. So when the river level is high, less water is moving at the ideal speed for holding steelhead—the speed of a comfortable walk. Fish that would normally hold in this tailout or that riffle are forced to new lies. Deep runs are often the last refuge on flooded rivers, some of the only places where the current still moves at a walking pace. And it just so happens the deep-water dead drift perfectly covers such water.

The length of the leader limits the achievable depth of the presentation. A 10-foot leader will allow the pattern to sink no more than ten feet, as the indicator will stop sliding at the connection point with the running line. Because the leader doesn't need to be turned over by a traditional casting motion, leaders as long as 20 feet are manageable with the deep-water dead drift. Line control becomes extremely difficult at such lengths, however. The maximum functional depth is about fifteen feet on most rivers for most anglers. Besides, once the indicator and pattern are more than fifteen feet apart, the variation between the fast water along the surface and the slow water along the bottom causes the indicator to drag the pattern through the strike zone—all but killing the technique's chances of success.

The deep-water dead drift consistently takes fish, period. The size of the steelhead's strike zone on a particular day will limit the slot size, of course, but fish move to the jig despite murky flows, cold water, and other detrimental conditions. As long as holding water exists and the water clarity is at a fishable level, the presentation stands a fine chance. The fluttering action of the marabou pattern as it hangs below the indicator dependably sparks the striking reflex in holding steelhead.

The Logistics

The deep-water dead drift is best performed downstream of you so that you can feed line into the drift, lengthening the size of the slot you cover on each cast. On big water, anglers frequently feed the entire running line.

As with other indicator tactics, the pattern is best suspended six to twelve inches from the bottom so that willing steelhead won't need to travel far to strike. To make sure you're fishing the right depth, try adjusting the position of the thread stop six inches at a time. If you're not dragging the bottom, move the thread stop up six inches, lowering the pattern. If you're dragging—as will be apparent by the compromised action of the indicator—move the thread stop down six inches, raising the pattern.

Position yourself at the top of the water to be covered and fifteen feet off to the side. Strip out all the line you'll need to complete the drift; on some rivers, you'll be stripping out all the running line. Ready the front 20 feet of line so that as the weighted terminal end flies toward the slot, the line can slip unhindered through the guides. To achieve this, many anglers place loops in their lips or in their line hand's fingers. Hang the indicator and pattern on a 3-foot leash off the end of the rod. Make an underhanded toss slightly upstream into the target slot, releasing the coiled slack (A), as shown on page 178. The ideal cast will sail high, like a rainbow between you and the target slot. This arch gives the pattern inertia and slack with which to begin the long sink toward the bottom.

As the indicator drifts past your position, make a line-flip mend upstream, positioning the line to reduce the likelihood of a drag-causing belly (B). In some situations, such as when you're trying to get the pattern down to lies more than twelve feet deep, stack mends that feed slack might be necessary. Because the running line has less mass than a normal fly line, more snap of the wrist is needed to deliver the stack mend accurately.

Once the indicator moves past your position, feed slack into the drift using slack tosses as the indicator's progress requires (C). A perfect dead drift is essential for success, so be sure to give an adequate amount of line. But beware of excessive slack fed into the drift. Too much and you'll be unable to come tight if a fish happens to take.

Steelhead—especially springtime bucks—frequently take at the end of the drift, as the pattern lifts from the bottom. When the indicator nears the end of the drift, allow the pattern to rise all the way to the top before stripping it back (D). Often fish will chase it up, sometimes even striking violently on the surface. Typically any take at the end of the drift is a solid one; as long as you come back firmly, the hook should find firm lodging in the top of the jaw.

Retrieving the pattern and indicator all the way back to the rod takes time—time when the pattern isn't fishing. To strip as quickly as possible, many anglers tuck the rod under an arm and strip with both hands.

To manage the coiled running line, some anglers employ stripping baskets, although the contraptions can be cumbersome protuberances while wading and hiking the river. The current will do a fine job of keeping the slack organized downstream of your position, if you allow it.

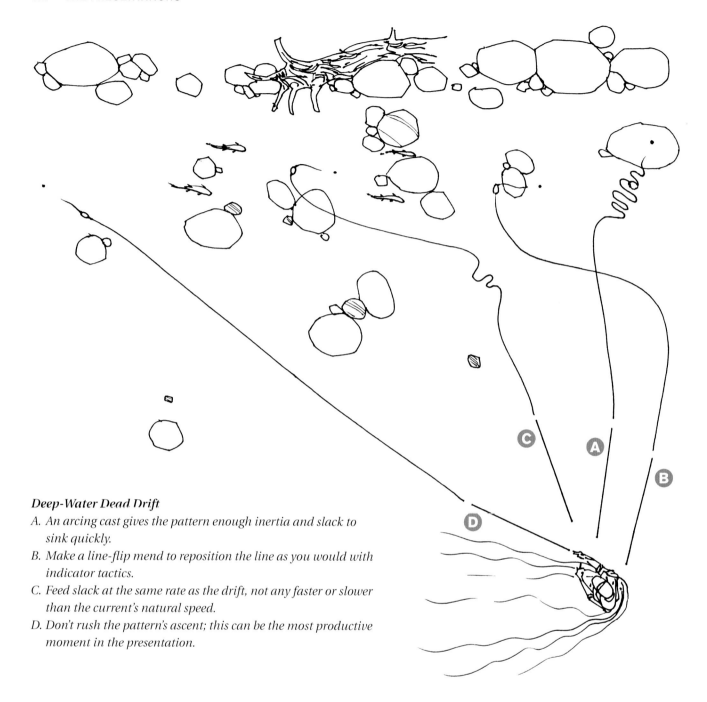

Deep-Water Dead Drift

A. *An arcing cast gives the pattern enough inertia and slack to sink quickly.*

B. *Make a line-flip mend to reposition the line as you would with indicator tactics.*

C. *Feed slack at the same rate as the drift, not any faster or slower than the current's natural speed.*

D. *Don't rush the pattern's ascent; this can be the most productive moment in the presentation.*

Perfecting the deep-water dead drift takes time, as does learning any new presentation. But the advantages offered by the tactic make the time a superb investment.

Rods, Lines, Leaders, Indicators, and Flies

The deep-water dead drift taxes fly rods. The heaving cast puts a healthy bend in the rod, and the distant hook sets can bend the cork under your fingertips. Rods lighter than a stout 8-weight aren't up to the job. Nine- and 10-weights are more suited to the work, the stiffer the better.

As with most steelheading presentations, rod length is important. The longer the rod, the more line can be kept off the water and controlled with precise mending techniques. The deep-water dead drift is no different. The longer the rod, the better. Flooded rivers limit the wading angler's ability to be ideally positioned for the presentation. Often the target slot will be on the far side of a fast tongue of current. To help maintain drag-free drifts, you'll need to hold the line above the fast water and deliver stack mends when necessary. Both tasks are completed quickly and efficiently with long rods.

Spey rods, especially those in the 12- to 13-foot range, are deadly deep-water dead-drifting tools. Their length helps control the line with precision. But more vitally, they're able to pick up huge amounts of slack with a single sweeping motion. When the indicator ducks, the Spey rod is capable of coming tight quickly, securing the hook solidly in the fish's mouth.

Running lines come in several forms. The deep-water dead drift is possible only with a floating version. An intermediate running line drops just below the surface, where it adamantly resists the finest attempts to mend it. To keep your floating running line mending and feeding effectively, treat it frequently with line cleaner. Steelhead fight brutally, often towing the line to the bottom, where it drags over rocks and submerged logs. Running lines rated for less than 30 pounds aren't up to the task.

Tapered leaders are by definition thick in the upper sections. Thick leaders slow the descent of a weighted fly and catch the river's twisting currents, causing the fly to lift prematurely from the bottom. The only reason fly fishers employ tapered leaders is to help turn the fly over during the casting stroke. But the deep-water dead drift doesn't require the fly line to turn over the indicator and pattern, and thus tapered leaders aren't necessary. To help sink the pattern as quickly as possible, most anglers use as thin a leader as possible with the presentation. Some use level leaders rated as light as 8-pound-test.

Most, however, find a 10-pound-test level leader to be the perfect balance between strength and sink rate. To allow the thread stop to slide up and down as needed, the leader must be free of knots.

The weighted jig is especially deadly when the pattern hangs directly below the indicator, causing the marabou to flutter enticingly. But for the pattern to hang ideally, the proper-size indicator is required. An indicator that is too small will sink under the surface, and one that is too big will be unnecessarily cumbersome. Also, because high-water steelhead often take subtly, the indicator must be sensitive, revealing the smallest abnormalities in the pattern's drift. Finally, the leader is made of delicate monofilament, so the indicator must not cause the line undue harm. After much experimentation, I've found that oval slip floats—the kind made of balsa or a similar synthetic—with a 1-inch diameter to be the ideal. I prefer those with elongated tops and bottoms for maximum sensitivity.

The deep-water dead drift doesn't require an array of jigs. Because the technique is relegated to certain conditions, namely high water, only patterns that match those conditions are needed. Most practitioners of the technique carry pink or flesh-colored jigs in two sizes: $1/8$ and

Complicated patterns aren't needed for the deep-water dead drift. Go big, go bright, and go heavy.

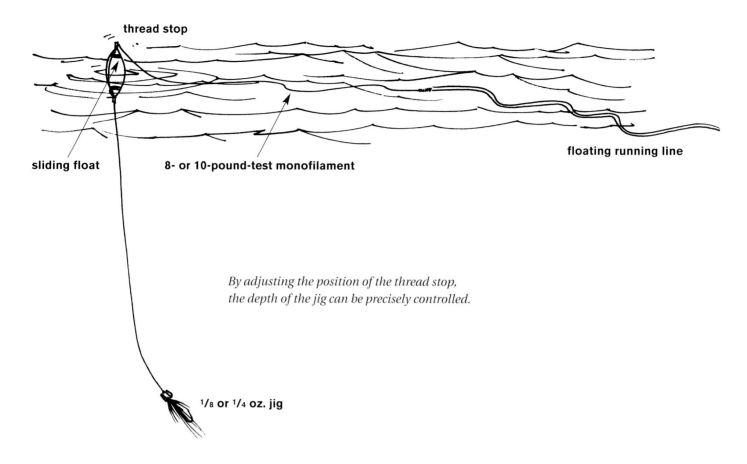

thread stop

sliding float

8- or 10-pound-test monofilament

floating running line

*By adjusting the position of the thread stop,
the depth of the jig can be precisely controlled.*

¹/₈ or ¹/₄ oz. jig

¹/₄ ounce. The smaller size is especially effective when the water is high yet clear, as is common in unlogged watersheds. The larger size is best suited to high and murky water. I prefer jigs made completely of marabou. These patterns have the most action underwater. The indicator riding the riffles on the surface causes the jig to flutter as it drifts; marabou heightens this effect. Many jigs are tied with rabbit strips, like the leeches we're used

Jig (peach)

to swinging. In my experience, however, rabbit fur doesn't sink as quickly as marabou. And when you're trying to reach a lie ten to fifteen feet down, small variations in sink rate make a big difference.

Variations

During times of high water, especially as it drops toward normal levels, steelhead typically become aggressive. Fish that may have been holding dourly for days become invigorated with the changing conditions. Such aggressive high-water fish usually aren't picky—if they see a fly that is remotely interesting, they'll nail it. Big patterns typically are all you'll need to move high-water fish.

Occasionally steelhead respond differently to increased flows, however, especially if the water is excessively cold. They'll take up a good lie and hold tight for days, their strike zones shrinking to mere inches. Under such conditions, the big patterns used with the deep-water dead drift might not spark the fish's striking reflex. A small dropper attached to the jig sometimes saves the day.

Attaching a dropper to the deep-water dead drift's point fly is a similar process used with indicator tactics. Clinch-knot a 6- to 8-inch section of tippet to the bend in the point fly's hook. At the end, attach a small dropper with an open clinch knot. A couple favorites include an

When the water becomes high and cold, as frequently happens during periods of snowmelt, attaching a small dropper can save the day.

Easy Egg or Lifter in size 6 or 8. Because the point fly plummets quickly through the water column, a limp section of tippet material between the point fly's hook bend and the dropper fly will wrap around the leader. To avoid this problem, use a heavy section of tippet. Twelve-pound-test isn't overkill.

Hooking Takers

When a steelhead takes the pattern below the deep-water dead drift, the indicator reacts in predictable ways. Usually it slowly slips under the surface, as if the hook snagged a rock. More infrequently, the indicator slams underwater as if attached to a diving whale. The least common take affects the indicator like a timid bluegill does a bobber—it twitches and bobs. You're wise to strike at any of these motions.

The indicator and pattern are likely to be downstream of your position when a fish takes, so the best striking angle is toward the downstream bank, as the motion will pull the hook toward the corner of the fish's jaw. The actual striking motion will be most suc-

cessful if done firmly and quickly, more a fast lift than a snappy cast.

To maintain a natural float as the indicator and fly move downstream, feed slack into the drift. Picking up all the slack with just a rod strike isn't always possible; the slack dilutes the power of the striking motion, often giving the steelhead a chance to spit out the suddenly alarming pattern. To eat up some of the slack, you can strip with your line hand as the rod hand strikes.

Once the rod comes up and you feel the head shakes of steelhead on the other end, you need to put any slack still in the water on the reel immediately. Running line has a special talent for wrapping itself around rod butts, reel seats, and anything else nearby. If the fish instantly takes to running, forget reeling in the slack. Instead, try to let the slack slip through the guides smoothly, applying an even and light drag pressure with your fingers.

The deep-water dead drift frequently hooks big, bright steelhead with a fondness for line-melting runs. When a fish takes, get to the shore fast—you might need to follow the brute downstream.

CHAPTER 17

Flies

Fly anglers are attached—maybe overly attached—to their fly patterns. Each of us has found a few patterns that we trust to take steelhead on our homewaters day in and day out. In the preceding presentation chapters, I listed the patterns I trust most with each technique, patterns that have proven themselves on the rivers I consistently fish. But because a single lifetime is far too short to explore every distinct strain of steelhead and adequately test every fly, a book on steelheading wouldn't be complete without an inventory of trusted patterns. So I called in some reinforcements.

The flies shown in the coming pages were donated by chromeheads throughout steelhead country, anglers who target a diverse swath of steelhead strains. Only the most trusted patterns have been included. But of course, no survey of steelhead patterns could ever include all the effective flies used throughout steelhead country. What follows is at best an incomplete list—but every fly here is a good one.

WET FLIES

Green Butt Skunk

Enlightened Green Butted Skunk

WET FLIES

Skunk

Fire Butted Skunk

Beach Bum

Undertaker

Coal Car

Silver Hilton

WET FLIES

Paris Hilton   MATT VANDER HEIDE

Green Butted Silver Hilton

Green Burlesque

Mack's Canyon

Green Butt Silver Hilton

Fly Dejur

WET FLIES

Freight Train

Purple Angel

Flash Dancer

Fiddle D

Purple Burlesque

Streetwalker

WET FLIES

Purple Peril

Smeraglio's September Sunset

Spawning Purple Peril

Red Wing Black Bird

Copper Train

Skykomish Sunrise

WET FLIES

Steelhead Scarlet Ibis

Steelhead Muddler

Silvey's Spey (orange)

Popsicle

Silvey's Spey (purple)

Cabero

WET FLIES

Glo-in-the-Dark Cabero

Motion Prawn (purple)

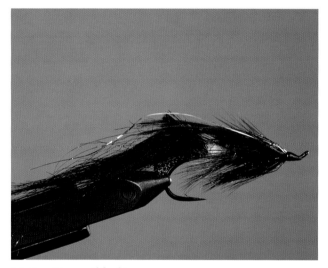

Motion Prawn (black)

Murdich's Wiggler

Motion Prawn (orange)

Poly-Wog

WET FLIES

Strung-Out in the Mud

Strung-Out Peril

Strung-Out Beach Bum

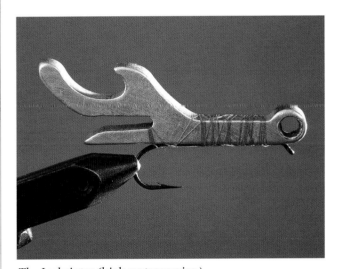

The Inebriator (high water version)

LEECHES

Strung-Out Politician

Thunderhead MOAL

LEECHES

Thunderhead MOAL (pink)

Fireball Leech (pink)

MOAL Rhoid

Fireball Leech (purple)

Fireball Leech (orange)

Hot Shot Leech (black)

LEECHES

Hot Shot Leech (purple)

Polar Cab (pink)

Squiggly Worm

Polar Cab (orange)

Marabou String Leech

Silvey's Poacher Prawn

LEECHES

Cabero Leech   NORM DOMAGALA

Articulated Marabou Leech

Nicholas Leech (pink)   JAY NICHOLAS

Double Articulated Leech (black)

Boss (orange)

DEAD-DRIFTING FLIES

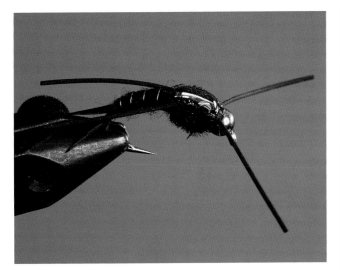

3-D Flashback Nymph (black)

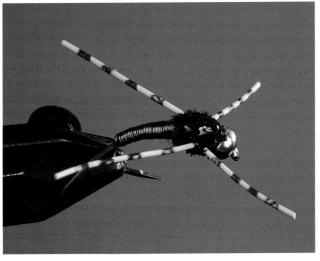

3-D Flashback Nymph (copper)

3-D Flashback Nymph (olive)

A. P. Spy Series Dr. Evil   MATT VANDER HEIDE

A. P. Spy Series Fat Bastard   MATT VANDER HEIDE

A. P. Spy Series Foxxy Brown   MATT VANDER HEIDE

DEAD-DRIFTING FLIES

A. P. Spy Series Goldmember   MATT VANDER HEIDE

Double Bitch Creek Nymph

A. P. Spy Series Shaggadelic   MATT VANDER HEIDE

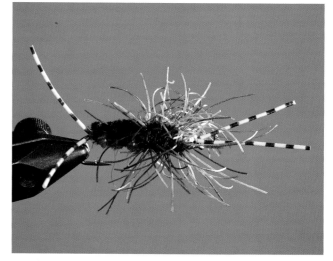

Beadhead Hefty Bitch Creek Nymph

Flashback Steelhead Stonefly

Loco Nymph

DEAD-DRIFTING FLIES

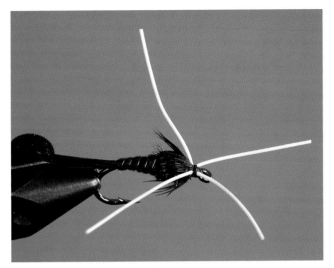

Steelhead Pheasant Tail

Vitamin D (black)

Steelhead Hare's Ear

Vitamin D (chartreuse)

Tungticker Black Stone

Vitamin D (orange)

DEAD-DRIFTING FLIES

Vitamin D (pink)

Steelhead October Caddis

Vitamin D (purple)

Steelhead October Pupa (tungsten bead)

Beadhead Steelie Stone

Beadhead Steelhead October Pupa

DEAD-DRIFTING FLIES

Steelhead Scud (chartreuse)

Skunk Shrimp

Steelhead Scud (orange)

Bottom Licker Nymph

Steelhead Scud (red)

Steelhead Dart

DEAD-DRIFTING FLIES

Rock Hopper (purple)

Kilowatt (pink)

Rock Hopper (pink)

Candy Dropper Jig   OVER-THE-EDGE

Steelhead Squid

Jig (pink)

DEAD-DRIFTING FLIES

Jig (pink and white)

Glo-Bug (orange)

Jig (peach)

Glo-Bug (pink)

Jig (flesh)

Clown Egg

DEAD-DRIFTING FLIES

Burnt Egg

Easy Egg (pink)

Easy Egg (fire)

Low Water Easy Egg (red)

Easy Egg (orange)

Low Water Easy Egg (orange)

DEAD-DRIFTING FLIES

Low Water Easy Egg (pink)

Roe Buggar   JAY NICHOLAS

Eggo

Tango Egg (green)

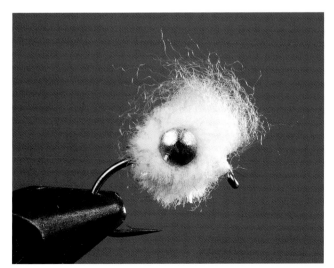

Creamball (chartreuse)

Tango Egg (pink)

DEAD-DRIFTING FLIES

Trilogy Egg (cherise)   DARIAN HYDE

Whipped Cream (orange)

Trilogy Egg (hot orange)   DARIAN HYDE

Whipped Cream (pink)

Trilogy Egg (shrimp pink)   DARIAN HYDE

Hot Bead Cab Egg

DEAD-DRIFTING FLIES

Gorman's Beadhead Cab Egg (fluorescent orange)

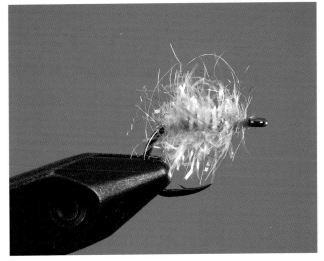

Low Water Lifter

Lifter (pink)

Deep Water Lifter

Lifter (peach)

Beadhead Lifter (blue)

DEAD-DRIFTING FLIES

Beadhead Lifter (cream)

Beadhead Lifter (pink)

Beadhead Lifter (fire)

Beadhead Lifter (red)

Beadhead Lifter (orange)

DRY FLIES

Arctic Fox Purple Muddler　　　　　　　NEIL RAY

Quigley's Gurgler

Green Butted Bomber

Strung-Out Skater

Waller Waker

Spot Top Skated Green Butt Skunk

DRY FLIES

Weapon of Mass Deception   NATE KOENIGSKNECHT

Steelhead Bee

October Skating Caddis

Chromer Caddis

CHAPTER 18

Managing a Hooked Steelhead

One of the few things I love more than catching chromers is taking a die-hard trout angler to my homewater and watching as the person sets the hook, feels the bucking steelhead on the other end, and promptly dives headlong off the sane train. In that moment—so often punctuated by swear words, incomplete thoughts, and references to a long-haired sandal-wearing icon from a couple thousand years ago—the horizons of the trout angler's world expand into the dawn and dust, and the person falls rapidly into the abyss between. The angler's first complete sentence comes out between adrenaline pants: "What have I been doing my whole life?"

Steelhead bend a fly rod like no other fish. As the salt water builds a metallic plating on their sides, it also injects their veins with pelagic jet fuel. Once a fish feels the sting of the hook and the building torque of a distant fly rod, the steelie points its aerodynamic head toward the moon and kicks on the afterburners. Fish-fighting techniques learned on the trout stream can't bring it back to earth. Beaching a hot steelhead requires advanced tools.

Even the finest steelheaders lose about 50 percent of the fish they hook. Sure they'll have streaks of landed fish—five in a row here, ten there—but they'll also have streaks of missed fish. I once lost twelve straight. But by setting the hook properly and then getting the fish to the beach as fast as possible, your odds of success go up dramatically.

For those anglers who fish for wild steelhead, mastering the delicate art of the quick beaching has moral implications as well as practical ones. Every minute a chromer spends fighting you, it is using vital energy that it could use to fight the currents of the river. Studies that tracked released fish show that as long as a steelhead is landed quickly, revived completely, and treated delicately throughout, the risks to the creature are minimal. But when anglers dillydally, callously lift the fish from the water to show their buddies, or toss back a still-tired fish, they put the steelhead at extreme jeopardy. Too often wild steelhead are subjected to all three disgraces.

No battle with a steelhead should ever last longer than one minute per pound of fish. Fifty years ago, such a fight time was impressive, but leaders weren't as strong then, nor were rods as forgiving. Today's technology ensures that even the toughest fish can be landed in less time. Most chromeheads land their fish in about thirty seconds per pound of fish. They achieve this feat by employing fighting techniques designed for big fish in a river environment.

I recently had the pleasure of fishing with a serious big-fish addict. Peter is known for his ability to land hogs quickly. The winter river flowed high and green, but our favorite lies were still in reach of traditional steelheading presentations. We chose to fish our way downstream,

Above: Hooking a steelhead is the easy part. Getting one to the beach—especially a wild fish fresh from the salt—is another matter entirely. Luckily, learning a few simple maneuvers can drastically improve your hooked-to-landed ratio.

hitting every slot of known holding water along the way. He'd go first, using downstream indicator tactics; I'd follow behind, swinging with a sink-tip. Halfway through our first run, Peter's indicator ducked with a splash. He raised the rod toward the downstream bank, and a good fish thrashed on the other end. During the fight that ensued, Peter employed every steelhead fighting technique in the book, landing the twelve-pound chromer in less than six minutes.

At the hook set, the steelhead rose to the surface and thrashed its thick body. Peter kept tight and steady ten-sion, reeling in the slack dangling from his line hand. By the time the fish decided to run, it was already smoothly connected to the reel. The steelhead burst into high gear, racing upstream at reel-melting velocity. Peter held the rod high, at a forty-five-degree angle, allowing the reel to apply steady and even pressure on the fish while the flex in the rod protected the tippet from any sudden jolts. Once the fish began to slow, Peter dropped his rod toward the upstream bank, changing the angle of pressure. The new rod position turned the fish off-balance, allowing the current to catch the side of its body—ending the

Landing steelhead is significantly easier with the help of a fellow chromehead. Here Matt Vander Heide, owner of the Scarlet Ibis Fly Shop, helps Tom Christensen land an especially feisty winter fish.

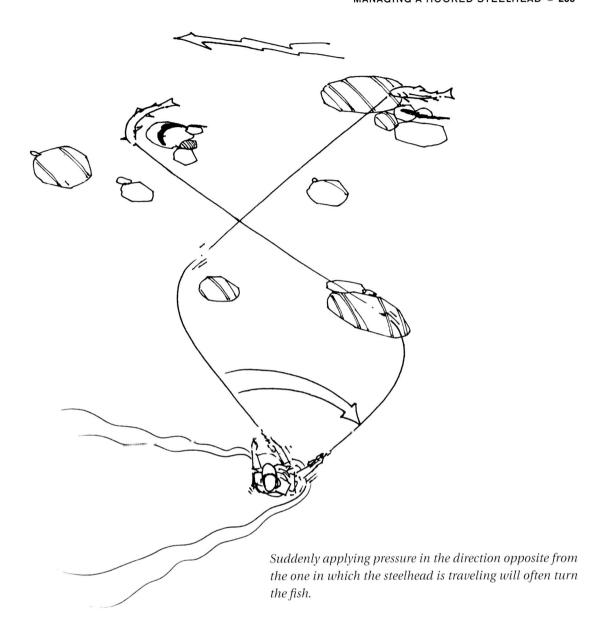

Suddenly applying pressure in the direction opposite from the one in which the steelhead is traveling will often turn the fish.

run. Immediately, the steelhead came back downstream. As it did, Peter quickly reeled in the slack, keeping steady tension on the fish.

The tactic Peter employed next is likely the most important steelhead fighting tool. To change the steelhead's direction of travel, he dropped the rod toward the water in the opposite direction from which the fish was traveling (see above). Instantly, the fish followed the rod, turning upstream and stopping directly in front of Peter.

Knowing that the big fish had a few more calories to burn, Peter didn't try to force him to the bank. Instead, he double-checked his drag setting and found firmer footing nearer the bank. Then he lowered the rod toward the downstream bank, again throwing the fish off-balance, and pumped in a few extra turns of line. Suddenly—but predictably—the fish broke for water downstream on

what would be its longest and last run. Peter raised the rod into the running position and began to pick his way down the bank. As the backing knot slipped through the guides, he lessened the drag setting slightly to counteract the drag applied by the current on the fly line. At this moment—as in all moments during the battle—he kept the maximum amount of tension possible on the fish without risking the tippet. Drag adjustments are a necessary part of fighting steelhead. When a hundred feet of line enters the water—or when the fish moves across a heavy current—the river works to dramatically increase the tension. If the reel's drag setting is left tight, the fish can frequently snap the tippet with a single head shake.

The steelhead stopped its run, as is typical, in the tailout of the run and turned to face upstream once again. Unfortunately, a cliff along the bank wouldn't allow Peter to follow all the way down to the fish's level. If descending

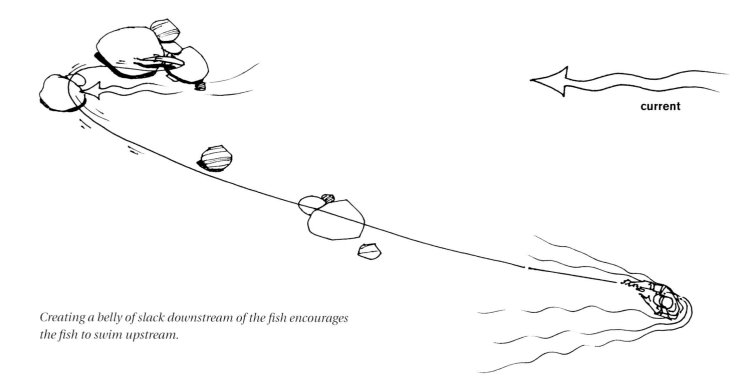

current

Creating a belly of slack downstream of the fish encourages the fish to swim upstream.

that far had been possible, Peter would have found a fish ready for a quick and easy beaching. But instead, he couldn't get any closer than sixty feet. Despite Peter's best efforts, dropping the rod to the downstream bank and leaning in hard, he couldn't move the fish from behind a rock. After almost a minute, it became clear that the fish wasn't going to be brought up from that tailout by simple pulling. Trusting the hook's place in the fish's jaw, Peter stripped out ten feet of slack with his line hand and fed the line into the current. For a tense moment, he couldn't feel the steelhead, but as the current carried the belly downstream of the fish, the tension returned. This time the directional pressure on the steelhead came from below (see above), a gentle pressure that the fish couldn't help but resist. Slowly the fish swam back into the pool, closing the distance to forty feet. Peter reeled up the slack and came tight to the fish again.

By now the steelhead couldn't hide its exhaustion. The runs tired it out—as is typical. But Peter still needed to persuade the fish to swim upstream and to come ashore. A steelhead hanging downstream of an angler is a problem; the hook is susceptible to slipping cleanly out of the fish's mouth. To move the fish upstream as quickly as possible, Peter used a technique known in steelheading circles as "swimming". He dropped his rod from a high position to the downstream bank, throwing the fish off-balance. While the steelhead struggled to re-produce its direct-upstream heading, Peter gained a few turns of line. Once the fish regained its position and line

stopped coming in, Peter flipped the rod toward the other bank and gained a few more turns of line (see page 211). By going back and forth, he forced the fish to swim toward his position.

Once the fish got within thirty feet, Peter tightened the drag, knowing the violent head shakes and runs characterizing the first phase of the fight were over. By tightening the drag, he'd be able to stop the slow bull-dogging runs so typical of the final phase of a steelhead's fight.

Once the steelhead came within seven feet of the shore, Peter readied for the beaching. He found a spot that had a smooth gravel bottom with a few inches of water over it. By changing the rod position, he turned the fish toward the far bank and immediately walked quickly up the beach. The fish turned in a circle, gained momentum, and slid into the shallows (page 211). Its best tail strokes couldn't counteract the inertia produced by the circle. Peter waited for the steelhead to flop over onto its side—the sign the battle is over—and quickly rushed to the steelhead's side to begin reviving it.

The key to Peter's quick success with a tough steel-head was his constant attention to rod position. When the fish ran, he kept the rod high, letting the creature tire itself against the reel's drag. When the fish held, he used a low rod position, turning the fish off-balance. Many beginning steelheaders maintain a high rod position throughout, thinking that only a high rod can provide adequate protection for the tippet. But steelhead quickly

current

To "swim" a fish upstream, drop the rod to one side and pump in line, until the fish regains its balance and line can't be cranked in. Then drop the rod to the other side and do the same.

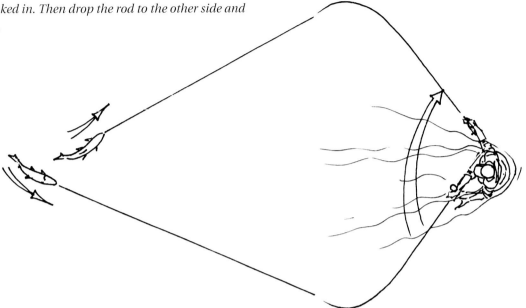

To give the fish enough momentum to get into shallow water, turn it in a circle and walk quickly up the beach. Once it is on its side, it can be easily tailed.

adjust to the angle of pressure applied by the rod, and once a fish has adjusted, it takes control of the fight. A steelhead in control of the battle will beat itself to death.

Peter's fish didn't jump, as is common with bigger bucks. But if it had, he'd have quickly dropped his rod to the water, throwing slack to the fish. If an airborne steel-head lands on a taut tippet, odds are good the fish will never make it to the shore.

If a suitable beach isn't available for landing the fish and you have no catch-and-release net on hand, the steel-head must be tailed while still in the water. Tailing a hot chromer is no easy task. Such a fish has a preternatural ability to snap alive and swim loops around a stunned angler—occasionally zipping through the angler's open legs.

Tailing a steelhead is best done by bringing the tired fish immediately upstream of your position. Before the fish can get its bearings, release a little tension, allowing the fish to slip downstream, and as it passes, grab the fish at the tail joint with your thumb and middle finger. Be sure to keep the rod handy in case you miss and the fish decides to head to a new watershed. Also, pinch your knees together to stop the fish from swimming between your legs.

The tail joint on most strains of steelhead can't be gripped firmly with an entire hand; your hand simply slips down over the tail. But most strains can be gripped securely with a robust thumb and middle finger. (This tail joint is the only place a steelhead should ever be squeezed.) Once the fish is tailed, you can tuck away the rod and use your free hand to cradle the fish just behind the pectoral fins.

As with all fish, steelhead should never be touched with dry hands. A dry hand scrapes the mucus from the fish's scales, making it susceptible to a potentially fatal fungus. For identical reasons, steelhead should never be pressed against a pair of waders, a fishing vest, or any other piece of clothing. If the fish is to be beached, don't bring it onto dry stones. Instead, bring it into shallow water, between one and three inches deep. Despite the ferocity of their fight, steelhead are delicate creatures that require tender treatment.

While you work to free the fly, leave the fish in the current, allowing it to catch its breath. Once the fly is free and the fish is ready for release, lay it upright and face-first into the river's current, which helps deliver oxygen back into its bloodstream. The ideal current speed moves at the pace of a comfortable walk. Any slower, and not enough oxygen will make it through the gills. Any faster, and the fish will have trouble staying righted in the current. If no proper current is readily available, options still

Notice how this eighteen-pound buck is being cradled with the front hand and held firmly with the back hand. This is the safest way to hold a fish while reviving it. The moment this fish kicked, it was released.

Measuring the length and girth of a wild steelhead is an indulgent bonus, one that should never come before the health of the fish. If a steelhead shows signs of stress, forget about the tape and release the fish immediately.

exist. In slow currents, you can pump the fish forward and back. In fast currents, you can use the lee created behind your waders.

Depending on the strain inflicted by the battle, the steelhead may be ready to swim on its own in a few seconds or several minutes. When your fish is ready, you'll know. It will kick repeatedly with its tail in gentle but robust strokes. Loosen your grasp slowly, remaining ready to regrip the fish and continue reviving it if necessary. When the fish is ready, it will kick away and disappear back into the green currents.

Estimating Weight

For years, steelheaders who have wanted to know the weight of a fish without killing it have used a standard equation generated by the International Game Fish Association (IGFA). The formulas use length and girth measurements and a knowledge of the general shape of fish to produce weight estimates that are within about 12 percent of the actual weight. But 12 percent is a lot. It could

make your twenty pound chromer eighteen pounds. As it turns out, the IGFA's formula was determined by studying the corpses of yellowfin tuna—a fish that hardly resembles a steelhead.

At the behest of anglers, a University of Portland mathematician named Lewis Lum recently devoted time to developing a new formula, one based on steelhead instead of tuna. Lum studied the data from seventy steelhead long ago killed and sent to the IGFA. From this data, he created a formula that produces estimated weights within 8 percent of the steelhead's actual live weight—the most accurate formula to date.

His equation, length × length × girth × 0.0007 = weight, is dependent on accurate in-field measurements. The length measurement is done from the crotch of the fish's tail to the tip of its nose. The girth measurement is done at the fish's widest point, usually just in front of the dorsal fin. Both dimensions can be determined quickly without lifting the steelhead from the current.

Common Lengths and Girths

	10	11	12	13	14	15	16	17	18	19	20	21	22	23	24	25	26
24	4.0	4.4	4.8	5.2	5.6	6.0	6.5	6.9	7.3	7.7	8.1	8.5	8.9	9.3	9.7	10.1	10.5
25	4.4	4.8	5.3	5.7	6.1	6.6	7.0	7.4	7.9	8.3	8.8	9.2	9.6	10.1	10.5	10.9	11.4
26	4.7	5.3	5.7	6.1	6.6	7.1	7.6	8.0	8.5	9.0	9.5	9.9	10.4	10.9	11.4	11.8	12.3
27	5.1	5.6	6.1	6.6	7.1	7.7	8.2	8.7	9.2	9.7	10.2	10.7	11.2	11.7	12.2	12.8	13.3
28	5.5	6.0	6.6	7.1	7.7	8.2	8.8	9.3	9.9	10.4	11.0	11.5	12.1	12.6	13.2	13.7	14.3
29	5.9	6.5	7.1	7.7	8.2	8.8	9.4	10.0	10.6	11.2	11.8	12.4	13.0	13.5	14.1	14.7	15.3
30	6.3	6.9	7.6	8.2	8.8	9.5	10.1	10.7	11.3	12.0	12.6	13.2	13.9	14.5	15.1	15.8	16.4
31	6.7	7.4	8.1	8.7	9.4	10.1	10.8	11.4	12.1	12.8	13.5	14.1	14.8	15.5	16.1	16.8	17.5
32	7.2	7.9	8.6	9.3	10.0	10.8	11.5	12.2	12.9	13.6	14.3	15.1	15.8	16.5	17.2	17.9	18.6
33	7.6	8.4	9.1	9.9	10.7	11.4	12.2	13.0	13.7	14.5	15.2	16.0	16.8	17.5	18.3	19.1	19.8
34	8.1	8.9	9.7	10.5	11.3	12.1	12.9	13.8	14.6	15.4	16.2	17.0	17.8	18.6	19.4	20.2	21.0
35	8.6	9.4	10.3	11.1	12.0	12.9	13.7	14.6	15.4	16.3	17.2	18.0	18.9	19.7	20.6	21.4	22.3
36	9.1	10.0	10.9	11.8	12.7	13.6	14.5	15.4	16.3	14.2	18.1	19.1	20.0	20.9	21.8	22.7	23.6
37	9.6	10.5	11.5	12.5	13.4	14.4	15.3	16.3	17.2	18.2	19.2	20.1	21.2	22.0	23.0	24.0	24.9
38	10.1	11.1	12.1	13.1	14.2	15.2	16.2	17.2	18.2	19.2	20.2	21.2	22.2	23.2	24.3	25.3	26.3
39	10.6	11.7	12.8	13.8	14.9	16.0	17.0	18.1	19.2	20.2	21.3	22.4	23.4	24.5	25.6	26.6	27.7
40	11.2	12.3	13.4	14.6	15.7	16.8	17.9	19.0	20.2	21.3	22.4	23.5	24.6	25.8	26.9	28.0	29.1
41	11.8	12.9	14.4	15.3	16.5	17.7	18.8	20.0	21.2	22.4	23.5	24.7	25.9	27.1	28.2	29.4	30.6
42	12.3	13.6	14.8	16.1	17.3	18.5	19.8	21.0	22.2	23.5	24.7	25.9	27.2	28.4	29.6	30.9	32.1

Though using Lum's formula produces the most accurate estimates of a steelhead's live weight, most steelhead between twenty-five and thirty-four inches don't need to have their weight calculated at all. The old length-minus-twenty trick will produce an estimate within about 10 percent of its actual weight. If a fish is thirty inches long, it'll be about ten pounds. A twenty-five-inch fish will be about five pounds. It isn't until a steelhead is longer than thirty-four inches that its girth starts to drastically affect its weight.

Of course, determining the weight of a wild steelhead is a superficial luxury, one that should never come before the health of the fish. If the big steelhead on the end of your fly line needs to be released immediately, hesitating for a few measurements may put its life in jeopardy. That's a risk steelheaders can't afford to take.

PART IV
Conservation

"The How is the shape of the What."

DAVID KEPLINGER

An angler—who likely bought food, flies, and other supplies in Maupin—works a Spey rod down a Deschutes run.

Fly fishing, as practiced by modern anglers, *is* a conservation movement. Persuading a perfectly happy fish to take a fly requires painstaking work. And this labor, though hardly benevolent from a single fish's point of view, does benefit the entire species and the watershed on which the fish depend.

Most of us don't live on the banks of our favorite rivers. Instead, by the malicious conspiring of the capitalist system, we've come to live in bigger towns ten, twenty, a hundred miles away. When we go fishing, we travel to the river's edge, bringing with us an influx of money. Businesses appear near the water—fly shops, guides, gas stations, motels, ice cream stands, coffee shops, and pubs. But these businesses aren't like those of similar character elsewhere; this riverside industry is directly tied to the health of the local fishery. If the river falls on hard times, the anglers will stop coming, and the businesses will stop turning profits. The river's entrepreneurs know their success depends on a stable, healthy fishery, and they aren't shy about putting their time and resources into local conservation efforts.

Plus, the anglers know that their happiness—their sanity, even—depends on having a healthy river to fish. When a mining company wants to crack open a mountain, when a logging company wants to scalp a delicate hillside, when a fish and game commission wants to double the number of hatchery steelhead, the businesses and anglers come together to save the river from certain disaster. In the last twenty years, fly fishing has protected rivers in just this manner throughout North America.

For fly-fishing steelheaders, conservation has seeped into the very fabric of our sport. Our quarry is especially susceptible to watershed abuse and fishery mismanagement. And our angling success depends on forming an observant homewater relationship with the rivers we fish. An entire run of fish can nearly disappear thanks to a single insensitive logging operation, as the example of Washington's Deer Creek shows. Or as we learned from so many of the hatchery programs on small coastal streams throughout the steelhead's range, a few years of irresponsible stocking can forever degrade the river's wild stocks. When enough anglers cherish a river and its

Two anglers work together to quickly unpin and release a wild steelhead.

217

Removing hatchery fish from the river ensures that wild steelhead will have less competition for redd space.

fish, we can rally together and make our voices heard. The future of our passion depends on our committed and continual awareness—and our willingness to stand up and yell when disgraces are approaching. And more disgraces are approaching now than at any time in the past twenty years.

While habitat degradation is a serious threat to wild steelhead populations, many informed anglers believe that the most urgent threat to wild fish is hatchery steelhead. Since the construction of the dams along the Columbia more than sixty years ago, politicians have seen hatcheries as an easy solution to the loss of native fish stocks. When a dam blocked fish from their spawning grounds and a whole generation of steelhead died,

the government built a hatchery to mitigate the losses. When abusive logging practices buried the spawning gravel, the government built a hatchery instead of forcing the responsible company to clean up its act. If hatcheries were able to create steelhead identical to the wild fish, we chromeheads would have been fine with the mitigation. But hatchery fish are deficient creatures. A hatchery steelhead is not the same as a wild steelhead. They stole our bread and gave us cardboard in return.

But many anglers eagerly took the cardboard and asked politely for more. So hatcheries have spread—and continue to spread—throughout steelhead country. Their dangers can't be underestimated. Hatchery steelhead compete for redd space. Every river has a limited amount of redd space; many ichthyologists believe the amount of spawning gravel to be the limiting factor in determining a river's holding capacity. When a hatchery hen digs a redd, it steals that space from a wild hen.

Moreover, hatchery steelhead breed readily with wild fish. Because hatchery fish are protected from risks during their early lives by hatchery managers, the adult fish on the redd are more likely to be inferior, and their offspring are more likely not to survive to return as adults. In just a few years of dumping smolts in the river, a hatchery can forever alter the watershed's wild steelhead. In countless Northwest rivers, the wild runs have been lost forever to hatchery clones. It's time we anglers said enough is enough. It's time we threw the cardboard at the feet of fisheries managers and demanded that they give us back our bread. It's time we demanded that they strive not to create a functional fish farm, but instead a healthy run of wild steelhead—a run that matches the carrying capacity of the watershed.

But some of us anglers are hesitant to get rid of hatchery fish altogether. We like to eat a fresh steelhead here and there. If we didn't have hatcheries, there wouldn't be enough steelhead to go around, right? On many streams, this is likely the case. The carrying capacity of the watershed isn't great enough to support the harvest of wild steelhead. But on other rivers, especially those with healthy headwaters, the carrying capacity would be high enough to allow a limited harvest. Of course, even with the best-case scenario, we couldn't kill as many fish as we can now. But we should ask ourselves, What's more important, killing a dozen hatchery steelhead a year or watching our homewater's wild steelhead stocks rebound to healthy levels?

It's time our steelhead streams were nurtured for the health of their wild stocks—not managed for the mass production of hatchery fish.

If steelhead rivers, like the remote stream pictured here, are to survive the twenty-first century, steelheaders must stand up and protect their homewaters.

The health of wild steelhead stocks requires us to do more than simply send our dues to conservation groups like Trout Unlimited and the Native Fish Society. The time for aggressive action is now. Steelheading is experiencing a boom of popularity. If we can each adamantly defend our own homewater, if we can stand together as a community of riverkeepers, if we can unite our voices into a single deafening roar, we might finally be able to give wild steelhead the chance they deserve. ■

Bibliography

Arnold, Bob. *Steelhead Water*. Portland, OR: Frank Amato Publications, 1993.

Arnold, Bob. *Steelhead and the Floating Line: A Meditation*. Portland, OR: Frank Amato Publications, 1995.

Bakke, Bill. *Conservation Report*. Native Fish Society. December 2006–January 2007.

Bakke, Bill. *Conservation Report*. Native Fish Society. October 2006.

Behnke, Robert J. *Trout and Salmon of North America*. New York: The Free Press, 2002.

Combs, Trey. *Steelhead Fly Fishing*. New York: Lyons & Burford Publishers, 1991.

Duncan, David James. *My Story As Told By Water: Confessions, Druidic Rants, Reflections, Bird-Watchings, Fish-Stalkings, Visions, Songs and Prayers Refracting Light, From Living Rivers, In the Age of the Industrial Dark*. San Francisco: Sierra Club Books, 2001.

Freeman, Mark. "Transmitters to Help State Create Steelhead Road Map." *The Register-Guard*. January 1, 2006.

Haig-Brown, Roderick L., and Ted Leeson. *The Seasons of a Fisherman*. New York: Lyons Press, 2001.

Hogan, Dec. *A Passion for Steelhead*. Bothell, WA: Wild River Press, 2006.

Hoglund, Pat. "Cure for 'Big-Fish-Itis.'" *Salmon and Steelhead Journal*. Spring 2006.

Kostow, K. E., and S. Zhou. "The Effect of an Introduced Summer Steelhead Hatchery Stock on the Productivity of a Wild Winter Steelhead Population." *Transactions of the American Fisheries Society*. 135: 825–841, 2006.

Law, Glenn. *A Concise History of Fly Fishing*. Guilford, CT: The Lyons Press, 2003.

Leeson, Ted. *The Habit of Rivers: Reflections on Trout Streams and Fly Fishing*. New York: Penguin Books, 1994.

Light, J. T., S. Fowler, and M. L. Dahlberg. "High Seas Distribution of North American Steelhead as Evidenced by Recoveries of Marked or Tagged Fish." *Fisheries Research Institute*. University of Washington, Seattle, 1988.

McGuane, Thomas. *The Longest Silence: A Life in Fishing*. New York: Vintage Books, 1999.

McMillan, Bill. *Dry Line Steelhead and Other Subjects*. Portland, OR: Frank Amato Publications, 1987.

Meyer, Deke. *Advanced Fly Fishing for Steelhead*. Portland, OR: Frank Amato Publications, 1992.

Nelson, T. C., M. L. Rosenau, and N. T. Johnston. "Behavior and Survival of Wild and Hatchery-Origin Winter Steelhead Spawners Caught and Released in a Recreational Fishery." *North American Journal of Fisheries Management*. 25: 931–942. 2005.

Pobst, Dick. *Trout Stream Insects: An Orvis Streamside Guide*. New York: The Lyons Press, 1990.

Rose, Doug. *The Color of Winter: Steelhead Fly Fishing on the Olympic Peninsula*. Portland, OR: Frank Amato Publications, 2003.

Rosenbauer, Tom. *Prospecting for Trout: Fly Fishing Secrets from a Streamside Observer*. New York: Delta Books, 1993.

Scott, Jock. *Greased Line Fishing for Salmon: Compiled from the Fishing Papers of the late A.H.E. Wood, of Glassel*. Portland, OR: Frank Amato Publications, 1982.

Index

Index of Fly Patterns